ALEXANDER KINGLAKE

EOT

TRACES OF TRAVEL

BROUGHT HOME

FROM THE EAST

With an introduction by
JAN MORRIS

Oxford New York
OXFORD UNIVERSITY PRESS
1982

Oxford University Press, Walton Street, Oxford OX2 6DP

London Glasgow New York Toronto
Delhi Bombay Calcutta Madras Karachi
Kuala Lumpur Singapore Hong Kong Tokyo
Nairobi Dar es Salaam Cape Town
Melbourne Auckland

and associates in
Beirut Berlin Ibadan Mexico City Nicosia

Introduction © Jan Morris 1982

First published by Oxford University Press 1906
First issued as an Oxford Paperback 1982

British Library Cataloguing in Publication Data

Kinglake, Alexander
Eothen, or, Traces of travel brought home from the
East.—(Oxford paperbacks)
1. Near East—Description and travel
I. Title
915.6'041 DS48
ISBN 0-19-281361-7

Library of Congress Cataloging in Publication Data

Kinglake, Alexander William, 1809–1891.
Eothen, or, Traces of travel brought home from the East.
(Oxford paperback)
Originally published: Oxford, Oxfordshire:
Oxford University Press, 1906.
1. Near East—Description and travel.
2. Kinglake, Alexander William, 1809–1891.
I. Title. II. Title: Eothen. III. Title:
Traces of travel brought home from the East.
DS48.K5 1982 915.6'041 82-6462
ISBN 0-19-281361-7 (pbk.) AACR2

Printed in Great Britain by
Richard Clay (The Chaucer Press) Ltd
Bungay, Suffolk

INTRODUCTION

BY JAN MORRIS

Eothen, ἠῶθεν, is a Greek word meaning 'from the East', but to readers of this book it means much more than that. Thanks to its inspired adoption by Alexander William Kinglake as a title for his masterpiece ('almost the only hard word in the book') it has come to represent in its very syllables the qualities of the work itself: the fun, the elegance, the youthfulness, the Englishness, what John Murray the publisher called the 'wicked spirit of jesting at everything'—qualities which Herodotus, from whom Kinglake borrowed the word, certainly never perceived in it. Kinglake was thirty-five when the book came out in 1844, and though its first edition was published anonymously, for the rest of his long life he was to be known as 'Eothen' Kinglake. Today *aficionados* of his merry genius have only to hear the word to be cheered by the sound of it.

Kinglake was one of God's Englishmen, at a time when Englishry had reached a climax of confidence and prestige. In 1809, four years after Trafalgar, six years before Waterloo, Mary Kinglake of Taunton in Somerset brought her first-born son Alex into the happiest of English circumstances, those of the well-heeled upper-middle classes. Her husband

William was not only a prosperous Taunton lawyer and banker, but also Lord of the Manor of Saltmoor, eleven miles out of town, where the Kinglakes had been settled for 400 years. If the family was never wildly rich, it was never hard-up either: and the young Alexander, though slight of build, pale and diffident, grew up into an amiable archetype of your early Victorian English gentleman.

He was brought up, as a gentleman must be, on Homer and the classics, and out of them evolved a cheerful paganism which he freely declared all his life. He went to a gentlemanly Devon crammer, kept by the poet Coleridge's brother, and thence to Eton. He graduated from one of the best Cambridge colleges, Trinity, and then, denied an army career by his short-sightedness, instead followed his father into the law, reading for the Chancery Bar with a tutor, Bryan Proctor, who was a poet as well as a barrister.

Kinglake was said to be rather a dandyish young man, meticulously dressed and coiffeured. In London he struck up a wide acquaintance, not least among literary people who frequented the Proctor house, but he most admired men of action, especially great commanders, and his closest friends remained high-spirited Eton contemporaries. He was very much one of them, for all his shyness. He was a bit of a snob, and if hardly a chauvinist, at least a convinced advocate of the theory that all things English were, on the whole, best. He admired Napoleon and La Grande Armée indeed, but then

many such Englishmen did: what was the point
of having a Wellington, if there was not a Napoleon
to beat?

It is a remarkable demonstration of the workings
of art—perhaps of Englishness, too—that a young
man of such background and instinct, whose
interests were chiefly in military matters and who
felt himself always a frustrated soldier, should have
written one of the most original, graceful and creative
of all travel books, which has cast a sort of spell
over the *genre* from that day to this.

It was a time of travel. The European wars were
over at last, and the monied English were free to
resume their practice of the Grand Tour, that leisurely
peregrination which was part of a gentleman's
education, and which had so affected the culture,
the manners and the self-image of the islanders.
Besides, though the British had lost their American
colonies, they still possessed a sizeable overseas
empire, and this gave to the families of the upper
bourgeoisie, in particular, a half-proprietorial attitude to the world at large. It was natural that a
young man in Kinglake's position, about to enter his
life's career, inspired by tales of war and dominion,
would wish to take a few months off to wander in
foreign parts: and so in the autumn of 1834 he
interrupted his law studies, arranged letters of
credit from his father's bank, and left London for
what was then called the Near East.

The conventional Grand Tour did not generally take its voyagers beyond the familiar round of France, Germany, Italy, Austria, Greece and possibly Egypt. Kinglake, though, aspired to travel of a less decorous kind. He was not, it seems, very interested in buildings, or literary remains, or works of art, or ruins. He was more or less tone-deaf. He wanted travel that would take him beyond the range of guide-books and drawing-room introductions, travel tinged with exotic sounds and smells, and enlivened perhaps with danger. He wanted, despite his myopia, to go campaigning. He felt the nameless lawyer's round creeping up on him, and he wanted an hour or two of glorious life.

His intentions had been fired by the return from foreign parts, in 1834, of one of those school friends, Lord Pollington, son of the second Earl of Mexborough. Pollington had travelled adventurously through Russia and Persia to India, and he had come home with splendid tales of his experiences. There was one great slab of the Near East, however, which he had circumvented: the Ottoman Empire, extending from what is now Yugoslavia in a great swathe through Turkey and the Levant to Egypt. He had time to spare still, like most young noblemen of the day, and so he and Kinglake conceived the idea of another journey together, from one end to the other of the Turkish Near East—from the Danube to the Nile.

Both were especially attracted by that part of the world. Politically it was of compelling interest:

the power of the Ottoman Sultans was waning, and the future of their empire was one of the great imponderables of world diplomacy. Historically it was fascinating, containing as it did not only sites of the Homeric epics, but the Holy Places of Christendom too. And since the Near East seemed to span the border between the civilized and the untamed, the settled and the nomadic, the fertile and the barren, it seemed likely to satisfy Kinglake's hunger for life, if only for a few months, more absolutely in the raw.

He had never been further from Somerset than Brittany. Never mind: in high fettle he set off in the autumn of 1834, joining up with Pollington at Hamburg and travelling across Europe, via Prague and Vienna, to begin the journey proper at the frontier of the Ottoman Empire at Semlin, now Zemun, just over the Sava river from Belgrade. At once, within the hour, the adventure began in earnest: for in crossing the frontier between Christianity and Islam the two Englishmen were crossing into another world, vividly symbolized that very first day by the elaborate precautions taken to prevent the germs of the plague, then endemic in the Ottoman domains, from crossing into the west. The idea of the plague greeted them across the frontier, and the fact of the plague was to hang always, sometimes suggestively, sometimes terrifyingly, over the whole of Kinglake's journey.

Besides Kinglake, Pollington and their various attendants there crossed the river that morning an interpreter called Mysseri. He too would have an

allegorical part to play in events, for the moment
they entered Ottoman territory he became almost a
spirit of cosmopolitanism, an airy, volatile figure,
fluent in seven languages, vividly foreign, cunning
and un-gentlemanly, floating always through the
narrative, fixing things, worrying, in pointed contrast to Kinglake's own insular, self-amused and
often escapist presence. Only the two of them indeed
last the book out: Pollington returns home at the
end of Chapter 4, and a series of other companions
and attendants come and go in the course of the
journey: but together the Englishman and the
Foreigner stick it out to the end, while around them,
like a shifting stage behind a pair of actors, the
scenes of Eastern travel unfold.

From Belgrade they went via Adrianople (now
Ederne) to Constantinople, where they stayed in
the Christian quarter of Pera, on the north side of
the Golden Horn. Then they travelled through the
country of the Troiad to Smyrna, where Pollington
left them to go home, but Kinglake and Mysseri took
ship first to Cyprus, then to Beirut. There Kinglake
made a detour to call upon the remarkable Lady
Hestor Stanhope, a childhood friend of his mother,
who was living in old age and extreme eccentricity
in a half-derelict former convent near Sidon.

Next they went down into Palestine, and after
visiting Tiberias and Nazareth, and losing their
way rather on the wrong side of Jordan, they came
to Jerusalem early in 1835. Gaza next, the eight-
day camel crossing of the Sinai desert, and by April

they were in Cairo, then in the depths of a particularly terrible visitation of the plague. This was the southern limit of the journey. By early summer Kinglake and Mysseri had started for home, crossing Sinai once more and travelling by way of Nablus and the Lake of Galilee to Damascus in Syria.

Finally, descending into Lebanon again by way of Baalbec, they took passage for Turkey: and landing at the little port of Satalieh, now Attaliyah, they reached the end of their adventure. 'The Pasha now gave us a generous feast', as the closing words of *Eothen* say, 'and as the moon got up and touched the heights of Taurus, we were joyfully winding our way through one of his defiles'—home after fifteen months of wandering to Europe, to England, and to 24 Old Buildings, Lincoln Inn, at which sedate legal address Kinglake would, over the next seven years, put it all down on paper.

Such was the journey this book describes—or rather, does not describe, for there was never a travel book more intensely subjective and selective, more immune to the orthodox demands of descriptive reportage. The journey was not really much in itself. Wild it might seem to Kinglake, and undeniably uncomfortable it was, but the countries were all familiar enough, other travellers were everywhere, and even in the middle of the Sinai Desert, the only truly hazardous part of the journey, Kinglake was half-disconcerted, half perhaps secretly delighted, to meet a fellow-Englishman coming the other way. *Eothen* is sub-titled *Traces of Travel*, but it is not the travel that is important in this work, only the traces it left upon its author's very particular sensibility.

Travel writing was not, of course, a new literary form. Not only had travellers' chronicles been widely read in England at least since the time of Hakluyt in the sixteenth century, but numbers of eminent writers—Defoe, Fielding, Sterne, Smollett— had written travel books of one kind or another. By Kinglake's day conventional accounts of the Grand Tour were two a penny, and all the countries he had visited had been thoroughly described already. His achievement was to make something altogether new out of a relatively commonplace experience, and he did it in three ways: in form, in selection, and above all in style.

The form came to him fortuitously. Another Eton contemporary, Eliot Warburton, was planning a similar journey: he was a fellow-pupil of Brian Proctor, too, and on Kinglake's return from the East he asked him for advice. Kinglake responded with a map and a suggested itinerary, but then decided to expand his advice into a book, based upon the ample notes and sketch-books he had kept during his travels. Warburton had long since left on his own adventure when *Eothen*, after two false starts, was finished at last, but the work retains its epistolary form. It is addressed 'By the Author to One of his Friends', its tone is intimate throughout, and it is full of semi-private allusions. Kinglake speaks to Warburton: but through him he speaks to *all* the Warburtons, all the English men and women of similar origins and similar tastes.

Addressing himself in this way so directly to his own kind, Kinglake could write without inhibitions. He did not, for instance, disguise his paganism. 'I am heathen', he once wrote. 'If I had my way I would write in every church, chapel and cathedral only one line: Important if true.' This was a risky attitude to take at a moment when England was about to enter its great period of evangelical self-righteousness, and indeed startled many of *Eothen's* original readers—even Warburton himself was put out. Not for long, though; Kinglake knew his audience, and he knew too that his general contempt for foreign arrangements, his conviction of English gentlemanly superiority, his unhappy bigotry towards Jews and Americans, would all find ready acceptance among his class and kind.

As for the selection, this was a matter of what came naturally. It is true that earlier writers, notably Sterne, had responded to travel more as an imaginative stimulus than a physical experience: but one feels in *Eothen* that its author was not making conscious literary decisions, in his choice of what to write about, but was simply expressing his own preferences. Those preferences were, in a word, adolescent—but adolescent generally in the best and freshest kind, the adolescence of the poet or the adventurer. *Eothen* is a thoroughly self-centred book, and that is half its charm. Youth is necessarily narrow, and Kinglake at twenty-five had a fairly limited range of analogy or comparison to draw upon. His mind goes back constantly to Eton—to Keate its notorious headmaster, to the river, to his friends there—and part of his pride in the status of the English gentleman may be ascribed to his distinctly limited knowledge of gentlemen of any other kind.

But more constructively, it was the combination of frankness and wonderment, youthful qualities both, that made his book unlike all others. Kinglake skipped what did not interest him. Bethlehem is described in thirteen lines, the Great Mosque of Damascus is not mentioned at all, and eight throw-way lines on Baalbec are concluded endearingly: 'Come! Baalbec is over; I got "rather well" out of that.' Nor did Kinglake much concern himself with local crafts and industries, those tedious favourites of travel-writers from his day to our own: when he wants to describe the Arab way of making bread, he simply compares it with roasting chestnuts.

He rarely offers us descriptions, as such. He is seldom concerned with the look of a place, but with the impression it makes on him. The effect of a scene or an experience is transmuted by his own personality: seldom into generalities, almost never into useful information, but into his own gay, reckless, sometimes unfair, sometimes moving, often hilarious artistic interpretation. He is hardly a reliable reporter—some of his stories are distinctly tall. He is nearer a parodist perhaps, a parodist of life itself, who applies to everything he sees, and everything he does, his own standards of amusement and emotion.

But it was the style that was to make *Eothen* famous. There is no pretending that Kinglake was a profound thinker, or for that matter a great descriptive writer. It was not so much what he said, more the way he said it. His style was described by a contemporary as 'lively, brilliant and rather insolent', and the adjectives are just. Unconventional in punctuation, cavalier in grammar, it is nevertheless an exceedingly polished style. Though Kinglake was naturally fluent, as his notebooks show, clearly during the seven years in which *Eothen* was gestating he wrote and rewrote it, refined its punctuation, adjusted its rhythms, weeded out its adjectives ever more precisely, and so gave it the ironic and immaculate sparkle which has always captivated its readers. *Eothen* is not a short book—it is nearly 100,000 words long—but it leaves behind it a sensation of compactness and completeness without satiety, like a very good meal. It is an oysters-and-Chablis book.

It could be accused of mannerism. Kinglake's style is certainly contrived. Just as his jokes depend upon careful timing, so his wider effects depend upon a calculated use of pace and contrast. The supreme example is the whole chapter he devotes to the Sphinx—or rather, to the responses and speculations aroused in him by his *contemplation* of the Sphinx— but there are countless lesser instances of subtly developed climax, bathos deliberately prepared, or calculated soarings of fancy.

But then if Kinglake's prose was buffed and self-conscious, so was he. *Le style est l'homme même*—and, one might add, the man's background too. In the urbanity, confidence, humour, arrogance and imperturbability of *Eothen* we see the condition of the English gentry at a splendid moment of its history, sublimated disarmingly into art.

Eothen did not immediately find a publisher. It was turned down by John Murray, the most famous publisher of travel literature, who thought its iconoclastic tone would scare off his respectable readership (though later, learning otherwise, he bought its copyright). When in 1844 John Ollivier of Pall Mall accepted it, he stipulated that Kinglake must contribute £50 to the cost of publication, Once in print, however, the book became an instant success. It ran through six editions almost at once. and has been in print ever since, going into paperback for the first time 120 years after its original appearance. Its effect upon the art of travel writing has been profound, and its influence may be traced down the generations from Robert Curzon's *Monasteries of the Levant* (1849) to Robert Byron's *Road to Oxiana* (1937) or Paul Theroux's *Great Railway Bazaar* (1975).

Its author did not remain anonymous for long, and 'Eothen' Kinglake became both rich and famous. Though he went on an adventurous trip to Algeria in 1845, he never wrote another travel book. Except for one or two reviews, his only other published work was a magisterial and much-admired history, published in successive volumes in the 1860s, of the opening phases of the Crimean War, which in his lasting enthusiasm for things military he had gone to witness for himself. He never achieved much distinction as a lawyer, but entered Parliament in 1857 as member for Bridgwater in Somerset, remaining there until 1868 when he was unseated because of the peculations of his agent—no blame being attached to Kinglake himself. Thereafter he lived the life of a popular and celebrated bachelor, with many friends and a reputation for gentle wit. He was a well-known member of the Travellers' and Athenaeum clubs, a familiar diner at grand tables, and some of his youthful prejudices, at least, he grew out of: by 1882 he was willing to subscribe to the fund for the defence of Arabi Pasha, the Egyptian nationalist who had dared to oppose the imperial power of Britain in the Near East.

A certain opacity surrounds his person in later years. He was 'Eothen' Kinglake to the very end, and to the end too he seems to have retained the personality that shines so engagingly through the pages of the book: a little shy even in old age, courteous, having about him an air of thoughtful polish and control—but somehow elusive. In life as in print, he was never a spontaneous man, but seemed to be holding something always in reserve:

the National Portrait Gallery picture of him, painted by Harriet Haviland in about 1863, shows him pale and somewhat melancholy, with a fine high brow and an expression of knightly tristesse. Henry James, in the last years of Kinglake's life, described him as 'old, deaf, delicate, distinguished, perfect, infinitely silent', while after his death one of his oldest friends, Janet Ross, said of him that his writing would live for ever, but that 'he himself . . . will never be known'.

Certainly his private life is largely closed to us. Though there were rumours that in the late 1840s he coveted the mistress of the future Emperor Louis-Napoléon, then living in London, there are no reports of any permanent liaison. Kinglake loved women, and they loved him, but perhaps not sexually: his closest friends included Lady Gregory, the Irish woman of letters, Olga Novikoff the political activist and Caroline Norton who was Lord Melbourne's lover, but he seems never to have been tempted towards the marriage-bonds he made so much fun of in *Eothen*. There was something virginal to him always, even innocent perhaps: when he died, in 1891, at 26 Lancaster Gate, London, he left his Somerset estate to two nieces, and asked his nurse Alice Dumper to distribute his trinkets and souvenirs among his friends.

Such was the man whom, by turning a page or two of this book, you may now accompany on one of the most hugely entertaining and exhilarating of all expeditions: into the East with Kinglake.

EOTHEN

A CAST OF CHARACTERS

in the order of their first appearance

Page 1. *'One of his friends'*: Eliot Warburton (1810–52), himself about to embark upon the eastern journey which resulted in his book *The Crescent and the Cross*. He went on to write several other books, and was drowned when the steamship *Amazon*, taking him to Cuba, foundered off Land's End. Until his own death nearly forty years later Kinglake wore a ring which Warburton had given him.

Page 1. *'Our lady of bitterness'*: Anne Proctor (died 1888), wife of Kinglake's law tutor Brian Proctor, a well-known literary hostess at whose house Kinglake met many eminent writers. Aciduous and sharp-tongued, she broke with Kinglake in middle life, and was said to have declined to speak to him for twenty-five years: but he went to her funeral, nevertheless, in the company of Browning and Henry James.

Page 5. *Lady Hester Stanhope* (1776–1839): grand-daughter of the elder Pitt and former housekeeper to the younger, who settled in Lebanon in 1812 and established a remarkable ascendancy over the local Bedouin tribes. She died at her hilltop home at Djoun, near Sidon, heavily in debt and attended only by one black servant, and there she is buried.

Page 10. *Methley*: John Savile, Lord Pollington (1809–60), later 3rd Earl of Mexborough, who lived at Methley Park in Yorkshire. He left Kinglake at Smyrna and in 1835 was elected a member of Parliament for Pontefract in Yorkshire. Though the two friends, who had known each other since Eton, were temporarily estranged after the publication of *Eothen*, they presently made it up, and Kinglake left Mexborough a pair of sabres in his will.

Page 18. *Mysseri*: Kinglake's servant, of indeterminate nationality but many tongues, who stayed with him throughout the journey described in *Eothen*, and later became a prosperous hotelier in Constantinople.

Page 25. *John Keate* (1773–1852): headmaster of Eton from 1809 to 1834, and a notorious disciplinarian.

Page 25. *Larrey Miller*: a tailor at Eton during Kinglake's time there.

Page 25. *Richard Okes* (1797–1888): an Eton master from 1823 to 1850, and later Provost of King's College, Cambridge.

Page 27. *Sabalkansky*: Count Hans Diebitsch (1785–1831), Prussian general in the Russian service, called by the Russians 'Sabalkansky' after his brilliant crossing of the Balkans in the Russian-Turko war of 1829.

Page 27. *George Keppell* (1799–1891): later 6th Earl of Albermarle, an adventurous soldier who had visited the Russian armies during their campaigns against Turkey in 1829, and wrote a book about the experience.

Page 32. *Giuseppini*: a well-known Italian inn-keeper in Pera, the Christian quarter of Constantinople.

Page 50. *Carrigaholt*: Henry Stuart Burton (born *c.*1809) of Castle Carrigaholt, County Clare, an Eton contemporary of Kinglake: Burton went home to Ireland in the following year, married a Dean's daughter and became Deputy Lieutenant for County Clare.

Page 81. *Dthemetri*: Kinglake's Arabic interpreter from Zante, in the Ionian Islands, then part of the British Empire.

Page 87. *Sir Sydney Smith*: Sir William Sidney Smith (1764–1840), admiral whose defence of Acre in 1799 led to Napoleon's humiliating retreat from Syria.

Page 88. *Richard Monckton Milnes* (1809–85): later 1st Baron Houghton, a Cambridge contemporary of Kinglake, poet, politician, traveller and patron of letters.

Page 93. *Ibrahim Pasha* (1789–1848): son of Mohammed Ali, Ottoman viceroy of Egypt, who on behalf of his rebellious father defeated an Ottoman army in Syria, later himself becoming Governor-General of Egypt and Syria.

Page 95. *Mehemet Ali* (1769–1849): Mohammed Ali, Ottoman Viceroy of Egypt who, after a war against the Sultan, won the hereditary right to rule Egypt, his dynasty surviving until the deposition of King Farouk in 1952.

Page 96. *Lord Hardwicke*: Charles Philip Yorke (1799–1873), admiral, MP and Postmaster-General.

Page 104. *William Paley* (1743–1805): theologian, author of *A View of the Evidences of Christianity*.

Page 111. *Bishop Alexander*: Michael Solomon Alexander (1799–1845) Jewish-born first Anglican Bishop of Jerusalem.

Page 131. *Sir Howard Douglas* (1776–1861): general, later Governor of New Brunswick, and author of *An Essay on the Principle and Construction of Military Bridges and the Passage of Rivers in Military Operations.*

Page 132. *William Hamilton* (1729–96): politician who, though he became Chancellor of the Exchequer, was remembered always for his brilliant maiden speech as Member for Petersfield in 1755.

Page 149. *Count Horace Sebastiani* (1772–1851): French marshal and diplomatist who as Ambassador in Constantinople from 1805 to 1807 exerted a powerful influence on the policies of the Porte.

Page 188. *Osman Effendi*: John McLeod (d. 1837), a former drummer-boy of the 78th Highlanders who had been captured by Turkish forces during the British invasion of Egypt in 1809, and eventually turned up as a slave in Arabia. There he was rescued by the explorer J.-L. Burckhardt, who obtained his liberty and found him employment in Cairo. He prospered, acquired several lodging houses in Cairo and provided all kinds of services for European travellers in Egypt. When he died, of the plague, two years after Kinglake's visit he was buried in a Muslim cemetery beneath the same stone as his benefactor Burckhardt.

Page 200. *Mamelukes*: descendants of Caucasian slaves who ruled Egypt from 1250 until the Ottoman conquest in 1517, and whose last descendants were virtually exterminated by Mohammed Ali in 1811.

Page 226. *Henry Milman* (1791–1868): poet, playwright and Dean of St. Paul's (though never in fact an Oxford professor).

Page 260 footnote. *Edward Everett* (1794–1865): American statesman and politician who served as United States Minister to Great Britain from 1841 to 1845. When in 1843 Oxford University proposed to confer an honorary degree upon him it was discovered just before the ceremony that he was a Unitarian by faith, and therefore ineligible. He is chiefly remembered now for having delivered the speech *before* President Lincoln's at Gettysburg in 1863.

CONTENTS

PREFACE TO THE FIRST EDITION

ADDRESSED BY THE AUTHOR TO ONE OF HIS FRIENDS

WHEN you first entertained the idea of travelling in the East, you asked me to send you an outline of the tour which I had made, in order that you might the better be able to choose a route for yourself. In answer to this request, I gave you a large French map, on which the course of my journey had been carefully marked; but I did not conceal from myself, that this was rather a dry mode for a man to adopt, when he wished to impart the results of his experience to a dear, and intimate friend. Now, long before the period of your planning an Oriental tour, I had intended to write some account of my Eastern Travels. I had, indeed, begun the task, and had failed; I had begun it a second time, and failing again, had abandoned my attempt with a sensation of utter distaste. I was unable to speak out, and chiefly, I think, for this reason—that I knew not to whom I was speaking. It might be you, or, perhaps, our Lady of Bitterness, who would read my story; or it might be some member of the Royal Statistical Society, and how on earth was I to write in a way that would do for all three?

Well—your request for a sketch of my tour suggested to me the idea of complying with your wish by a revival of my twice abandoned attempt.

I tried; and the pleasure and confidence which I felt in speaking to you soon made my task so easy, and even amusing, that after a while (though not in time for your tour), I completed the scrawl from which this book was originally printed.

The very feeling, however, which enabled me to write thus freely, prevented me from robing my thoughts in that grave and decorous style which I should have maintained if I had professed to lecture the public. Whilst I feigned to myself that you, and you only, were listening, I could not by possibility speak very solemnly. Heaven forbid that I should talk to my own genial friend, as though he were a great and enlightened Community, or any other respectable Aggregate !

Yet I well understood that the mere fact of my professing to speak to you rather than to the public generally, could not perfectly excuse me for printing a narrative too roughly worded, and accordingly, in revising the proof-sheets, I have struck out those phrases which seemed to be less fit for a published volume than for intimate conversation. It is hardly to be expected, however, that correction of this kind should be perfectly complete, or that the almost boisterous tone in which many parts of the book were originally written should be thoroughly subdued. I venture, therefore, to ask, that the familiarity of language still possibly apparent in the work, may be laid to the account of our delightful intimacy, rather than to any presumptuous motive; I feel, as you know, much too timidly, too distantly, and too respectfully towards the Public, to be capable of seeking to put myself on terms of easy fellowship with strange and casual readers.

It is right to forewarn people (and I have tried to do this as well as I can, by my studiously unpromising title-page [1]) that the book is quite superficial in its character. I have endeavoured to discard from it all valuable matter derived from the works of others, and it appears to me that my efforts in this direction have been attended with great success; I believe I may truly acknowledge, that from all details of geographical discovery, or antiquarian research—from all display of 'sound learning, and religious knowledge'—from all historical and scientific illustrations—from all useful statistics—from all political disquisitions—and from all good moral reflections, the volume is thoroughly free.

My excuse for the book is its truth: you and I know a man, fond of hazarding elaborate jokes, who, whenever a story of his happens not to go down as wit, will evade the awkwardness of the failure, by bravely maintaining that all he has said is pure fact. I can honestly take this decent though humble mode of escape. My narrative is not merely righteous in matters of fact (where fact is in question), but it is true in this larger sense—it conveys, not those impressions which *ought to have been* produced upon any 'well constituted mind', but those which were really and truly received at the time of his rambles, by a headstrong and not very amiable traveller, whose prejudices in favour of other people's notions were then exceedingly slight. As I have felt so I have written; and the result is, that there will often be found in my narrative a jarring discord between the associations properly belonging to interesting sites, and the tone in which I speak of them. This seemingly perverse mode of treating the

---

[1] 'Eōthen' is, I hope, almost the only hard word to be found in the book: it is written in Greek ἠῶθεν,—(Atticè, with an aspirated ε instead of η),—and signifies, 'from the early dawn', —'from the East'.—*Donn. Lex.* 4th edition.

subject is forced upon me by my plan of adhering to
sentimental truth, and really does not result from
any impertinent wish to tease or trifle with readers.
I ought, for instance, to have felt as strongly in
Judæa, as in Galilee, but it was not so in fact: the
religious sentiment (born in solitude) which had
heated my brain in the Sanctuary of Nazareth was
rudely chilled at the foot of Zion, by disenchanting
scenes, and this change is accordingly disclosed by
the perfectly worldly tone in which I speak of
Jerusalem and Bethlehem.

My notion of dwelling precisely upon those matters
which happened to interest me, and upon none other,
would of course be intolerable in a regular book of
travels. If I had been passing through countries not
previously explored, it would have been sadly perverse to withhold careful descriptions of admirable
objects, merely because my own feelings of interest in
them may have happened to flag; but where the
countries which one visits have been thoroughly and
ably described, and even artistically illustrated by
others, one is fully at liberty to say as little (though
not quite so much) as one chooses. Now a traveller
is a creature not always looking at sights—he re-
members (how often!) the happy land of his birth—
he has, too, his moments of humble enthusiasm about
fire, and food—about shade, and drink; and if he
gives to these feelings anything like the prominence
which really belonged to them at the time of his
travelling, he will not seem a very good teacher;
once having determined to write the sheer truth
concerning the things which chiefly have interested
him, he must, and he will, sing a sadly long strain
about Self; he will talk for whole pages together
about his bivouac fire, and ruin the Ruins of Baalbec
with eight or ten cold lines.

But it seems to me that this egotism of a traveller, however incessant—however shameless and obtrusive, must still convey some true ideas of the country through which he has passed. His very selfishness— his habit of referring the whole external world to his own sensations, compels him, as it were, in his writings, to observe the laws of perspective;—he tells you of objects, not as he knows them to be, but as they seemed to him. The people, and the things that most concern him personally, however mean and insignificant, take large proportions in his picture, because they stand so near to him. He shows you his Dragoman, and the gaunt features of his Arabs— his tent—his kneeling camels—his baggage strewed upon the sand :—but the proper wonders of the land —the cities—the mighty ruins and monuments of bygone ages, he throws back faintly in the distance. It is thus that he felt, and thus he strives to repeat, the scenes of the Elder World. You may listen to him for ever without learning much in the way of Statistics ; but, perhaps, if you bear with him long enough, you may find yourself slowly and faintly impressed with the realities of Eastern Travel.

My scheme of refusing to dwell upon matters which failed to interest my own feelings, has been departed from in one instance—namely, in my detail of the late Lady Hester Stanhope's conversation on supernatural topics ; the truth is, that I have been much questioned on this subject, and I thought that my best plan would be to write down at once all that I could ever have to say concerning the personage whose career has excited so much curiosity amongst Englishwomen. The result is, that my account of the lady goes to a length which is not justified either by the importance of the subject, or by the extent to which it interested the narrator.

You will see that I constantly speak of 'my People', 'my Party', 'my Arabs', and so on, using terms which might possibly seem to imply that I moved about with a pompous retinue. This, of course, was not the case. I travelled with the simplicity proper to my station, as one of the industrious class, who was not flying from his country because of ennui, but was strengthening his will, and tempering the metal of his nature for that life of toil and conflict in which he is now engaged. But an Englishman, journeying in the East, must necessarily have with him Dragomen capable of interpreting the Oriental languages ; the absence of wheeled-carriages obliges him to use several beasts of burthen for his baggage, as well as for himself and his attendants ; the owners of the horses or camels, with *their* slaves or servants, fall in as part of his train, and altogether the cavalcade becomes rather numerous, without, however, occasioning any proportionate increase of expense. When a traveller speaks of all these followers in mass, he calls them his 'people', or his 'troop', or his 'party', without intending to make you believe that he is therefore a Sovereign Prince.

You will see that I sometimes follow the custom of the Scots in describing my fellow countrymen by the names of their paternal homes.

Of course all these explanations are meant for casual readers. To you, without one syllable of excuse or deprecation, and in all the confidence of a friendship that never yet was clouded, I give the long promised volume, and add but this one 'Good-bye!' for I dare not stand greeting you here.

EOTHEN

CHAPTER I

OVER THE BORDER

At Semlin I still was encompassed by the scenes
and the sounds of familiar life; the din of a busy
world still vexed and cheered me; the unveiled faces
of women still shone in the light of day. Yet, whenever I chose to look southward, I saw the Ottoman's
fortress—austere, and darkly impending high over
the vale of the Danube—historic Belgrade. I had
come, as it were, to the end of this wheel-going
Europe, and now my eyes would see the Splendour
and Havoc of The East.

The two frontier towns are less than a gun-shot
apart, yet their people hold no communion. The
Hungarian on the North, and the Turk and the
Servian on the Southern side of the Save, are as
much asunder as though there were fifty broad provinces that lay in the path between them. Of the
men that bustled around me in the streets of Semlin,
there was not, perhaps, one who had ever gone down
to look upon the stranger race dwelling under the
walls of that opposite castle. It is the Plague, and
the dread of the Plague, that divide the one people
from the other. All coming and going stands forbidden by the terrors of the yellow flag. If you
dare to break the laws of the quarantine, you will
be tried with military haste; the court will scream
out your sentence to you from a tribunal some fifty
yards off; the priest, instead of gently whispering
to you the sweet hopes of religion, will console you

at duelling distance, and after that you will find yourself carefully shot, and carelessly buried in the ground of the Lazaretto.

When all was in order for our departure, we walked down to the precincts of the Quarantine Establishment, and here awaited us the 'compromised[1]' officer of the Austrian Government, whose duty it is to superintend the passage of the frontier, and who for that purpose lives in a state of perpetual excommunication. The boats with their 'compromised' rowers were also in readiness.

After coming in contact with any creature or thing belonging to the Ottoman Empire it would be impossible for us to return to the Austrian territory without undergoing an imprisonment for fourteen days in the Lazaretto. We felt therefore that before we committed ourselves, it was important to take care that none of the arrangements necessary for the journey had been forgotten; and in our anxiety to avoid such a misfortune we managed the work of departure from Semlin with nearly as much solemnity as if we had been departing this life. Some obliging persons from whom we had received civilities during our short stay in the place, came down to say their farewell at the river's side ; and now, as we stood with them at the distance of three or four yards from the 'compromised' officer, they asked if we were perfectly certain that we had wound up all our affairs in Christendom, and whether we had no parting requests to make. We repeated the caution to our servants, and took anxious thought lest by any possibility we might

---

[1] A 'compromised' person is one who has been in contact with people or things supposed to be capable of conveying infection. As a general rule, the whole Ottoman empire lies constantly under this terrible ban. The 'yellow flag' is the ensign of the Quarantine Establishment.

be cut off from some cherished object of affection :—
were they quite sure that nothing had been forgotten
— that there was no fragrant dressing-case with its
gold-compelling letters of credit from which we might
be parting for ever ?—No—every one of our treasures
lay safely stowed in the boat, and we—we were ready
to follow. Now, therefore, we shook hands with our
Semlin friends, and they immediately retreated for
three or four paces, so as to leave us in the centre of
a space between them and the 'compromised' officer ;
the latter then advanced, and asking once more if we
had done with the civilized world, held forth his hand
—I met it with mine, and there was an end to Christendom for many a day to come.

We soon neared the southern bank of the river, but
no sounds came down from the blank walls above,
and there was no living thing that we could yet see,
except one great hovering bird of the vulture race
flying low and intent, and wheeling round and round
over the Pest-accused city.

But presently there issued from the postern a group
of human beings,—beings with immortal souls, and
possibly some reasoning faculties, but to me the grand
point was this, that they had real, substantial, and
incontrovertible turbans ; they made for the point
towards which we were steering ; and when at last I
sprang upon the shore, I heard and saw myself now
first surrounded by men of Asiatic blood : I have
since ridden through the land of the Osmanlees—
from the Servian Border to the Golden Horn—from
the Gulf of Satalieh to the Tomb of Achilles ; but
never have I seen such hyper-Turk looking fellows as
those who received me on the banks of the Save ;
they were men in the humblest order of life, having
come to meet our boat in the hope of earning something by carrying our luggage up to the city ; but, poor

though they were, it was plain that they were Turks of
the proud old school, and had not yet forgotten the
fierce, careless bearing of their once victorious race.

Though the province of Servia generally has obtained a kind of independence, yet Belgrade, as being
a place of strength on the frontier, is still garrisoned
by Turkish troops under the command of a Pasha.
Whether the fellows who now surrounded us were
soldiers or peaceful inhabitants I did not understand;
they wore the old Turkish costume; vests and jackets
of many and brilliant colours divided from the loose
petticoat-trowsers by heavy volumes of shawl, so
thickly folded around their waists as to give the
meagre wearers something of the dignity of true cor-
pulence. This cincture enclosed a whole bundle of
weapons; no man bore less than one brace of immensely long pistols and a yataghan (or cutlass), with
a dagger or two of various shapes and sizes; most of
these arms were inlaid with silver highly burnished,
and they shone all the more lustrously for being worn
along with garments decayed and even tattered (this
carefulness of his arms is a point of honour with the
Osmanlee; he never allows his bright yataghan to
suffer from his own adversity): then the long drooping
mustachios, and the ample folds of the once white
turbans that lowered over the piercing eyes, and the
haggard features of the men, gave them an air of
gloomy pride, and that appearance of trying to be
disdainful under difficulties which one almost always
sees in those of the Ottoman people who live and
remember old times; they looked as if they would
have thought themselves more usefully, more honour-
ably, and more piously employed in cutting our
throats than in carrying our portmanteaus. The
faithful Steel (Methley's Yorkshire servant) stood
aghast for a moment at the sight of his master's lug-

gage upon the shoulders of these warlike porters, and
when at last we began to move, he could scarcely
avoid turning round to cast one affectionate look
towards Christendom, but quickly again he marched
on with the steps of a man—not frightened exactly,
but sternly prepared for death, or the Koran, or even
for plural wives.

The Moslem quarter of a city is lonely and desolate ;
you go up, and down, and on, over shelving and
hillocky paths through the narrow lanes walled in by
blank, windowless dwellings ; you come out upon an
open space strewed with the black ruins that some
late fire has left ; you pass by a mountain of cast-
away things, the rubbish of centuries, and on it you
see numbers of big, wolf-like dogs lying torpid under
the sun, with limbs outstretched to the full, as if they
were dead ; storks or cranes, sitting fearless upon the
low roofs, look gravely down upon you ; the still air
that you breathe is loaded with the scent of citron and
pomegranate rinds scorched by the sun, or (as you
approach the Bazaar) with the dry, dead perfume of
strange spices.   You long for some signs of life, and
tread the ground more heavily, as though you would
wake the sleepers with the heel of your boot ; but the
foot falls noiseless upon the crumbling soil of an
eastern city, and Silence follows you still.   Again and
again you meet turbans, and faces of men, but they
have nothing for you—no welcome—no wonder—no
wrath—no scorn—they look upon you as we do upon
a December's fall of snow—as a 'seasonable', unac-
countable, uncomfortable work of God that may have
been sent for some good purpose, to be revealed
hereafter.

Some people had come down to meet us with an
invitation from the Pasha, and we wound our way up
to the castle.   At the gates there were groups of

soldiers, some smoking, and some lying flat like corpses upon the cool stones. We went through courts, ascended steps, passed along a corridor, and walked into an airy, white-washed room, with an European clock at one end of it, and Moostapha Pasha at the other : the fine, old, bearded potentate looked very like Jove—like Jove, too, in the midst of his clouds, for the silver fumes of the Narguilè [1] hung lightly circling round him.

The Pasha received us with the smooth, kind, gentle manner that belongs to well-bred Osmanlees ; then he lightly clapped his hands, and instantly the sound filled all the lower end of the room with slaves : a syllable dropped from his lips ; it bowed all heads, and conjured away the attendants like ghosts (their coming and their going was thus swift and quiet, because their feet were bare, and they passed through no door, but only by the yielding folds of a purder). Soon the coffee-bearers appeared, every man carrying separately his tiny cup in a small metal stand ; and presently to each of us there came a pipe-bearer—a grave and solemn functionary, who first rested the bowl of the tchibouque at a measured distance on the floor, and then, on this axis, wheeled round the long cherry tube, and gracefully presented it on half-bended knee : already the fire (well kindled beforehand) was glowing secure in the bowl, and so, when I pressed the amber lip to mine, there was no coyness to conquer ; the willing fume came up, and answered my slightest sigh, and followed softly every breath inspired, till it touched me with some faint sense and understanding of Asiatic contentment.

Asiatic contentment ! Yet hardly, perhaps, one

[1] The Narguilè is a water-pipe upon the plan of the Hookah, but more gracefully fashioned ; the smoke is drawn by a very long flexible tube that winds its snake-like way from the vase to the lips of the beatified smoker.

hour before I had been wanting my bill, and ringing for waiters in a shrill and busy hotel.

In the Ottoman dominions there is scarcely any hereditary influence except that belonging to the family of the Sultan, and wealth, too, is a highly volatile blessing, not easily transmitted to the descendants of the owner. From these causes it results, that the people standing in the place of nobles and gentry are official personages; and though many (indeed the greater number) of these potentates are humbly born and bred, you will seldom, I think, find them wanting in that polished smoothness of manner and those well undulating tones which belong to the best Osmanlees. The truth is, that most of the men in authority have risen from their humble station by the arts of the courtier, and they keep in their high estate those gentle powers of fascination to which they owe their success. Yet, unless you can contrive to learn a little of the language, you will be rather bored by your visits of ceremony; the intervention of the Dragoman is fatal to the spirit of conversation. I think I should mislead you if I were to attempt to give the substance of any particular conversation with Orientals. A traveller may write and say that, 'the Pasha of So-and-So was particularly interested in the vast progress which has been made in the application of steam, and appeared to understand the structure of our machinery—that he remarked upon the gigantic results of our manufacturing industry—showed that he possessed considerable knowledge of our Indian affairs, and of the constitution of the Company, and expressed a lively admiration of the many sterling qualities for which the people of England are distinguished'. But the heap of commonplaces thus quietly attributed to the Pasha will have been founded perhaps on some such talking as this:—

Pasha. The Englishman is welcome ; most blessed among hours is this, the hour of his coming.

Dragoman (to the Traveller). The Pasha pays you his compliments.

Traveller. Give him my best compliments· in return, and say I'm delighted to have the honour of seeing him.

Dragoman (to the Pasha). His Lordship, this Englishman, Lord of London, Scorner of Ireland, Suppressor of France, has quitted his governments, and left his enemies to breathe for a moment, and has crossed the broad waters in strict disguise, with a small but eternally faithful retinue of followers, in order that he might look upon the bright countenance of the Pasha among Pashas—the Pasha of the everlasting Pashalik of Karagholookoldour.

Traveller (to his Dragoman). What on earth have you been saying about London ? The Pasha will be taking me for a mere cockney. Have not I told you *always* to say, that I am from a branch of the family of Mudcombe Park, and that I am to be a magistrate for the county of Bedfordshire, only I've not qualified, and that I should have been a Deputy-Lieutenant, if it had not been for the extraordinary conduct of Lord Mountpromise, and that I was a candidate for Boughton-Soldborough at the last election, and that I should have won easy if my committee had not been bribed. I wish to heaven that if you *do* say any thing about me, you'd tell the simple truth.

Dragoman—[is silent].

Pasha. What says the friendly Lord of London ? is there aught that I can grant him within the Pashalik of Karagholookoldour ?

Dragoman (growing sulky and literal). This friendly Englishman—this branch of Mudcombe— this head purveyor of Boughton-Soldborough—this possible policeman of Bedfordshire is recounting his achievements and the number of his titles.

Pasha. The end of his honours is more distant than the ends of the earth, and the catalogue of his glorious deeds is brighter than the firmament of heaven!

Dragoman (to the Traveller). The Pasha congratulates your Excellency.

Traveller. About Boughton-Soldborough? The deuce he does!—but I want to get at his views in relation to the present state of the Ottoman Empire; tell him the Houses of Parliament have met, and that there has been a speech from the throne pledging England to maintain the integrity of the Sultan's dominions.

Dragoman (to the Pasha). This branch of Mudcombe, this possible policeman of Bedfordshire, informs your Highness that in England the talking houses have met, and that the integrity of the Sultan's dominions has been assured for ever and ever by a speech from the velvet chair.

Pasha. Wonderful chair! Wonderful houses!— whirr! whirr! all by wheels!—whiz! whiz! all by steam!—wonderful chair! wonderful houses! wonderful people!—whirr! whirr! all by wheels!—whiz! whiz! all by steam!

Traveller (to the Dragoman). What does the Pasha mean by that whizzing? he does not mean to say, does he, that our Government will ever abandon their pledges to the Sultan?

Dragoman. No, your Excellency, but he says the English talk by wheels and by steam.

Traveller. That's an exaggeration; but say that the English really have carried machinery to great perfection; tell the Pasha (he'll be struck with that) that whenever we have any disturbances to put down, even at two or three hundred miles from London, we can send troops by the thousand to the scene of action in a few hours.

Dragoman (recovering his temper and freedom of speech). His Excellency, this Lord of Mudcombe, observes to your Highness, that whenever the Irish, or the French, or the Indians rebel against the English, whole armies of soldiers and brigades of artillery are dropped into a mighty chasm called Euston Square, and, in the biting of a cartridge, they rise up again in Manchester, or Dublin, or Paris, or Delhi, and utterly exterminate the enemies of England from the face of the earth.

Pasha. I know it—I know all—the particulars have been faithfully related to me, and my mind comprehends locomotives. The armies of the English ride upon the vapours of boiling cauldrons, and their horses are flaming coals!—whirr! whirr! all by wheels!—whiz! whiz! all by steam!

Traveller (to his Dragoman). I wish to have the opinion of an unprejudiced Ottoman gentleman as to the prospects of our English commerce and manufactures; just ask the Pasha to give me his views on the subject.

Pasha (after having received the communication of the Dragoman). The ships of the English swarm like flies; their printed calicoes cover the whole earth, and by the side of their swords the blades of Damascus are blades of grass. All India is but an item in the Ledger-books of the Merchants whose lumber-rooms are filled with ancient thrones!—whirr! whirr! all by wheels!—whiz! whiz! all by steam!

Dragoman. The Pasha compliments the cutlery of England, and also the East India Company.

Traveller. The Pasha's right about the cutlery: I tried my scimitar with the common officers' swords belonging to our fellows at Malta, and they cut it like the leaf of a Novel. Well (to the Dragoman), tell the Pasha I am exceedingly gratified to find that he entertains such a high opinion of our manufacturing energy, but I should like him to know, though, that we have got something in England besides that. These foreigners are always fancying that we have nothing but ships and railways, and East India Companies; do just tell the Pasha, that our rural districts deserve his attention, and that even within the last two hundred years there has been an evident improvement in the culture of the turnip; and if he does not take any interest about that, at all events you can explain that we have our virtues in the country—that we are a truth-telling people, and, like the Osmanlees, are faithful in the performance of our promises. Oh! and by the by, whilst you are about it, you may as well just say at the end that the British yeoman is still, thank God! the British yeoman.

Pasha (after hearing the Dragoman). It is true, it is true:—through all Feringhistan the English are foremost and best, for the Russians are drilled swine, and the Germans are sleeping babes, and the Italians are the servants of Songs, and the French are the sons of Newspapers, and the Greeks are the weavers of lies, but the English and the Osmanlees are brothers together in righteousness; for the Osmanlees believe in one only God, and cleave to the Koran, and destroy idols; so do the English worship one God, and abominate graven images, and tell the truth, and believe in a book, and though they drink the juice of the grape, yet to say that they worship their prophet as God, or to say that they are eaters of pork, these are lies—lies born of Greeks, and nursed by Jews!

Dragoman. The Pasha compliments the English.

Traveller (rising). Well, I've had enough of this.

Tell the Pasha I am greatly obliged to him for his
hospitality, and still more for his kindness in furnishing
me with horses, and say that now I must be off.

Pasha (after hearing the Dragoman, and standing
up on his Divan).[1]   Proud are the sires, and blessed
are the dams of the horses, that shall carry his Excellency to the end of his prosperous journey.   May the
saddle beneath him glide down to the gates of the
happy city like a boat swimming on the third river of
Paradise.   May he sleep the sleep of a child, when
his friends are around him; and the while that his
enemies are abroad may his eyes flame red through
the darkness—more red than the eyes of ten tigers !—
farewell !

Dragoman.   The Pasha wishes your Excellency a
pleasant journey.

So ends the visit.

CHAPTER II

TURKISH TRAVELLING

In two or three hours our party was ready; the
servants, the Tatar, the mounted Suridgees, and the
baggage-horses altogether made up a strong cavalcade.
The accomplished Mysseri, of whom you have heard
me speak so often, and who served me so faithfully
throughout my Oriental journeys, acted as our interpreter, and was, in fact, the brain of our corps.   The
Tatar, you know, is a government courier properly
employed in carrying despatches, but also sent with
travellers to speed them on their way and answer with

---

[1] That is, if he stands up at all: Oriental etiquette would not
warrant his rising, unless his visitor were supposed to be at least
his equal in point of rank and station.

his head for their safety. The man whose head was
thus pledged for our precious lives was a glorious
looking fellow, with that regular and handsome cast
of countenance which is now characteristic of the
Ottoman race.[1] His features displayed a good deal
of serene pride, self-respect, fortitude, a kind of ingenuous sensuality, and something of instinctive wisdom, without any sharpness of intellect. He had been
a Janissary (as I afterwards found), and he still kept
up the old praetorian strut which used to affright the
Christians in former times—a strut so comically
pompous, that any close imitation of it, even in the
broadest farce, would be looked upon as a very rough
over-acting of the character. It is occasioned in part
by dress and accoutrements. The weighty bundle of
weapons carried upon the chest throws back the body
so as to give it a wonderful portliness, and, moreover,
the immense masses of clothes that swathe his limbs
force the wearer in walking to swing himself heavily
round from left to right, and from right to left. In
truth, this great edifice of woollen, and cotton, and
silk, and silver, and brass, and steel, is not at all fitted
for moving on foot; it cannot even walk without
frightfully discomposing its fair proportions ; and as
to running—our Tatar ran *once* (it was in order to pick
up a partridge that Methley had winged with a pistol-
shot), and the attempt was one of the funniest mis-
directions of human energy that wondering man ever
saw. But put him in his stirrups, and then is the
Tatar himself again : there he lives at his pleasure,
reposing in the tranquillity of that true home (the
home of his ancestors), which the saddle seems to

[1] The continual marriages of these people with the chosen
beauties of Georgia and Circassia have overpowered the original
ugliness of their Tatar ancestors.

afford him, and drawing from his pipe the calm pleasures of his 'own fireside'; or else dashing sudden
over the earth, as though for a moment he felt the
mouth of a Turcoman steed, and saw his own Scythian
plains lying boundless and open before him.

It was not till his subordinates had nearly completed their preparations for the march that our Tatar,
'commanding the forces', arrived; he came sleek and
fresh from the bath (for so is the custom of the Otto-
mans when they start upon a journey), and was carefully accoutred at every point. From his thigh to his
throat he was laden with arms and other implements
of a campaigning life. There is no scarcity of water
along the whole road from Belgrade to Stamboul, but
the habits of our Tatar were formed by his ancestors,
and not by himself, so he took good care to see that
his leathern water-flask was amply charged and properly strapped to the saddle along with his blessed
tchibouque. And now, at last, he has cursed the
Suridgees, in all proper figures of speech, and is ready
for a ride of a thousand miles; but before he comforts
his soul in the marble baths of Stamboul he will be
another and a lesser man—his sense of responsibility,
his too strict abstemiousness, and his restless energy,
disdainful of sleep, will have worn him down to a
fraction of the sleek Moostapha who now leads out
our party from the gates of Belgrade.

The Suridgees are the men employed to lead the
baggage-horses. They are most of them Gipsies.
Their lot is a sad one: they are the last of the human
race, and all the sins of their superiors (including the
horses) can safely be visited on them. But the
wretched look often more picturesque than their
betters; and though all the world despise these poor
Suridgees, their tawny skins and their grisly beards
will gain them honourable standing in the foreground

of a landscape. We had a couple of these fellows
with us, each leading a baggage-horse, to the tail of
which last another baggage-horse was attached. There
was a world of trouble in pursuading the stiff angular
portmanteaus of Europe to adapt themselves to their
new condition, and sit quietly on pack-saddles, but all
was right at last, and it gladdened my eyes to see our
little troop file off through the winding lanes of the
city, and show down brightly in the plain beneath:
the one of our party most out of keeping with the
rest of the scene was Methley's Yorkshire servant, who
always rode doggedly on in his pantry jacket, looking
out for 'gentlemen's seats'.

Methley and I had English saddles, but I think we
should have done just as well (I should certainly have
seen more of the country) if we had adopted saddles
like that of our Tatar, who towered so loftily over the
scraggy little beast that carried him. In taking
thought for the East, whilst in England, I had made
one capital hit which you must not forget—I had
brought with me a pair of common spurs; these were
a great comfort to me throughout my horseback
travels, by keeping up the cheerfulness of the many
unhappy nags that I had to bestride: the angle of
the oriental stirrup is a very poor substitute for spurs.

The Ottoman horseman, raised by his saddle to a
great height above the humble level of the back that
he bestrides, and using a very sharp bit, is able to lift
the crest of his nag, and force him into a strangely
fast shuffling walk, the orthodox pace for the journey.
My comrade and I, using English saddles, could not
easily keep our beasts up to this peculiar amble:
besides, we thought it a bore to be *followed* by our
attendants for a thousand miles, and we generally,
therefore, did duty as the rear guard of our 'grand
army': we used to walk our horses till the party in

front had got into the distance, and then retrieve the
lost ground by a gallop.

We had ridden on for some two or three hours—the
stir and bustle of our commencing journey had ceased
—the liveliness of our little troop had worn off with the
declining day, and the night closed in as we entered
the great Servian forest.   Through this our road was
to last for more than a hundred miles.   Endless and
endless now on either side the tall oaks closed in their
ranks, and stood gloomily lowering over us, as grim
as an army of giants with a thousand years' pay in
arrear.   One strived, with listening ear, to catch some
tidings of that Forest World within—some stirring of
beasts, some night bird's scream ; but all was quite
hushed, except the voice of the cicalas that peopled
every bough, and filled the depths of the forest
through and through with one same hum everlasting
—more stilling than very silence.

At first our way was in darkness, but after a while
the moon got up, and touched the glittering arms and
tawny faces of our men with light so pale and mystic,
that the watchful Tatar felt bound to look out for
Demons, and take proper means for keeping them off :
forthwith he determined that the duty of frightening
away our ghostly enemies (like every other troublesome work) should fall upon the poor Suridgees ;
they accordingly lifted up their voices, and burst upon
the dreaded stillness of the forest with shrieks and
dismal howls.   These precautions were kept up inces-
santly, and were followed by the most complete
success, for not one demon came near us.

Long before midnight we reached the hamlet in
which we were to rest for the night ; it was made up
of about a dozen clay huts standing upon a small
tract of ground hardly won from the forest.   The
peasants living there spoke a Slavonic dialect, and

Mysseri's knowledge of the Russian tongue enabled him to talk with them freely. We took up our quarters in a square room with white walls and an earthen floor, quite bare of furniture and utterly void of women. They told us, however, that these Servian villagers lived in happy abundance, but that they were careful to conceal their riches, as well as their wives.

The burdens unstrapped from the pack-saddles very quickly furnished our den : a couple of quilts spread upon the floor with a carpet bag at the head of each, became capital sofas—portmanteaus, and hat-boxes, and writing-cases, and books, and maps, and gleaming arms, soon lay strewed around us in pleasant confusion. Mysseri's canteen, too, began to yield up its treasures, but we relied upon finding some provisions in the village. At first the natives declared that their hens were mere old maids, and all their cows unmarried ; but our Tatar swore such a grand sonorous oath, and fingered the hilt of his yataghan with such persuasive touch, that the land soon flowed with milk, and mountains of eggs arose.

And soon there was tea before us, with all its welcome fragrance ; and as we reclined on the floor we found that a portmanteau was just the right height for a table ; the duty of candlesticks was ably performed by a couple of intelligent natives ; the rest of the villagers stood by the open door-way at the lower end of the room, and watched our banquet with grave and devout attention.

The first night of your first campaign (though you be but a mere peaceful campaigner) is a glorious time in your life. It is so sweet to find oneself free from the stale civilization of Europe ! Oh my dear ally, when first you spread your carpet in the midst of these eastern scenes, do think for a moment of those your fellow-creatures that dwell in squares, and streets,

and even (for such is the fate of many!) in actual
country houses; think of the people that are 'presenting their compliments', and 'requesting the
honour', and 'much regretting',—of those that are
pinioned at dinner tables, or stuck up in ball-rooms,
or cruelly planted in pews—ay, think of these, and so
remembering how many poor devils are living in a
state of utter respectability, you will glory the more
in your delightful escape.

But, with all its charms, a mud floor, (like a mercenary match) does certainly promote early rising.
Long before day-break we were up, and had breakfasted; afterwards there was nearly a whole tedious
hour to endure, whilst the horses were laden by torch-
light; but this had an end, and then our day's journey
began. Cloaked, and sombre, at first we made our
sullen way through the darkness with scarcely one
barter of words, but soon the genial morn burst down
from Heaven, and stirred the blood so gladly through
our veins that the very Suridgees, with all their
troubles, could now look up for an instant, and almost
seem to believe in the temporary goodness of God.

The actual movement from one place to another, in
Europeanised countries, is a process so temporary—it
occupies, I mean, so small a proportion of the traveller's
entire time, that his mind remains unsettled so long
as the wheels are going; he may be alive enough
to external objects of interest, and to the crowding
ideas which are often invited by the excitement of a
changing scene, but he is still conscious of being in a
provisional state, and his mind is for ever recurring
to the expected end of his journey; his ordinary ways
of thought have been interrupted, and before any new
mental habits can be formed he is quietly fixed in his
hotel. It will be otherwise with you when you journey
in the East. Day after day, perhaps week after week,

and month after month, your foot is in the stirrup.
To taste the cold breath of the earliest morn, and to
lead or follow your bright cavalcade till sunset through
forests and mountain passes, through valleys and
desolate plains, all this becomes your MODE OF
LIFE, and you ride, eat, drink, and curse the mos-
quitoes as systematically as your friends in England
eat, drink, and sleep. If you are wise, you will not look
upon the long period of time thus occupied in actual
movement, as the mere gulf dividing you from the
end of your journey, but rather as one of those rare
and plastic seasons of your life, from which, perhaps,
in after times, you may love to date the moulding of
your character—that is, your very identity. Once
feel this, and you will soon grow happy and contented
in your saddle home. As for me and my comrade,
however, in this part of our journey we often forgot
Stamboul, forgot all the Ottoman Empire, and only
remembered old times. We went back, loitering on
the banks of the Thames—not grim old Thames, of
' after life ', that washes the Parliament houses, and
drowns despairing girls,—but Thames the ' old Eton
fellow ' that wrestled with us in our boyhood till he
taught us to be stronger than he. We bullied Keate,
and scoffed at Larrey Miller, and Okes; we rode along
loudly laughing, and talked to the grave Servian forest,
as though it were the ' Brocas clump '.

Our pace was commonly very slow, for the baggage-
horses served us for a drag, and kept us to a rate of
little more than five miles in the hour ; but now and
then, and chiefly at night, a spirit of movement would
suddenly animate the whole party ; the baggage-
horses would be teased into a gallop, and when once
this was done, there would be such a banging of portmanteaus, and such convulsions of carpet bags upon
their panting sides, and the Suridgees would follow

them up with such a hurricane of blows, and screams, and curses, that stopping or relaxing was scarcely possible ; then the rest of us would put our horses into a gallop, and so, all shouting cheerily, would hunt and drive the sumpter beasts, like a flock of goats, up hill and down dale, right on to the end of their journey.

The distances between our relays of horses varied greatly ; some were not more than fifteen or twenty miles, but twice, I think, we performed a whole day's journey of more than sixty miles with the same beasts.

When, at last, we came out from the forest, our road lay through scenes like those of an English park. The green sward unfenced, and left to the free pasture of cattle, was dotted with groups of stately trees, and here and there darkened over with larger masses of wood that seemed gathered together for bounding the domain, and shutting out some 'infernal' fellow creature in the shape of a newly made squire : in one or two spots the hanging copses look down upon a lawn below with such sheltering mien, that, seeing the like in England, you would have been tempted almost to ask the name of the spendthrift or the madman who had dared to pull down 'the old hall'.

There are few countries less infested by 'lions' than the provinces on this part of your route: you are not called upon to 'drop a tear' over the tomb of 'the once brilliant' any body, or to pay your 'tribute of respect' to any thing dead or alive ; there are no Servian or Bulgarian Litterateurs with whom it would be positively disgraceful not to form an acquaintance ; you have no staring, no praising to get through : the only public building of any interest that lies on the road is of modern date, but is said to be a good specimen of oriental architecture ; it is of a pyramidi-cal shape, and is made of thirty thousand skulls

contributed by the rebellious Servians in the early
part (I believe) of this century ; I am not at all sure
of my date, but I fancy it was in the year 1806 that
the first skull was laid. I am ashamed to say that, in
the darkness of the early morning, we unknowingly
went by the neighbourhood of this triumph of art,
and so basely got off from admiring 'the simple
grandeur of the architect's conception', and 'the
exquisite beauty of the fretwork'.

There being no 'lions', we ought, at least, to have
met with a few perils, but the only robbers we saw
anything of had been long since dead and gone ;
the poor fellows had been impaled upon high poles,
and so propped up by the transverse spokes beneath
them, that their skeletons, clothed with some white,
wax-like remains of flesh, still sat lolling in the
sunshine, and listlessly stared without eyes.

One day it seemed to me that our path was a little
more rugged than usual, and I found that I was
deserving for myself the title of Sabalkansky, or
'Transcender of the Balcan'. The truth is, that, as
a military barrier, the Balcan is a fabulous mountain ;
such seems to be the view of Major Keppell, who
looked on it towards the East with the eye of a
soldier ; and certainly in the Sophia pass there is no
narrow defile, and no ascent sufficiently difficult to
stop, or delay for a long time, a train of siege artillery.

Before we reached Adrianople, Methley had been
seized with we knew not what ailment, and when we
had taken up our quarters in the city he was cast to
the very earth by sickness. Adrianople enjoyed an
English Consul, and I felt sure that, in Eastern phrase,
his house would cease to be his house, and would
become the house of my sick comrade : I should have
judged rightly under ordinary circumstances, but the
levelling plague was abroad, and the dread of it had

dominion over the consular mind. So now (whether
dying or not, one could hardly tell,) upon a quilt
stretched out along the floor, there lay the best hope
of an ancient line, without the material aids to comfort of even the humblest sort, and (sad to say) without
the consolation of a friend, or even a comrade worth
having. I have a notion that tenderness and pity are
affections occasioned in some measure by living within
doors ; certainly, at the time I speak of, the open-air
life which I had been leading, or the wayfaring hardships of the journey, had so strangely blunted me,
that I felt intolerant of illness, and looked down upon
my companion, as if the poor fellow, in falling ill, had
betrayed a want of spirit : I entertained, too, a most
absurd idea—an idea that his illness was partly
affected. You see that I have made a confession :
this I hope—that I may hereafter look charitably
upon the hard, savage acts of peasants, and the
cruelties of a 'brutal' soldiery. God knows that I
strived to melt myself into common charity, and to
put on a gentleness which I could not feel ; but this
attempt did not cheat the keenness of the sufferer ; he
could not have felt the less deserted, because that I
was with him.

We called to aid a solemn Armenian (I think he
was), half soothsayer, half hakim or doctor, who, all
the while counting his beads, fixed his eyes steadily
upon the patient, and then suddenly dealt him a
violent blow on the chest. Methley bravely dissembled
his pain, for he fancied that the blow was meant to
try whether or not the plague were on him.

Here was really a sad embarrassment—no bed—
nothing to offer the invalid in the shape of food, save
a piece of thin, tough, flexible, drab-coloured cloth,
made of flour and mill-stones in equal proportions,
and called by the name of 'bread' ; then the patient,

of course, had no 'confidence in his medical man';
and, on the whole, the best chance of saving my comrade seemed to lie in taking him out of the reach of
his doctor, and bearing him away to the neighbourhood of some more genial consul. But how was this
to be done ? Methley was much too ill to be kept in
his saddle, and wheel carriages, as means of travelling,
were unknown. There is, however, such a thing as an
' Araba ', a vehicle drawn by oxen, in which the wives
of a rich man are sometimes dragged four or five miles
over the grass by way of recreation. The carriage is
rudely framed, but you recognize in the simple grandeur of its design a likeness to things majestic ; in
short, if your carpenter's son were to make a ' Lord
Mayor's coach ' for little Amy, he would build a
carriage very much in the style of a Turkish Araba.
No one had ever heard of horses being used for drawing a carriage in this part of the world, but Necessity
is the mother of Innovation as well as of Invention. I
was fully justified, I think, in arguing that there were
numerous instances of horses being used for that purpose in our own country—that the laws of nature are
uniform in their operation over all the world (except
Ireland) — that that which was true in Piccadilly, must
be true in Adrianople—that the matter could not
fairly be treated as an ecclesiastical question, for that
the circumstance of Methley's going on to Stamboul
in an Araba drawn by horses, when calmly and dis-
passionately considered, would appear to be perfectly
consistent with the maintenance of the Mahometan
religion, as by law established. Thus poor, dear,
patient Reason would have fought her slow battle
against Asiatic prejudice, and I am convinced that
she would have established the possibility (and perhaps
even the propriety) of harnessing horses in a hundred
and fifty years ; but, in the meantime, Mysseri, well

seconded by our Tatar, contrived to bring the controversy to a premature end, by having the horses put to.

It was a sore thing for me to see my poor comrade
brought to this, for young though he was, he was a
veteran in travel : when scarcely yet of age, he had
invaded India, from the frontiers of Russia, and that
so swiftly, that, measuring by the time of his flight,
the broad dominions of the King of Kings were
shrivelled up to a dukedom ; and now, poor fellow,
he was to be poked into an Araba, like a Georgian
girl ! He suffered greatly, for there were no springs
for the carriage, and no road for the wheels, and so the
concern jolted on over the open country, with such
twists, and jerks, and jumps, as might almost dis-
locate the supple tongue of Satan.

All day the patient kept himself shut up within the
lattice-work of the Araba, and I could hardly know
how he was faring until the end of the day's journey,
when I found that he was not worse, and was buoyed
up with the hope of some day reaching Constantinople.

I was always conning over my maps, and fancied
that I knew pretty well my line ; but after Adrianople
I had made more southing than I knew for, and it
was with unbelieving wonder and delight that I came
suddenly upon the shore of the sea : a little while, and
its gentle billows were flowing beneath the hoofs of my
beast.   But the hearing of the ripple was not enough
communion,—and the seeing of the blue Propontis
was not to know and possess it—I must needs plunge
into its depth, and quench my longing love in the
palpable waves ; and so when old Moostapha (defender
against demons) looked round for his charge, he saw
with horror and dismay, that he, for whose life his own
life stood pledged, was possessed of some devil who
had driven him down into the sea—that the rider and
the steed had vanished from earth, and that out

among the waves was the gasping crest of a post
horse, and the ghostly head of the Englishman moving
upon the face of the waters.

We started very early indeed, on the last day of
our journey, and, from the moment of being off, until
we gained the shelter of the imperial walls, we were
struggling face to face with an icy storm that swept
right down from the steppes of Tartary, keen, fierce,
and steady as a northern conqueror. Methley's
servant, who was the greatest sufferer, kept his saddle
until we reached Stamboul, but was then found to be
quite benumbed in limbs, and his brain was so much
affected, that when he was lifted from his horse, he
fell away in a state of unconsciousness, the first stage
of a dangerous fever.

Our Tatar, worn down by care and toil, and carrying seven heavens full of water in his manifold jackets
and shawls, was a mere weak and vapid dilution of the
sleek Moostapha, who, scarce more than one fortnight
before, came out like a bridegroom from his chamber,
to take the command of our party.

Mysseri seemed somewhat over-wearied, but he had
lost none of his strangely quiet energy ; he wore a
grave look, however, for he now had learnt that the
plague was prevailing at Constantinople, and he was
fearing that our two sick men, and the miserable looks
of our whole party, might make us unwelcome at Pera.

We crossed the Golden Horn in a caïque. As soon
as we had landed, some woe-begone looking fellows
were got together, and laden with our baggage. Then
on we went, dripping and sloshing, and looking very
like men that had been turned back by the Royal
Humane Society for being incurably drowned. Sup-
porting our sick, we climbed up shelving steps, and
threaded many windings, and at last came up into the
main street of Pera, humbly hoping that we might

not be judged guilty of the plague, and so be cast back with horror from the doors of the shuddering Christians.

Such was the condition of the little troop, which fifteen days before had filed away so gaily from the gates of Belgrade. A couple of fevers and a north-easterly storm had thoroughly spoiled our looks.

The interest of Mysseri with the house of Giuseppini was too powerful to be denied, and at once, though not without fear and trembling, we were admitted as guests.

CHAPTER III

CONSTANTINOPLE

EVEN if we don't take a part in the chant about 'Mosques and Minarets', we can still yield praises to Stamboul. We can chant about the harbour; we can say and sing that nowhere else does the sea come so home to a city: there are no pebbly shores—no sand bars—no slimy river-beds—no black canals—no locks nor docks to divide the very heart of the place from the deep waters. If being in the noisiest mart of Stamboul, you would stroll to the quiet side of the way amidst those cypresses opposite, you will cross the fathomless Bosphorus; if you would go from your hotel to the Bazaars, you must pass by the bright blue pathway of the Golden Horn, that can carry a thousand sail of the line. You are accustomed to the gondolas that glide among the palaces of St. Mark, but here, at Stamboul, it is a hundred-and-twenty-gun ship that meets you in the street. Venice strains out from the steadfast land, and in old times would send forth the Chief of the State to woo and wed the re-

luctant sea ; but the stormy bride of the Doge is the
bowing slave of the Sultan—she comes to his feet
with the treasures of the world—she bears him from
palace to palace—by some unfailing witchcraft, she
entices the breezes to follow her,[1] and fan the pale
cheek of her lord—she lifts his armed navies to the
very gates of his garden—she watches the walls of his
Serail—she stifles the intrigues of his Ministers—she
quiets the scandals of his Court— she extinguishes his
rivals and hushes his naughty wives all one by one.
So vast are the wonders of the Deep !

All the while that I stayed at Constantinople the
plague was prevailing, but not with any violence ; its
presence, however, lent a mysterious and exciting,
though not very pleasant, interest to my first knowledge of a great oriental city ; it gave tone and colour
to all I saw and all I felt—a tone and a colour sombre
enough, but true, and well befitting the dreary monuments of past power and splendour.   With all that is
most truly oriental in its character the plague is associated : it dwells with the faithful in the holiest quarters of their city.   The coats and the hats of Pera are
held to be nearly as innocent of infection as they are
ugly in shape and fashion ; but the rich furs and the
costly shawls, the broidered slippers and the gold-
laden saddle-cloths—the fragrance of burning aloes
and the rich aroma of patchouli—these are the signs
that mark the familiar home of plague.   You go out
from your queenly London—the centre of the greatest
and strongest amongst all earthly dominions—you go
out thence, and travel on to the capital of an Eastern
Prince—you find but a waning power, and a faded
splendour, that inclines you to laugh and mock ; but

[1] There is almost always a breeze either from the Marmora,
or from the Black Sea, that passes along the course of the
Bosphorus.

let the infernal Angel of Plague be at hand, and he, more mighty than armies, more terrible than Suleyman in his glory, can restore such pomp and majesty to the weakness of the imperial city, that if, *when HE is there*, you must still go prying amongst the shades of this dead empire, at least you will tread the path with seemly reverence and awe.

It is the firm faith of almost all the Europeans living in the East, that plague is conveyed by the touch of infected substances, and that the deadly atoms especially lurk in all kinds of clothes and furs : it is held safer to breathe the same air with a man sick of the plague, and even to come into contact with his skin, than to be touched by the smallest particle of woollen or of thread which may have been within the reach of possible infection. If this be a right notion, the spread of the malady must be materially aided by the observance of a custom prevailing amongst the people of Stamboul. It is this : when an Osmanlee dies, one of his dresses is cut up, and a small piece of it is sent to each of his friends as a memorial of the departed—a fatal present, according to the opinion of the Franks, for it too often forces the living not merely to remember the dead man, but to follow and bear him company.

The Europeans during the prevalence of the plague, if they are forced to venture into the streets, will carefully avoid the touch of every human being whom they pass : their conduct in this respect shows them strongly in contrast with the 'true believers'. The Moslem stalks on serenely, as though he were under the eye of his God, and were 'equal to either fate'. The Franks go crouching, and slinking from death, and some (those chiefly of French extraction) will fondly strive to fence out Destiny with shining capes of oilskin !

For some time you may manage by great care to thread your way through the streets of Stamboul without incurring contact; for the Turks, though scornful of the terrors felt by the Franks, are generally very courteous in yielding to that which they hold to be a useless and impious precaution, and will let you pass safe, if they can. It is impossible, however, that your immunity can last for any length of time, if you move about much through the narrow streets and lanes of a crowded city.

As for me, I soon got 'compromised'. After one day of rest the prayers of my hostess began to lose their power of keeping me from the pestilent side of the Golden Horn. Faithfully promising to shun the touch of all imaginable substances, however enticing, I set off very cautiously, and held my way uncompromised till I reached the water's edge; but before my caïque was quite ready, some rueful-looking fellows came rapidly shambling down the steps with a plague-stricken corpse, which they were going to bury amongst the faithful on the other side of the water. I contrived to be so much in the way of this brisk funeral, that I was not only touched by the men bearing the body, but also, I believe, by the foot of the dead man, as it hung lolling out of the bier. The accident gave me such a strong interest in denying the soundness of the contagion theory that I did in fact deny and repudiate it altogether: and from that time, acting upon my own convenient view of the matter, I went wherever I chose, without taking any serious pains to avoid a touch. It seems to me now very likely the Europeans are right, and that the plague may be really conveyed by contagion; but during the whole time of my remaining in the East my views on this subject more nearly approached to those of the fatalists; and so, when afterwards the

plague of Egypt came dealing his blows around me,
I was able to live amongst the dying without that
alarm and anxiety which would inevitably have
pressed upon my mind, if I had allowed myself to
believe that every passing touch was really a probable
death-stroke.

And perhaps as you make your difficult way
through a steep and narrow alley, shut in between
blank walls, and little frequented by passers, you
meet one of those coffin-shaped bundles of white
linen that implies an Ottoman lady. Painfully
struggling against the obstacles to progression
interposed by the many folds of her clumsy drapery,
by her big mud boots, and especially by her two
pairs of slippers, she works her way on full awkwardly enough, but yet there is something of
womanly consciousness in the very labour and effort
with which she tugs and lifts the burden of her
charms: she is closely followed by her women slaves.
Of her very self you see nothing, except the dark,
luminous eyes that stare against your face, and the
tips of the painted fingers depending like rosebuds
from out of the blank bastions of the fortress. She
turns, and turns again, and carefully glances around
her on all sides, to see that she is safe from the eyes
of Mussulmans, and then suddenly withdrawing the
yashmak [1], she shines upon your heart and soul with
all the pomp and might of her beauty. And this,
it is not the light, changeful grace that leaves you
to doubt whether you have fallen in love with a
body, or only a soul; it is the beauty that dwells
secure in the perfectness of hard, downright outlines,

---

[1] The yashmak, you know, is not a mere semi-transparent
veil, but rather a good substantial petticoat applied to the
face; it thoroughly conceals all the features except the eyes;
the way of withdrawing it is by pulling it down.

and in the glow of generous colour. There is fire, though, too—high courage, and fire enough in the untamed mind, or spirit, or whatever it is which drives the breath of pride through those scarcely parted lips.

You smile at pretty women—you turn pale before the beauty that is great enough to have dominion over you. She sees, and exults in your giddiness; she sees and smiles; then, presently, with a sudden movement, she lays her blushing fingers upon your arm, and cries out 'Yumourdjak!' (Plague! meaning, 'there is a present of the plague for you!') This is her notion of a witticism: it is a very old piece of fun, no doubt—quite an oriental Joe Miller; but the Turks are fondly attached not only to the institutions, but also to the jokes of their ancestors; so, the lady's silvery laugh rings joyously in your ears, and the mirth of her women is boisterous and fresh, as though the bright idea of giving the plague to a Christian had newly lit upon the earth.

Methley began to rally very soon after we had reached Constantinople, but there seemed at first to be no chance of his regaining strength enough for travelling during the winter; and I determined to stay with my comrade until he had quite recovered; so I bought me a horse and a 'pipe of tranquillity' [1], and took a Turkish phrase-master. I troubled myself a great deal with the Turkish tongue, and gained at last some knowledge of its structure: it is enriched, perhaps overladen, with Persian and Arabic words imported into the language, chiefly for the purpose of representing sentiments, and religious dogmas and

[1] The 'pipe of tranquillity' is a tchibouque too long to be conveniently carried on a journey: the possession of it therefore implies that its owner is stationary, or at all events that he is enjoying a long repose from travel.

terms of art and luxury, entirely unknown to the Tatar ancestors of the present Osmanlees; but the body and the spirit of the old tongue are yet alive, and the smooth words of the shopkeeper at Constantinople can still carry understanding to the ears of the untamed millions who rove over the plains of Northern Asia. The structure of the language, especially in its more lengthy sentences, is very like to the Latin; the subject matters are slowly and patiently enumerated, without disclosing the purpose of the speaker until he reaches the end of his sentence, and then at last there comes the clenching word which gives a meaning and connection to all that has gone before. If you listen at all to speaking of this kind your attention, rather than be suffered to flag, must grow more and more lively as the phrase marches on.

The Osmanlees speak well. In countries civilized according to the European plan, the work of trying to persuade tribunals is almost all performed by a set of men, who seldom do anything else; but in Turkey, this division of labour has never taken place, and every man is his own advocate. The importance of the rhetorical art is immense, for a bad speech may endanger the property of the speaker as well as the soles of his feet, and the free enjoyment of his throat. So it results that most of the Turks whom one sees have a lawyer-like habit of speaking connectedly and at length. Even the treaties continually going on at the bazaar for the buying and selling of the merest trifles are carried on by speechifying, rather than by mere colloquies, and the eternal uncertainty as to the market value of things in constant sale gives room enough for discussion. The seller is for ever demanding a price immensely beyond that for which he sells at last, and so occasions un-

speakable disgust in many Englishmen, who cannot
see why an honest dealer should ask more for his
goods than he will really take:—the truth is,
however, that an ordinary tradesman of Constantinople has no other way of finding out the fair
market value of his property. His difficulty is
easily shown by comparing the mechanism of the
commercial system in Turkey with that of our own
people. In England, or in any other great mercantile country, the bulk of the things bought and
sold goes through the hands of a wholesale dealer,
and it is he who higgles and bargains with an entire
nation of purchasers by entering into treaty with
retail sellers. The labour of making a few large
contracts is sufficient to give a clue for finding the
fair market value of the goods sold throughout the
country; but in Turkey, from the primitive habits
of the people, and partly from the absence of great
capital and great credit, the important merchant,
the warehouseman, the wholesale dealer, the retail
dealer, and the shopman, are all one person. Old
Moostapha, or Abdallah, or Hadgi Mohamed waddles
up from the water's edge with a small packet of
merchandize, which he has bought out of a Greek
brigantine, and when at last he has reached his nook
in the bazaar, he puts his goods *before* the counter,
and himself *upon* it; then laying fire to his tchibouque he 'sits in permanence', and patiently waits
to obtain 'the best price that can be got in an open
market'. This is his fair right as a seller, but he
has no means of finding out what that best price is,
except by actual experiment. He cannot know the
intensity of the demand, or the abundance of the
supply otherwise than by the offers which may
be made for his little bundle of goods; so he
begins by asking a perfectly hopeless price, and

then descends the ladder until he meets a purchaser,
for ever

> striving to attain
> By shadowing out the unattainable.

This is the struggle which creates the continual
occasion for debate. The vendor perceiving that the
unfolded merchandise has caught the eye of a possible
purchaser, commences his opening speech. He covers
his bristling broadcloths and his meagre silks with the
golden broidery of oriental praises, and, as he talks,
along with the slow and graceful waving of his arms,
he lifts his undulating periods, upholds, and poises
them well till they have gathered their weight and
their strength, and then hurls them bodily forward,
with grave, momentous swing. The possible purchaser
listens to the whole speech with deep and serious
attention ; but when it is over, *his* turn arrives ; he
elaborately endeavours to show why he ought not to
buy the things at a price twenty times larger than
their value : bystanders attracted to the debate take
a part in it as independent members—the vendor is
heard in reply, and coming down with his price,
furnishes the materials for a new debate. Sometimes,
however, the dealer, if he is a very pious Mussulman,
and sufficiently rich to hold back his ware, will take
a more dignified part, maintaining a kind of judicial
gravity, and receiving the applicants who come to his
stall as if they were rather suitors than customers.
He will quietly hear to the end some long speech that
concludes with an offer, and will answer it all with
that bold monosyllable ('Yok') which means distinctly 'No'.

I caught one glimpse of the old Heathen world.
My habits of studying military subjects had been
hardening my heart against Poetry. For ever staring

at the flames of battle, I had blinded myself to the
lesser and finer lights that are shed from the imagina-
tions of men.   In my reading at this time, I delighted
to follow from out of Arabian sands the feet of the
armed believers, and to stand in the broad manifest
storm-tract of Tatar devastation; and thus, though
surrounded at Constantinople by scenes of much
interest to the 'classical scholar', I had cast aside
their associations like an old Greek grammar, and
turned my face to the 'shining Orient', forgetful of
old Greece, and all the pure wealth she left to this
matter-of-fact ridden world.   But it happened to me
one day to mount the high grounds overhanging the
streets of Pera.   I sated my eyes with the pomps of
the city and its crowded waters, and then I looked
over where Scutari lay half-veiled in her mournful
cypresses.   I looked yet farther, and higher, and saw
in the heavens a silvery cloud that stood fast and
still against the breeze: it was pure and dazzling
white as might be the veil of Cytherea, yet touched
with such fire, as though from beneath the loving eyes
of an immortal were shining through and through.
I knew the bearing, but had enormously misjudged
its distance and underrated its height, and so it was
as a sign and a testimony—almost as a call from the
neglected gods, that now I saw and acknowledged the
snowy crown of the Mysian Olympus!

CHAPTER IV

THE TROAD

METHLEY recovered almost suddenly, and we determined to go through the Troad together.

My comrade was a capital Grecian: it is true that
his singular mind so ordered and disposed his classic

lore as to impress it with something of an original and barbarous character—with an almost Gothic quaintness, more properly belonging to a rich native ballad than to the poetry of Hellas: there was a certain impropriety in his knowing so much Greek—an unfitness in the idea of marble fauns, and satyrs, and even Olympian gods, lugged in under the oaken roof and the painted light of an odd old Norman hall. But Methley, abounding in Homer, really loved him (as I believe) in all truth, without whim or fancy; moreover, he had a good deal of the practical sagacity

of a Yorkshireman hippodamoio,

and this enabled him to apply his knowledge with much more tact than is usually shown by people so learned as he.

I, too, loved Homer, but not with a scholar's love. The most humble and pious among women, was yet so proud a mother that she could teach her first-born son, no Watt's hymns—no collects for the day; she could teach him in earliest childhood, no less than this—to find a home in his saddle, and love old Homer, and all that Homer sung. True it is, that the Greek was ingeniously rendered into English—the English of Pope, but not even a mesh like that can screen an earnest child from the fire of Homer's battles.

I pored over the Odyssey as over a story-book, hoping and fearing for the hero whom yet I partly scorned. But the Iliad—line by line, I clasped it to my brain with reverence as well as with love. As an old woman deeply trustful sits reading her Bible because of the world to come, so, as though it would fit me for the coming strife of this temporal world, I read, and read the Iliad. Even outwardly it was not like other books; it was throned in towering folios. There

was a preface or dissertation printed in type still
more majestic than the rest of the book; this I read,
but not till my enthusiasm for the Iliad had already
run high. The writer compiling the opinions of
many men, and chiefly of the ancients, set forth,
I know not how quaintly, that the Iliad was all in
all to the human race—that it was history—poetry
—revelation—that the works of men's hands were
folly and vanity, and would pass away like the
dreams of a child, but that the kingdom of Homer
would endure for ever and ever.

I assented with all my soul. I read, and still read;
I came to know Homer. A learned commentator
knows something of the Greeks, in the same sense as
an oil and colour man may be said to know something
of painting; but take an untamed child, and leave
him alone for twelve months with any translation of
Homer, and he will be nearer by twenty centuries to
the spirit of old Greece: *he* does not stop in the
ninth year of the siege to admire this or that group
of words—*he* has no books in his tent, but he shares
in vital counsels with the 'King of men', and knows
the inmost souls of the impending gods; how profanely he exults over the powers divine when they
are taught to dread the prowess of mortals! and
most of all how he rejoices when the God of War
flies howling from the spear of Diomed, and mounts
into heaven for safety! Then the beautiful episode
of the 6th book: the way to feel this is not to go
casting about, and learning from pastors and masters
how best to admire it: the impatient child is not
grubbing for beauties, but pushing the siege; the
women vex him with their delays and their talking—
the mention of the nurse is personal, and little
sympathy has he for the child that is young enough
to be frightened at the nodding plume of a helmet;

but all the while that he thus chafes at the pausing of the action, the strong vertical light of Homer's poetry is blazing so full upon the people and things of the Iliad, that soon to the eyes of the child they grow familiar as his mother's shawl; yet of this great gain he is unconscious, and on he goes, vengefully thirsting for the best blood of Troy, and never remitting his fierceness, till almost suddenly it is changed for sorrow—the new and generous sorrow that he learns to feel, when the noblest of all his foes lies sadly dying at the Scaean gate.

Heroic days are these, but the dark ages of school-boy life come closing over them. I suppose it's all right in the end, yet, at first sight, it does seem a sad intellectual fall from your mother's dressing-room to a buzzing school. You feel so keenly the delights of early knowledge! you form strange mystic friendships with the mere names of mountains, and seas, and continents, and mighty rivers; you learn the ways of the planets, and transcend their narrow limits, and ask for the end of space; you vex the electric cylinder till it yields you, for your toy to play with, that subtle fire in which our earth was forged; you know of the nations that have towered high in the world, and the lives of the men who have saved whole empires from oblivion. What more will you ever learn? Yet the dismal change is ordained, and then, thin meagre Latin (the same for every body), with small shreds and patches of Greek, is thrown like a pauper's pall over all your early lore; instead of sweet knowledge, vile, monkish, doggerel grammars, and graduses, dictionaries, and lexicons, and horrible odds and ends of dead languages are given you for your portion, and down you fall, from Roman story to a three-inch scrap of 'Scriptores Romani',—from Greek poetry, down, down to the cold rations of

'Poetae Graeci', cut up by commentators, and served out by schoolmasters!

It was not the recollection of school nor college learning, but the rapturous and earnest reading of my childhood which made me bend forward so longingly to the plains of Troy.

Away from our people and our horses, Methley and I went loitering along, by the willowy banks of a stream that crept in quietness through the low, even plain. There was no stir of weather over-head —no sound of rural labour—no sign of life in the land, but all the earth was dead and still, as though it had lain for thrice a thousand years under the leaden gloom of one unbroken sabbath.

Softly and sadly the poor, dumb, patient stream went winding, and winding along, through its shifting pathway; in some places its waters were parted, and then again, lower down, they would meet once more. I could see that the stream from year to year was finding itself new channels, and flowed no longer in its ancient track, but I knew that the springs which fed it were high on Ida—the springs of Simois and Scamander!

It was coldly, and thanklessly, and with vacant unsatisfied eyes that I watched the slow coming, and the gliding away, of the waters. I tell myself now, as a profane fact, that I did indeed stand by that river (Methley gathered some seeds from the bushes that grew there), but, since that I am away from his banks, 'divine Scamander' has recovered the proper mystery belonging to him as an unseen deity; a kind of indistinctness, like that which belongs to far antiquity, has spread itself over my memory of the winding stream that I saw with these very eyes. One's mind regains in absence that dominion over earthly things which has been shaken by the rude contact; you force yourself hardily into the material presence of a mountain or a river, whose name belongs to poetry and ancient religion, rather than to the external world ; your feelings, wound up and kept ready for some sort of half-expected rapture, are chilled and borne down for the time under all this load of real earth and water, but, let these once pass out of sight, and then again the old fanciful notions are restored, and the mere realities which you have just been looking at are thrown back so far into distance, that the very event of your intrusion upon such scenes begins to look dim and uncertain as though it belonged to mythology.

It is not over the plain before Troy that the river now flows; its waters have edged away far towards the north, since the day that 'divine Scamander' (whom the gods call Xanthus) went down to do battle for Ilion, 'with Mars, and Phoebus, and Latona, and Diana glorying in her arrows, and Venus the lover of smiles'.

And now, when I was vexed at the migration of Scamander, and the total loss or absorption of poor dear Simois, how happily Methley reminded me that Homer himself had warned us of some such changes ! The besiegers in beginning their wall had neglected the hecatombs due to the gods, and so after the fall of Troy, Apollo turned the paths of the rivers that flow from Ida, and sent them flooding over the wall till all the beach was smooth, and free from the unhallowed works of the Greeks. It is true I see now, on looking to the passage, that Neptune, when the work of destruction was done, turned back the rivers to their ancient ways :

$$. \ . \ . \ \pi o \tau a \mu o \dot{v} s \ \delta' \ \ddot{\epsilon} \tau \rho \epsilon \psi \epsilon \ \nu \acute{\epsilon} \epsilon \sigma \theta a \iota$$
$$K \grave{a} \rho \ \dot{\rho} \acute{o} o \nu \ \mathring{\eta} \ \pi \epsilon \rho \ \pi \rho \acute{o} \sigma \theta \epsilon \nu \ \ddot{\iota} \epsilon \nu \ \kappa a \lambda \lambda \acute{\iota} \rho \rho o o \nu \ \ddot{v} \delta \omega \rho,$$

but their old channels, passing through that light, pervious soil, would have been lost in the nine days'

flood, and perhaps the god, when he willed to bring
back the rivers to their ancient beds, may have done
his work but ill: it is easier, they say, to destroy
than it is to restore.

We took to our horses again, and went southward
towards the very plain between Troy and the tents
of the Greeks, but we rode by a line at some distance
from the shore. Whether it was that the lay of the
ground hindered my view towards the sea, or that I
was all intent upon Ida, or whether my mind was in
vacancy, or whether, as is most like, I had strayed
from the Dardan plains, all back to gentle England,
there is now no knowing, nor caring, but it was—not
quite suddenly indeed, but rather, as it were, in the
swelling and falling of a single wave, that the reality
of that very sea-view which had bounded the sight of
the Greeks, now visibly acceded to me, and rolled full
in upon my brain. Conceive how deeply that eternal
coast-line—that fixed horizon—those island rocks,
must have graven their images upon the minds of the
Grecian warriors by the time that they had reached
the ninth year of the siege! conceive the strength and
the fanciful beauty of the speeches with which a whole
army of imagining men must have told their weariness,
and how the sauntering chiefs must have whelmed
that daily, daily scene with their deep Ionian curses!

And now it was that my eyes were greeted with
a delightful surprise. Whilst we were at Constantinople, Methley and I had pored over the map
together; we agreed that whatever may have been
the exact site of Troy, the Grecian camp must have
been nearly opposite to the space betwixt the islands
of Imbros and Tenedos:

Μεσσηγὺς Τενέδοιο καὶ Ἴμβρου παιπαλοέσσης,

but Methley reminded me of a passage in the Iliad

in which Neptune is represented as looking at the scene of action before Ilion from above the island of Samothrace. Now, Samothrace, according to the map, appeared to be not only out of all seeing distance from the Troad, but to be entirely shut out from it by the intervening Imbros, a larger island, which stretches its length right athwart the line of sight from Samothrace to Troy. Piously allowing that the dread Commotor of our globe might have seen all mortal doings, even from the depths of his own cerulean kingdom, I still felt that if a station were to be chosen from which to see the fight, old Homer, so material in his ways of thought, so averse from all haziness and overreaching, would have *meant* to give the god for his station some spot within reach of men's eyes from the plains of Troy. I think that this testing of the poet's words by map and compass may have shaken a little of my faith in the completeness of his knowledge. Well, now I had come; there to the south was Tenedos, and here at my side was Imbros, all right, and according to the map, but aloft over Imbros,—aloft in a far away heaven was Samothrace, the watchtower of Neptune!

So Homer had appointed it, and so it was: the map was correct enough, but could not, like Homer, convey *the whole truth*. Thus vain and false are the mere human surmises and doubts which clash with Homeric writ!

Nobody, whose mind had not been reduced to the most deplorably logical condition, could look upon this beautiful congruity betwixt the Iliad and the material world, and yet bear to suppose that the poet may have learned the features of the coast from mere hearsay; now then, I believed—now I knew that Homer had *passed along here*,—that this vision

of Samothrace over-towering the nearer island was
common to him and to me.

After a journey of some few days by the route of
Adramiti and Pergamo, we reached Smyrna. The
letters which Methley here received obliged him to
return to England.

CHAPTER V

INFIDEL SMYRNA

SMYRNA, or Giaour Izmir, 'Infidel Smyrna', as
the Mussulmans call it, is the main point of commercial contact betwixt Europe and Asia; you are
there surrounded by the people and the confused
customs of many and various nations—you see the
fussy European adopting the East, and calming his
restlessness with the long Turkish 'pipe of tranquillity'—you see Jews offering services, and receiving
blows [1]—on one side you have a fellow whose dress
and beard would give you a good idea of the true
oriental, if it were not for the gobemouche expression
of countenance with which he is swallowing an article
in a French newspaper; and there, just by, is a
genuine Osmanlee, smoking away with all the majesty

---

[1] The Jews of Smyrna are poor, and having little merchandise
of their own to dispose of, they are sadly importunate in offering
their services as intermediaries; their troublesome conduct has
led to the custom of beating them in the open streets. It is
usual for Europeans to carry long sticks with them for the
express purpose of keeping off the chosen people. I always
felt ashamed to strike the poor fellows myself, but I confess to
the amusement with which I witnessed the observance of this
custom by other people. The Jew seldom got hurt much, for
he was always expecting the blow, and was ready to recede
from it the moment it came; one could not help being rather
gratified at seeing him bound away so nimbly with his long
robes floating out in the air, and then again wheel round, and
return with fresh importunities.

of a Sultan; but before you have time to admire sufficiently his tranquil dignity, and his soft Asiatic repose, the poor old fellow is ruthlessly 'run down' by an English midshipman, who has set sail on a Smyrna hack. Such are the incongruities of the 'infidel city', at ordinary times; but when I was there, our friend Carrigaholt had imported himself, and his oddities, as an accession to the other and inferior wonders of Smyrna.

I was sitting alone in my room one day at Constantinople, when I heard Methley approaching my door with shouts of laughter and welcome, and presently I recognized that peculiar cry by which our friend Carrigaholt expresses his emotions; he soon explained to us the final causes by which the Fates had worked out their wonderful purpose of bringing him to Constantinople. He was always, you know, very fond of sailing, but he had got into such sad scrapes (including, I think, a lawsuit) on account of his last yacht, that he took it into his head to have a cruise in a merchant vessel; so he went to Liverpool, and looked through the craft lying ready to sail till he found a smart schooner that perfectly suited his taste: the destination of the vessel was the last thing he thought of, and when he was told that she was bound for Constantinople, he merely assented to that as a part of the arrangement to which he had no objection. As soon as the vessel had sailed, the hapless passenger discovered that his skipper carried on board an enormous wife with an inquiring mind, and an irresistible tendency to impart her opinions. She looked upon her guest as upon a piece of waste intellect that ought to be carefully tilled. She tilled him accordingly. If the Dons of Oxford could have seen poor Carrigaholt thus absolutely 'attending lectures' in the bay of

Biscay, they would surely have thought him sufficiently punished for all the wrongs he did them,
whilst he was preparing himself under their care
for the other and more boisterous University. The
voyage did not last more than six or eight weeks,
and the philosophy inflicted on Carrigaholt was not
entirely fatal to him; certainly he was somewhat
emaciated, and for aught I know, he may have
subscribed too largely to the 'Feminine-right-of-
reason Society'; but it did not appear that his
health had been seriously affected. There was a
scheme on foot, it would seem, for taking the passenger back to England in the same schooner—a
scheme, in fact, for keeping him perpetually afloat,
and perpetually saturated with arguments; but when
Carrigaholt found himself a'shore, and remembered
that the skipperina (who had imprudently remained
on board) was not there to enforce her suggestions,
he was open to the hints of his servant (a very
sharp fellow), who arranged a plan for escaping,
and finally brought off his master to Giuseppini's
Hotel.

Our friend afterwards went by sea to Smyrna, and
there he now was in his glory. He had a good, or
at all events a gentleman-like judgement in matters
of taste, and as his great object was to surround
himself with all that his fancy could dictate, he
lived in a state of perpetual negotiation; he was for
ever on the point of purchasing, not only the material
productions of the place, but all sorts of such fine
ware as 'intelligence', 'fidelity', and so on. He
was most curious, however, as the purchaser of the
'affections'. Sometimes he would imagine that he
had a marital aptitude, and his fancy would sketch
a graceful picture in which he appeared reclining on
a divan, with a beautiful Greek woman fondly couched

at his feet, and soothing him with the witchery of
her guitar; having satisfied himself with the ideal
picture thus created, he would pass into action ; the
guitar he would buy instantly, and would give such
intimations of his wish to be wedded to a Greek as
could not fail to produce great excitement in the
families of the beautiful Smyrniotes. Then, again
(and just in time, perhaps, to save him from the
yoke), his dream would pass away, and another
would come in its stead ; he would suddenly feel the
yearnings of a father's love, and willing by force of
gold to transcend all natural preliminaries, he would
issue instructions for the purchase of some dutiful
child that could be warranted to love him as a parent.
Then at another time he would be convinced that
the attachment of menials might satisfy the longings
of his affectionate heart, and thereupon he would
give orders to his slave-merchant for something in
the way of eternal fidelity. You may well imagine
that this anxiety of Carrigaholt to purchase, not
only the scenery, but the many dramatis personae
belonging to his dreams, with all their goodness and
graces complete, necessarily gave an immense stimulus
to the trade and intrigue of Smyrna, and created a
demand for human virtues which the moral resources
of the place were totally inadequate to supply.
Every day after breakfast, this lover of the Good
and the Beautiful held a levee : in his ante-room
there would be not only the sellers of pipes, and
slippers, and shawls, and such like Oriental merchandise—not only embroiderers and cunning work-
men patiently striving to realize his visions of
Albanian dresses—not only the servants offering for
places, and the slave-dealer tendering his sable ware,
but there would be the Greek master waiting to
teach his pupil the grammar of the soft Ionian

tongue in which he was to delight the wife of his
imagination, and the music-master who was to teach
him some sweet replies to the anticipated tones
of the fancied guitar; and then, above all, and
proudly eminent with undisputed preference of entrée,
and fraught with the mysterious tidings on which
the realization of the whole dream might depend,
was the mysterious match-maker[1], enticing, and
postponing the suitor, yet ever keeping alive in
his soul the love of that pictured virtue, whose
beauty (unseen by eyes) was half revealed to the
imagination.

You would have thought that this practical dreaming must have soon brought Carrigaholt to a bad end,
but he was in much less danger than might be supposed: for besides that the new visions of happiness
almost always came in time to counteract the fatal
completion of the preceding scheme, his high breed-
ing and his delicately sensitive taste almost always
befriended him at times when he was left without
any other protection; and the efficacy of these
qualities in keeping a man out of harm's way is
really immense. In all baseness and imposture there
is a coarse, vulgar spirit, which, however artfully
concealed for a time, must sooner or later show itself
in some little circumstance sufficiently plain to
occasion an instant jar upon the mind of those
whose taste is lively and true; to such men a shock
of this kind, disclosing the *ugliness* of a cheat,
is more effectively convincing than any mere proofs
could be.

Thus guarded from isle to isle, and through Greece
and through Albania, this practical Plato with a
purse in his hand, carried on his mad chase after the

[1] Marriages in the East are arranged by professed match-
makers; many of these, I believe, are Jewesses.

Good and the Beautiful, and yet returned in safety to
his home. But now, poor fellow, the lowly grave
that is the end of men's romantic hopes has closed
over all his rich fancies, and all his high aspira-
tions; he is utterly married! No more hope, no
more change for him—no more relays—he must
go on Vetturiniwise to the appointed end of his
journey.

Smyrna, I think, may be called the chief town and
capital of that Grecian race against which you will
be cautioned so carefully as soon as you touch the
Levant. You will say that I ought not to confound
as one people the Greeks living under a constitutional
government with the unfortunate Rayahs who 'groan
under the Turkish yoke', but I can't see that political
events have hitherto produced any strongly marked
difference of character. If I could venture to rely
(this I feel that I cannot at all do) upon my own
observation, I should tell you that there were more
heartiness and strength in the Greeks of the Ottoman
Empire than in those of the new kingdom: the truth
is that there is a greater field for commercial enterprise, and even for Greek ambition, under the
Ottoman sceptre than is to be found in the dominions
of Otho. Indeed the people, by their frequent migrations from the limits of the constitutional kingdom,
to the territories of the Porte, seem to show, that, on
the whole, they prefer 'groaning under the Turkish
yoke', to the honour of 'being the only true source
of legitimate power', in their own land.

For myself I love the race; in spite of all their
vices, and even in spite of all their meannesses, I
remember the blood that is in them, and still love the
Greeks. The Osmanlees are, of course, by nature,
by religion, and by politics, the strong foes of the
Hellenic people; and as the Greeks, poor fellows!

happen to be a little deficient in some of the virtues
which facilitate the transaction of commercial business
(such as veracity, fidelity, etc.), it naturally follows
that they are highly unpopular with the European
merchants. Now these are the persons through
whom, either directly or indirectly, is derived the
greater part of the information which you gather in
the Levant, and therefore you must make up in your
mind to hear an almost universal and unbroken
testimony against the character of the people, whose
ancestors invented Virtue. And strange to say, the
Greeks themselves do not attempt to disturb this
general unanimity of opinion by any dissent on their
part. Question a Greek on the subject, and he will
tell you at once that the people are 'traditori', and
will then, perhaps, endeavour to shake off his fair
share of the imputation, by asserting that his father
had been dragoman to some foreign embassy, and
that he (the son), therefore, by the law of nations,
had ceased to be Greek.

'E dunque no siete traditore?'

'Possible, Signor, ma almeno Io no sono Greco.'

Not even the diplomatic representatives of the
Hellenic kingdom are free from the habit of depreciating their brethren. I recollect, that at one of the
ports in Syria, a Greek vessel was rather unfairly
kept in quarantine by order of the Board of Health,
a board which consisted entirely of Europeans. A
consular agent from the kingdom of Greece had lately
hoisted his flag in the town, and the captain of the
vessel drew up a remonstrance, and requested his
consul to lay it before the Board.

'Now, *is* this reasonable?' said the consul, 'is it
reasonable that I should place myself in collision with
all the principal European gentlemen of the place for
the sake of you, a Greek?' The skipper was greatly

vexed at the failure of his application, but he scarcely even questioned the justice of the ground which his consul had taken. Well, it happened some time afterwards, that I found myself at the same port, having gone thither with the view of embarking for the port of Syra. I was anxious, of course, to elude as carefully as possible the quarantine detentions which threatened me on my arrival, and hearing that the Greek consul had a brother who was a man in authority at Syra, I got myself presented to the former, and took the liberty of asking him to give me such a letter of introduction to his relative at Syra as might possibly have the effect of shortening the term of quarantine. He acceded to this request with the utmost kindness and courtesy ; but when he replied to my thanks by saying that ' in serving an Englishman he was doing no more than his strict duty commanded', not even my gratitude could prevent me from calling to mind his treatment of the poor captain who had the misfortune of *not* being an alien in blood to his consul and appointed protector.

I think that the change which has taken place in the character of the Greeks, has been occasioned, in great measure, by the doctrines and practice of their religion. The Greek Church has animated the Muscovite peasant, and inspired him with hopes and ideas which, however humble, are still better than none at all ; but the faith, and the forms, and the strange ecclesiastical literature which act so advantageously upon the mere clay of the Russian serf, seem to hang like lead upon the ethereal spirit of the Greek. Never, in any part of the world, have I seen religious performances so painful to witness as those of the Greeks. The horror, however, with which one shudders at their worship, is attributable, in some

measure, to the mere effect of costume. In all the
Ottoman dominions, and very frequently too, in the
kingdom of Otho, the Greeks wear turbans, or other
head-dresses, and shave their heads, leaving only a
rat's- tail at the crown of the head; they of course
keep themselves covered within doors as well as
abroad, and they never remove their head-gear,
merely on account of being in a church: but when
the Greek stops to worship at his proper shrine, then,
and then only, he always uncovers; and as you see
him thus with shaven skull, and savage tail depending from his crown, kissing a thing of wood and glass,
and cringing with base prostrations and apparent
terror before a miserable picture, you see superstition
in a shape, which, outwardly at least, is sadly abject
and repulsive.

The fasts, too, of the Greek Church produce an ill
effect upon the character of the people, for they are
not a mere farce, but are carried to such an extent as
to bring about a real mortification of the flesh. The
febrile irritation of the frame, operating in conjunc-
tion with the depression of the spirits occasioned by
abstinence, will so far answer the objects of the rite,
as to engender some religious excitement, but this is
of a morbid and gloomy character; and it seems to
be certain, that along with the increase of sanctity,
there comes a fiercer desire for the perpetration of
dark crimes. The number of murders committed
during Lent is greater, I am told, than at any other
time of the year. A man under the influence of a
bean dietary (for this is the principal food of the
Greeks during their fasts) will be in an apt humour
for enriching the shrine of his saint, and passing a
knife through his next-door neighbour. The moneys
deposited upon the shrines are appropriated by priests.
The priests are married men, and have families to.

provide for ; they ' take the good with the bad ', and
continue to recommend fasts.

Then, too, the Greek Church enjoins her followers
to keep holy such a vast number of saints' days, as
practically to shorten the lives of the people very
materially. I believe that one-third out of the
number of days in the year are ' kept holy ', or rather
kept stupid, in honour of the saints. No great portion of the time thus set apart is spent in religious
exercises, and the people don't betake themselves to
any such animating pastimes as might serve to
strengthen the frame, or invigorate the mind, or
exalt the taste. On the contrary, the saints' days of
the Greeks in Smyrna are passed in the same manner
as the Sabbaths of well-behaved Protestant house-
maids in London—that is to say, in a steady and
serious contemplation of street scenery. The men
perform this duty *at the doors* of their houses,—the
women *at the windows*. Windows, indeed, by the
custom of Greek towns, are so decidedly appropriated
to the gentle sex, that a man would be looked upon
as utterly effeminate if he ventured to choose such
a position for the keeping of his saints' days. I was
present one day at a treaty for the hire of some
apartments at Smyrna which was carried on between
Carrigaholt and the Greek woman to whom the
rooms belonged. Carrigaholt objected that the
windows commanded no view of the street ; immediately the brow of the majestic matron was
clouded, and with all the scorn of a Spartan mother she
coolly asked Carrigaholt, and said, ' Art thou a tender
damsel that thou wouldst sit, and gaze from windows ? '
The man whom she addressed, however, had not gone
to Greece with any intention of placing himself under
the laws of Lycurgus, and was not to be diverted
from his views by a Spartan rebuke, so he took care

to find himself windows after his own heart, and there, I believe, for many a month, he kept the saints' days, and all the days intervening, after the fashion of Grecian women.

Oh! let me be charitable to all who write, and to all who lecture, and to all who preach, since even I, a lay-man not forced to write at all, can hardly avoid chiming in with some tuneful cant! I have had the heart to talk about the pernicious effects of the Greek holidays; and yet to these I owe most gracious and beautiful visions! I will let the words stand, as a humbling proof that I am subject to that nearly immutable law which compels a man with a pen in his hand to be uttering every now and then some sentiment not his own. It seems as though the power of expressing regrets and desires by written symbols were coupled with a condition that the writer should from time to time express the regrets and desires of other people—as though, like a French peasant under the old régime, he were bound to perform a certain amount of work *upon the public highways*. I rebel as stoutly as I can against this horrible corvée—I try not to deceive you—I try to set down the thoughts which are fresh within me, and not to pretend any wishes or griefs which I do not really feel; but no sooner do I cease from watchfulness in this regard, than my right hand is, as it were, seized by some false angel, and even now, you see, I have been forced to put down such words and sentences as I ought to have written, if really and truly I had wished to disturb the Saints' days of the beautiful Smyrniotes!

Disturb their saints' days?—Oh, no! for as you move through the narrow streets of the city at these times of festival the transom-shaped windows suspended over your head on either side are filled with the beautiful descendants of the old Ionian race; all

(even yonder empress throned at the window of that
humblest mud cottage) are attired with seeming
magnificence; their classic heads are crowned with
scarlet and laden with jewels or coins of gold—the
whole wealth of the wearers[1];—their features are
touched with a savage pencil, hardening the outline
of eyes and eye-brows, and lending an unnatural fire
to the stern, grave looks, with which they pierce your
brain.   Endure their fiery eyes as best you may, and
ride on slowly and reverently, for, facing you from the
side of the transom that looks longwise through the
street, you see the one glorious shape transcendant in
its beauty; you see the massive braid of hair as it
catches a touch of light on its jetty surface—and the
broad, calm, angry brow—the large eyes deeply set,
and self-relying as the eyes of a conqueror, with all
their rich shadows of thought lying darkly around
them,—you see the thin fiery nostril, and the bold
line of the chin and throat disclosing all the fierceness,
and all the pride, passion, and power that can live
along with the rare womanly beauty of those sweetly
turned lips.   But then there is a terrible stillness in
this breathing image; it seems like the stillness of a
savage that sits intent and brooding day by day upon
some one fearful scheme of vengeance, and yet more
like it seems to the stillness of an Immortal whose
will must be known and obeyed without sign or speech.
Bow down!—Bow down and adore the young Perse-
phonie, transcendant Queen of Shades!

[1] A Greek woman wears her whole fortune upon her person,
in the shape of jewels or gold coins.   I believe that this mode
of investment is adopted in great measure for safety's sake.   It
has the advantage of enabling a suitor to *reckon*, as well as to
admire, the objects of his affection.

CHAPTER VI

GREEK MARINERS

I SAILED from Smyrna in the Amphitrite, a Greek brigantine, which was confidently said to be bound for the coast of Syria, but I knew that this announcement was not to be relied upon with positive certainty, for the Greek mariners are practically free from the stringency of ship's papers, and where they will, there they go. However, I had the whole of the cabin for myself and my attendant Mysseri, subject only to the society of the Captain at the hour of dinner. Being at ease in this respect, being furnished, too, with plenty of books, and finding an unfailing source of interest in the thorough Greekness of my Captain and my crew, I felt less anxious than most people would have been about the probable length of the cruise: I knew enough of Greek navigation to be sure that our vessel would cling to earth like a child to its mother's knee, and that I should touch at many an isle before I set foot upon the Syrian coast; but I had no invidious preference for Europe, Asia, or Africa (I was safe from all danger of America), and I felt that I could defy the winds to blow me upon a coast that was blank and void of interest. My patience was extremely useful to me, for the cruise altogether endured some forty days, and that in the midst of winter.

According to me, the most interesting of all the Greeks (male Greeks) are the mariners, because their pursuits and their social condition are so nearly the same as those of their famous ancestors. You will say that the occupation of commerce must have smoothed down the salience of their minds; and this would be so, perhaps, if their mercantile affairs were

conducted according to the fixed business-like routine
of Europeans ; but the ventures of the Greeks are
surrounded by such a multitude of imagined dangers,
and (from the absence of regular marts, in which the
true value of merchandize can be ascertained), are so
entirely speculative, and besides are conducted in a
manner so wholly determined upon by the wayward
fancies and wishes of the crew, that they belong to
Enterprise, rather than to Industry, and are very
far indeed from tending to deaden any freshness of
character.

The vessels in which war and piracy were carried
on during the years of the Greek Revolution, became
merchantmen at the end of the war, but the tactics
of the Greeks, as naval warriors, were so exceedingly
cautious, and their habits as commercial mariners are
so wild, that the change has been more slight than
you might imagine.   The first care of Greeks (Greek
Rayahs) when they undertake a shipping enterprise,
is to procure for their vessel the protection of some
European power.   This is easily managed by a little
intriguing with the dragoman of one of the embassies
at Constantinople, and the craft soon glories in the
ensign of Russia, or the dazzling Tricolour, or the
Union Jack.   Thus, to the great delight of her crew,
she enters upon the ocean world with a flaring lie at
her peak ; but the appearance of the vessel does no
discredit to the borrowed flag : she is frail, indeed,
but is gracefully built, and smartly rigged ; she
always carries guns, and, in short, gives good promise
of mischief and speed.

The privileges attached to the vessel and her crew
by virtue of the borrowed flag are so great as to
imply a liberty wider even than that which is often
enjoyed in our more strictly civilized countries, so
that there is no good ground for saying that the

development of the true character belonging to
Greek mariners is prevented by the dominion of the
Ottoman. These men are free, too, from the power
of the great Capitalist—a power more withering
than despotism itself to the enterprises of humble
venturers. The capital employed is supplied by
those whose labour is to render it productive; the
crew receive no wages, but have all a share in the
venture, and in general, I believe, they are the
owners of the whole freight; they choose a captain,
to whom they intrust just power enough to keep the
vessel on her course in fine weather, but not quite
enough for a gale of wind; they also elect a cook and
a mate. The cook whom we had on board was particularly careful about the ship's reckoning, and when, under
the influence of the keen sea-breezes, we grew fondly
expectant of an instant dinner, the great author of
pilafs would be standing on deck with an ancient
quadrant in his hands, calmly affecting to take an
observation. But then, to make up for this, the
captain would be exercising a controlling influence
over the soup, so that all in the end went well. Our
mate was a Hydriot, a native of that island rock
which grows nothing but mariners and mariners'
wives. His character seemed to be exactly that
which is generally attributed to the Hydriot race;
he was fierce, and gloomy, and lonely in his ways.
One of his principal duties seemed to be that of
acting as counter-captain, or leader of the opposition,
denouncing the first symptoms of tyranny, and protecting even the cabin-boy from oppression. Besides
this, when things went smoothly, he would begin to
prognosticate evil, in order that his more light-
hearted comrades might not be puffed up with the
seeming good fortune of the moment.

It seemed to me that the personal freedom of these

sailors, who own no superiors except those of their
own choice, is as like as may be to that of their sea-
faring ancestors.   And even in their mode of navigation they have admitted no such an entire change as
you would suppose probable ; it is true that they have
so far availed themselves of modern discoveries as to
look to the compass instead of the stars, and that they
have superseded the immortal gods of their forefathers
by St. Nicholas in his glass case [1], but they are not
yet so confident either in their needle, or their saint,
as to love an open sea, and they still hug their shores
as fondly as the Argonauts of old.   Indeed, they have
a most unsailor-like love for the land, and I really
believe that in a gale of wind they would rather have
a rock-bound coast on their lee than no coast at all.
According to the notions of an English seaman, this
kind of navigation would soon bring the vessel on
which it might be practised to an evil end.   The
Greek, however, is unaccountably successful in escaping the consequences of being 'jammed in ', as it is
called, upon a lee shore.

These seamen, like their forefathers, rely upon no
winds unless they are right astern, or on the quarter ;
they rarely go *on* a wind if it blows at all fresh, and if
the adverse breeze approaches to a gale, they at once
fumigate St. Nicholas, and put up the helm.   The
consequence of course is, that under the ever-varying
winds of the Ægean they are blown about in the most
whimsical manner.   I used to think that Ulysses with
his ten years' voyage had taken his time in making
Ithaca, but my experience in Greek navigation soon
made me understand that he had had, in point of
fact, a pretty good 'average passage'.

---

[1] St. Nicholas is the great patron of Greek sailors ; a small
picture of him, enclosed in a glass case, is hung up like a
barometer at one end of the cabin.

Such are now the mariners of the Ægean: free, equal amongst themselves, navigating the seas of their fore-fathers with the same heroic and yet childlike spirit of venture, the same half-trustful reliance upon heavenly aid, they are the liveliest images of true old Greeks that time and the new religions have spared to us.

With one exception, our crew were a 'solemn company', and yet, sometimes, if all things went well, they would relax their austerity, and show a disposition to fun, or rather to quiet humour. When this happened, they invariably had recourse to one of their number who went by the name of 'Admiral Nicolou'; he was an amusing fellow, the poorest, I believe, and the least thoughtful of the crew, but full of rich humour. His oft-told story of the events by which he had gained the soubriquet of 'Admiral' never failed to delight his hearers, and when he was desired to repeat it for my benefit the rest of the crew crowded round with as much interest as if they were listening to the tale for the first time. The tale was this :—A number of Greek brigs and brigantines were at anchor in the bay at Beyrout; a festival of some kind particularly attractive to the sailors was going on in the town, and (whether with or without leave I know not) the crews of all the craft, except that of Nicolou, had gone ashore : on board this vessel (she carried dollars) there was, it would seem, a more careful or more influential captain,—a man who was able to enforce his determination that at least one of the crew should be left on board. Nicolou's good nature was with him so powerful an impulse that he could not resist the delight of volunteering to stay with the vessel, whilst his comrades went ashore; his proposal was accepted, and the crew and captain soon left him alone on the deck of his vessel. The sailors, gathering together from their several ships, were

amusing themselves in the town, when suddenly
there came down from betwixt the mountains one of
those sudden hurricanes which sometimes occur in
southern climes. Nicolou's vessel, together with four
of the craft which had been left unmanned, broke
from her moorings, and all five of the vessels were
carried out seaward. The town is on a salient point
at the southern side of the bay, so that 'the Admiral'
was close under the eyes of the inhabitants and the
shore-gone sailors, when he gallantly drifted out at
the head of his little fleet. If Nicolou could not
entirely control the manœuvres of the squadron,
there was at least no human power to divide his
authority, and thus it was that he took rank as
'Admiral'. Nicolou cut his cable, and so for the
time saved his vessel ; the rest of the fleet under his
command were quickly wrecked, whilst 'the Admiral'
got away clear to the open sea. The violence of the
squall soon passed off, but Nicolou felt that his
chance of one day resigning his high duties as an
admiral for the enjoyments of private life on the
steadfast shore mainly depended upon his success in
working the brig with his own hands ; so, after
calling on his namesake, the saint (not for the first
time, I take it), he got up some canvas and took the
helm ; he became equal, he told us, to a score of
Nicolous, and the vessel, as he said, was 'manned
with his terrors'. For two days, it seems, he cruised
at large, but at last, either by his seamanship, or by
the natural instinct of the Greek mariners for finding
land, he brought his craft close to an unknown shore
that promised well for his purpose of running in the
vessel, and he was preparing to give her a good berth
on the beach, when he saw a gang of ferocious-looking
fellows coming down to the point for which he was
making. Poor Nicolou was a perfectly unlettered

and untutored genius, and for that reason, perhaps,
a keen listener to tales of terror; his mind had been
impressed with some horrible legend of cannibalism,
and he now did not doubt for a moment that the
men awaiting him on the beach were the monsters at
whom he had shuddered in the days of his childhood.
The coast on which Nicolou was running his vessel
was somewhere, I fancy, at the foot of the Anzairie
mountains, and the fellows who were preparing to
give him a reception were probably very rough
specimens of humanity. It is likely enough that
they might have given themselves the trouble of
putting 'the Admiral' to death, for the purpose of
simplifying their claim to the vessel, and preventing
litigation, but the notion of their cannibalism was of
course utterly unfounded. Nicolou's terror had, however, so graven the idea on his mind, that he could
never after dismiss it. Having once determined the
character of his expectant hosts, the Admiral naturally
thought that it would be better to keep their dinner
waiting any length of time, than to attend their feast
in the character of a roasted Greek, so he put about
his vessel, and tempted the deep once more. After
a further cruise the lonely commander ran his vessel
upon some rocks at another part of the coast; there
she was lost with all her treasures, and Nicolou was
but too glad to scramble ashore, though without one
dollar in his girdle. These adventures seem flat
enough as I repeat them, but the hero expressed his
terrors by such odd terms of speech, and such
strangely humorous gestures, that the story came
from his lips with an unfailing zest, so that the
crew who had heard the tale so often could still
enjoy to their hearts the rich fright of the Admiral,
and still shudder with unabated horror when he came
to the loss of the dollars.

The power of listening to long stories (and for this, by the by, I am giving you large credit) is common, I fancy, to most sailors; and the Greeks have it to a high degree, for they can be perfectly patient under a narrative of two or three hours' duration. These long stories are mostly founded upon Oriental topics, and in one of them I recognized, with some alteration, an old friend of the 'Arabian Nights'. I inquired as to the source from which the story had been derived, and the crew all agreed that it had been handed down unwritten from Greek to Greek. Their account of the matter does not, perhaps, go very far towards showing the real origin of the tale, but when I afterwards took up the 'Arabian Nights', I became strongly impressed with a notion that they must have sprung from the brain of a Greek. It seems to me that these stories, whilst they disclose a complete and habitual *knowledge* of things Asiatic, have about them so much of freshness and life, so much of the stirring and volatile European character, that they cannot have owed their conception to a mere Oriental, who, for creative purposes, is a thing dead and dry—a mental mummy that may have been a live King just after the flood, but has since lain balmed in spice. At the time of the Caliphat the Greek race was familiar enough to Bagdad; they were the merchants, the pedlers, the barbers and intriguers-general of south-western Asia, and therefore the Oriental materials with which the Arabian tales were wrought must have been completely at the command of the inventive people to whom I would attribute their origin.

We were nearing the isle of Cyprus, when there arose half a gale of wind, with a heavy chopping sea. My Greek seamen considered that the weather amounted, not to a half, but to an integral gale of

wind at the very least; so they put up the helm, and
scudded for twenty hours. When we neared the
main land of Anadoli, the gale ceased, and a favourable breeze springing up, soon brought us off Cyprus
once more. Afterwards the wind changed again, but
we were still able to lay our course by sailing close-
hauled.

We were at length in such a position, that by
holding on our course for about half an hour, we
should get under the lee of the island, and find ourselves in smooth water, but the wind had been
gradually freshening; it now blew hard, and there
was a heavy sea running.

As the grounds for alarm arose, the crew gathered
together in one close group; they stood pale and
grim under their hooded capotes like monks awaiting
a massacre, anxiously looking by turns along the
pathway of the storm, and then upon each other, and
then upon the eye of the Captain, who stood by the
helmsman. Presently the Hydriot came aft, more
moody than ever, the bearer of fierce remonstrance
against the continuing of the struggle; he received
a resolute answer, and still we held our course.
Soon there came a heavy sea that caught the bow
of the brigantine as she lay jammed in betwixt the
waves; she bowed her head low under the waters,
and shuddered through all her timbers, then gallantly
stood up again over the striving sea with bowsprit
entire. But where were the crew?—It was a crew
no longer, but rather a gathering of Greek citizens;
—the shout of the seamen was changed for the
murmuring of the people—the spirit of the old
Demos was alive. The men came aft in a body, and
loudly asked that the vessel should be put about,
and that the storm be no longer tempted. Now,
then, for speeches:—the Captain, his eyes flashing

fire, his frame all quivering with emotion—wielding his every limb, like another and a louder voice—pours forth the eloquent torrent of his threats, and his reasons, his commands, and his prayers; he promises—he vows—he swears that there is safety in holding on—safety, *if Greeks will be brave!* The men hear and are moved, but the gale rouses itself once more, and again the raging sea comes trampling over the timbers that are the life of all. The fierce Hydriot advances one step nearer to the Captain, and the angry growl of the people goes floating down the wind; but they listen, they waver once more, and once more resolve, then waver again, thus doubtfully hanging between the terrors of the storm and the persuasion of glorious speech, as though it were the Athenian that talked, and Philip of Macedon that thundered on the weather-bow.

Brave thoughts winged on Grecian words gained their natural mastery over Terror; the Brigantine held on her course, and reached smooth water at last.

I landed at Limesol, the westernmost port of Cyprus, leaving the Brigantine to sail for Larnecca, and there await my arrival.

CHAPTER VII

CYPRUS

THERE was a Greek at Limesol, who hoisted his flag as an English Vice-Consul, and he insisted upon my accepting his hospitality. With some difficulty, and chiefly by assuring him that I could not delay my departure beyond an early hour in the afternoon, I induced him to allow my dining with

his family, instead of banqueting all alone with the
representative of my sovereign, in consular state and
dignity. The lady of the house, it seemed, had
never sat at table with an European; she was very
shy about the matter, and tried hard to get out of
the scrape, but the husband, I fancy, reminded her
that she was theoretically an Englishwoman, by
virtue of the flag that waved over her roof, and that
she was bound to show her nationality by sitting at
meat with me. Finding herself inexorably condemned to bear with the dreaded gaze of European
eyes, she tried to save her innocent children from the
hard fate awaiting herself, but I obtained that all of
them (and I think there were four or five) should sit
at the table. You will meet with abundance of
stately receptions, and of generous hospitality too,
in the East, but rarely, very rarely in those regions
(or even, so far as I know, in any part of southern
Europe), does one gain an opportunity of seeing the
familiar and in-door life of the people.

This family party of the good Consul's (or rather
of mine, for I originated the idea, though he furnished
the materials) went off very well: the mamma was
shy at first, but she veiled her awkwardness by affecting to scold the children. These had all immortal
names—names, too, which they owed to tradition, and
certainly not to any classical enthusiasm of their
parents: every instant I was delighted by some such
phrases as these:—'Themistocles, my love, don't
fight.'—'Alcibiades, can't you sit still?'—'Socrates,
put down the cup.'—'Oh, fie! Aspasia, don't oh!
don't be naughty!' It is true that the names were
pronounced, Socrahtie, Aspahsie—that is, according
to accent, and not according to quantity, but I suppose it is scarcely now to be doubted that they were
so sounded in ancient times.

To me, it seems that of all the lands I know (you
will see in a minute how I connect this piece of prose
with the Isle of Cyprus), there is none in which mere
wealth—mere unaided wealth—is held half so cheaply,
none in which a poor devil of a millionaire without
birth or ability occupies so humble a place as in
England. My Greek host was chatting with me
(I think upon the roof of the house, for that is the
lounging place in Eastern climes), when suddenly he
assumed a serious air, and intimated a wish to talk
over the British Constitution,—a subject with which,
as he assured me, he was thoroughly acquainted.
He presently, however, remarked that there was one
anomalous circumstance attendant upon the practical
working of our political system which he had never
been able to hear explained in a manner satisfactory
to himself. From the fact of his having found a
difficulty in his subject, I began to think that my
host might really know rather more of it than his
announcement of a thorough knowledge had led me
to expect; I felt interested at being about to hear
from the lips of an intelligent Greek, quite remote
from the influence of European opinions, what might
seem to him the most astonishing and incomprehen-
sible of all those results which have followed from
the action of our political institutions. The anomaly
—the only anomaly which had been detected by the
Vice-Consular wisdom—consisted in the fact that
Rothschild (the late money-monger) had never been
the Prime Minister of England! I gravely tried to
throw some light upon the mysterious causes that
had kept the worthy Israelite out of the Cabinet, but
I think I could see that my explanation was not
satisfactory. Go and argue with the flies of summer
that there is a power divine yet greater than the sun
in the heavens, but never dare hope to convince the

people of the South that there is any other God
than Gold.

My intended journey was to the sight of the
Paphian temple. I take no antiquarian interest in
ruins, and care little about them unless they are
either striking in themselves, or else serve to mark
some spot very dear to my fancy. I knew that the
ruins of Paphos were scarcely, if at all, discernible,
but there was a will, and a longing, more imperious
than mere curiosity, that drove me thither.

For this, just then, was my Pagan soul's desire—
that (not forfeiting my inheritance for the life to
come) it had yet been given me to live through this
world—to live a favoured mortal under the old
Olympian dispensation—to speak out my resolves to
the listening Jove, and hear him answer with
approving thunder—to be blessed with divine
counsels from the lips of Pallas Athēnie—to believe
—ay, only to believe—to believe for one rapturous
moment that in the gloomy depths of the grove by
the mountain's side, there were some leafy pathway
that crisped beneath the glowing sandal of Aphrodētie
—Aphrodētie, not coldly disdainful of even a mortal's
love! And this vain, heathenish longing of mine
was father to the thought of visiting the scene of the
ancient worship.

The isle is beautiful: from the edge of the rich,
flowery fields on which I trod, to the midway sides of
the snowy Olympus, the ground could only here and
there show an abrupt crag or a high straggling ridge
that upshouldered itself from out of the wilderness of
myrtles, and of a thousand bright-leaved shrubs that
twined their arms together in lovesome tangles. The
air that came to my lips was warm and fragrant as
the ambrosial breath of the goddess, infecting me—
not (of course) with a faith in the old religion of the

isle, but with a sense and apprehension of its mystic
power—a power that was still to be obeyed—obeyed
by *me*; for why otherwise did I toil on with sorry
horses to 'where, for HER, the hundred altars glowed
with Arabian incense, and breathed with the fragrance
of garlands ever fresh ? ' [1]

I passed a sadly disenchanting night in the cabin
of a Greek priest—not a priest of the goddess, but
of the Greek Church; there was but one humble
room, or rather shed, for man, and priest, and beast.
The next morning I reached Baffa (Paphos), a village
not far distant from the site of the temple.   There
was a Greek husbandman there who (not for emolu-
ment, but for the sake of the protection and dignity
which it afforded) had got leave from the man at
Limesol to hoist his flag as a sort of Deputy-
provisionary-sub-vice-pro-acting-consul of the British
Sovereign. The poor fellow instantly changed his
Greek head-gear for the cap of consular dignity, and
insisted upon accompanying me to the ruins. I would
not have stood this, if I could have felt the faintest
gleam of my yesterday's pagan piety, but I had
ceased to dream, and had nothing to dread from any
new disenchanters.

The ruins (the fragments of one or two prostrate
pillars) lie upon a promontory bare and unmystified
by the gloom of surrounding groves. My Greek
friend in his consular cap stood by, respectfully
waiting to see what turn my madness would take
now that I had come at last into the presence of the
old stones. If you have no taste for research, and
can't affect to look for inscriptions, there is some
awkwardness in coming to the end of a merely

---

[1]   . . . ubi templum illi, centumque Sabaeo
    Thure calent arae, sertisque recentibus halant.
                                    ÆNEID, i. 415.

sentimental pilgrimage, when the feeling which
impelled you has gone : in such a strait you have
nothing to do but to laugh the thing off as well as
you can—and, by the by, it is not a bad plan to
turn the conversation (or rather allow the natives to
turn it) towards the subject of hidden treasures :
this is a topic on which they will always speak with
eagerness, and if they can fancy that you, too, take
an interest in such matters, they will not only begin
to think you perfectly sane, but will even perhaps
give you credit for some more than human powers of
forcing dark Earth to show you its hoards of gold.

When we returned to Baffa, the Vice-Consul seized
a club, with the quietly determined air of a brave
man, resolved to do some deed of note ; he went into
the yard adjoining his cottage where there were
some thin, thoughtful, canting cocks, and serious,
low-church-looking hens, respectfully listening, and
chickens of tender years so well brought up as
scarcely to betray in their conduct the careless levity
of youth. The Vice-Consul stood for a moment
quite calm—collecting his strength ; then suddenly
he rushed into the midst of the congregation, and
began to deal death and destruction on all sides ; he
spared neither sex nor age ; the dead and dying
were immediately removed from the field of slaughter,
and in less than an hour, I think, they were brought
to the table, deeply buried in mounds of snowy rice.

My host was in all respects a fine, generous fellow.
I could not bear the idea of impoverishing him by
my visit, and my faithful Mysseri not only assured
me that I might safely offer money to the Vice-
Consul, but recommended that I should give no
more to him than to 'the others', meaning any
other peasant. I felt, however, that there was something about the man, besides the flag and cap, which

made me shrink from offering coin, and, as I mounted
my horse on departing, I gave him the only thing
fit for a present that I happened to have with me,
a rather handsome clasp-dagger, brought from Vienna.
The poor fellow was ineffably grateful, and I had some
difficulty in tearing myself from out of the reach of
his thanks.   At last I gave him what I supposed to
be the last farewell, and rode on; but I had not
gained more than about a hundred yards, when my
host came bounding and shouting after me, with
a goats' milk cheese in his hand, and this (it was
rather a burthensome gift) he fondly implored me to
accept.   In old times the shepherd of Theocritus,
or (to speak less dishonestly) the shepherd of the
' Poetae Graeci ', sung his best song ; I in this latter
age presented my best dagger, and both of us received
the same rustic reward.

It had been known that I should return to Limesol,
and when I arrived there, I found that a noble old
Greek had been hospitably plotting to have me for
his guest.   I willingly accepted his offer.   The day
of my arrival happened to be my host's birthday, and
during all the morning there was a constant influx of
visitors who came to offer their congratulations.   A
few of these were men, but most of them were young
graceful girls.   Almost all of them went through the
ceremony with the utmost precision and formality :
each in succession spoke her blessing in the tone of
a person repeating a set formula,—then deferentially
accepted the invitation to sit,—partook of the proffered
sweetmeats and the cold, glittering water,—remained
for a few minutes either in silence or engaged in very
thin conversation—then arose, delivered a second
benediction, followed by an elaborate farewell, and
departed.

The bewitching power attributed at this day to

the women of Cyprus is curious in connection with
the worship of the sweet goddess who called their isle
her own. The Cypriot is not, I think, nearly so
beautiful in face as the Ionian queens of Izmir, but
she is tall, and slightly formed; there is a high-souled
meaning and expression—a seeming consciousness
of gentle empire that speaks in the wavy lines of the
shoulder, and winds itself like Cytherea's own cestus
around the slender waist; then the richly abounding
hair (not enviously gathered together under the
head-dress) descends the neck, and passes the waist
in sumptuous braids. Of all other women with
Grecian blood in their veins, the costume is graciously
beautiful, but these, the maidens of Limesol—their
robes are more gently, more sweetly imagined, and
fall like Julia's Cashmere in soft, luxurious folds. The
common voice of the Levant allows that in face the
women of Cyprus are less beautiful than their majestic
sisters of Smyrna, and yet, says the Greek, he may
trust himself to one and all the cities of the Ægean,
and may still weigh anchor with a heart entire, but
that so surely as he ventures upon the enchanted Isle
of Cyprus, so surely will he know the rapture or the
bitterness of Love. The charm, they say, owes its
power to that which the people call the astonishing
'politics' (πολιτική) of the women, meaning, I fancy,
their tact, and their witching ways; the word, however, plainly fails to express one-half of that which
the speakers would say. I have smiled to hear the
Greek with all his plenteousness of fancy, and all the
wealth of his generous language, yet vainly struggling
to describe the ineffable spell which the Parisians
dispose of in their own smart way, by a summary
'Je ne sçai quoi'.

I went to Larnecca, the chief city of the isle, and
over the water at last to Beyrout.

CHAPTER VIII

LADY HESTER STANHOPE

BEYROUT on its land side is hemmed in by mountains. There dwell the Druses.

Often enough I saw the ghostly images of the women with their exalted horns stalking through the streets, and I saw too in travelling the affrighted groups of the mountaineers as they fled before me, under the fear that my troop might be a company of Income-tax commissioners, or a press-gang enforcing the conscription for Mehemet Ali, but nearly all my knowledge of the people, except in regard of their mere costume and outward appearance, is drawn from books and despatches. To these last I have the honour to refer you.[1]

I received hospitable welcome at Beyrout, from the Europeans as well as from the Syrian Christians, and I soon discovered that in all society the standing topic of interest was an Englishwoman (Lady Hester Stanhope) who lived in an old convent on the Lebanon range, at the distance of about a day's journey from the town. The lady's habit of refusing to see Europeans added the charm of mystery to a character which, even without that aid, was sufficiently distinguished to command attention.

Many years of Lady Hester's early womanhood had been passed with Lady Chatham, at Burton Pynsent, and during that inglorious period of the heroine's life, her commanding character, and (as they would have called it, in the language of those days) her ' condescending kindness ' towards my mother's

---

[1] The papers laid before Parliament by the Foreign Office in 1840 and 1841.

family, had increased in them those strong feelings of
respect and attachment, which her rank and station
alone would have easily won from people of the middle
class.   You may suppose how deeply the quiet women
in Somersetshire must have been interested, when
they slowly learned by vague and uncertain tidings,
that the intrepid girl who had been used to break
their vicious horses for them was reigning in sovereignty over the wandering tribes of Western Asia!
I know that her name was made almost as familiar to
me in my childhood as the name of Robinson Crusoe ;
both were associated with the spirit of adventure, but
whilst the imagined life of the cast-away mariner
never failed to seem glaringly real, the true story of
the Englishwoman ruling over Arabs always sounded
to me like a fable.   I never had heard, nor indeed, I
believe, had the rest of the world ever heard anything
like a certain account of the heroine's adventures : all
I knew was, that in one of the drawers, the delight of
my childhood, along with atta of roses, and fragrant
wonders from Hindostan, there were letters carefully
treasured, and trifling presents which I was taught to
think valuable because they had come from the Queen
of the Desert—a Queen who dwelt in tents, and
reigned over wandering Arabs.

The subject, however, died away, and from the
ending of my childhood up to the period of my arrival
in the Levant, I had seldom even heard a mentioning
of the Lady Hester Stanhope ; but now wherever I
went I was met by the name so familiar in sound,
and yet so full of mystery, from the vague, fairy-tale
sort of idea which it brought to my mind : I heard it
too connected with fresh wonders, for it was said that
the woman was now acknowledged as an inspired being
by the people of the Mountains, and it was even hinted
with horror that she claimed to be *more than a prophet*.

I felt at once that my mother would be sorry to hear that I had been within a day's ride of her early friend without offering to see her, and I therefore despatched a letter to the Recluse, mentioning the maiden name of my mother (whose marriage was subsequent to Lady Hester's departure), and saying that if there existed on the part of her Ladyship any wish to hear of her old Somersetshire acquaintance, I should make a point of visiting her. My letter was sent by a foot messenger who was to take an unlimited time for his journey, so that it was not, I think, until either the third or the fourth day that the answer arrived. A couple of horsemen covered with mud suddenly dashed into the little court of the 'Locanda', in which I was staying, bearing themselves as ostentatiously as though they were carrying a cartel from the Devil to the Angel Michael; one of these (the other being his attendant) was an Italian by birth (though now completely orientalized), who lived in my Lady's establishment as doctor nominally, but practically as an upper servant; he presented me a very kind and appropriate letter of invitation.

It happened that I was rather unwell at this time, so that I named a more distant day for my visit than I should otherwise have done; and after all I did not start at the time fixed. Whilst still remaining at Beyrout I received another letter from Lady Hester; this I will give you, for it shows that whatever the eccentricities of the writer may have been, she could at least be thoughtful and courteous:—

Sir,
        I hope I shall be disappointed in seeing you on Wednesday, for the late rains have rendered the river Damoor, if not dangerous, at least very unpleasant to pass for a person who has been lately indisposed, for if the animal swims, you would be immerged in the waters. The weather will probably change after the 21st of the moon, and after a couple of

days the roads and the river will be passable, therefore I shall
expect you either Saturday or Monday.

It will be a great satisfaction to me to have an opportunity of
inquiring after your mother, who was a sweet, lovely girl when
I knew her.

> Believe me, Sir,
> Yours sincerely,
> HESTER LUCY STANHOPE.

Early one morning I started from Beyrout.   There
are no established relays of horses in Syria, at least
not in the line which I took, and you therefore hire
your cattle for the whole journey, or at all events
for your journey to some large town.   Under these
circumstances you don't of course require a functionary empowered to compel the supply of horses,
and you can therefore dispense with a Tatar.   In
other respects the mode of travelling through Syria
differs very little from that which I have described
as prevailing in Turkey.   I hired my horses and
mules for the whole of the journey from Beyrout to
Jerusalem.   The owner of the beasts (he had a
couple of fellows under him) was the most dignified
member of my party; he was, indeed, a magnificent
old man, and was called Shereef, or 'holy',—a title
of honour, which, with the privilege of wearing the
green turban, he well deserved, not only from the
blood of the Prophet that glowed in his veins, but
from the well-known sanctity of his life, and the
length of his blessed beard.

Mysseri, of course, still travelled with me, but the
Arabic was not one of the seven languages which he
spoke so perfectly, and I was, therefore, obliged to
hire another interpreter.   I had no difficulty in finding a proper man for the purpose—one Demetrius,
or, as he was always called, Dthemetri, a native of
Zante, who had been tossed about by fortune in all
directions.   He spoke the Arabic well, and com-

municated with me in Italian. The man was a very
zealous member of the Greek Church. He had been
a tailor. He had a thoroughly Tatar countenance,
—a countenance so odd and ugly that it expressed all
his griefs of body and mind in the most ludicrous
manner imaginable. He embellished the natural
caricature of his person by suspending about his neck
and shoulders and waist, quantities of little bundles
and bags filled with treasures, which he thought too
valuable to be entrusted to the jerking of pack-
saddles. The mule that fell to his lot on this journey
every now and then, forgetting that his rider was
a saint, and remembering that he was a tailor, took a
quiet roll upon the ground, and stretched his limbs
calmly and lazily, like a good man awaiting a sermon.
Dthmetri never got seriously hurt, but the subversion
and dislocation of his bundles made him for the
moment a sad spectacle of ruin, and when he regained
his legs, his wrath with the mule was sure to be very
amusing. He always addressed the beast in language
implying that he, a Christian and saint, had been
personally insulted and oppressed by a Mahometan
mule. Dthemetri however, on the whole, proved to
be a most able and capital servant. I suspected him
of now and then leading me out of my way, in order
that he might have the opportunity of visiting the
shrine of a saint, and on one occasion, as you will see
by and by, he was induced by religious motives to
commit a gross breach of duty ; but putting these
pious faults out of the question (and they were faults of
the right side), he was always faithful and true to me.

I left Saïde (the Sidon of ancient times) on my
right, and about an hour, I think, before sunset, began
to ascend one of the many low hills of Lebanon.   On
the summit before me was a broad, grey mass of
irregular building, which, from its position, as well as

from the gloomy blankness of its walls, gave the idea
of a neglected fortress; it had, in fact, been a convent
of great size, and, like most of the religious houses in
this part of the world, had been made strong enough
for opposing an inert resistance to any mere casual
band of assailants who might be unprovided with
regular means of attack: this was the dwelling-place
of Chatham's fiery grand-daughter.

The aspect of the first court I entered was such as
to keep one in the idea of having to do with a fortress,
rather than a mere peaceable dwelling-place. A
number of fierce-looking and ill-clad Albanian soldiers
were hanging about the place, inert, and striving, as
well as they could, to bear the curse of Tranquillity;
two or three of them were smoking their tchibouques,
but the rest were lying torpidly upon the flat stones,
like the bodies of departed brigands. I rode on to an
inner part of the building, and at last, quitting my
horses, was conducted through a doorway that led me
at once from an open court into an apartment on the
ground floor. As I entered, an Oriental figure in
male costume approached me from the further end of
the room, with many and profound bows; but the
growing shades of evening prevented me from dis-
tinguishing the features of the personage who was
receiving me with this solemn welcome. I had always,
however, understood that Lady Hester Stanhope wore
the male attire, and I began to utter in English the
common civilities that seemed to be proper on the
commencement of a visit by an uninspired mortal to
a renowned Prophetess; but the figure which I
addressed only bowed so much the more, prostrating
itself almost to the ground, but speaking to me never
a word. I feebly strived not to be outdone in gestures
of respect; but presently my bowing opponent saw
the error under which I was acting, and suddenly

convinced me that at all events I was not *yet* in the presence of a superhuman being, by declaring that he was far from being 'Miladi', and was, in fact, nothing more or less godlike than the poor Doctor who had brought his Mistress's letter to Beyrout.

Lady Hester, in the right spirit of hospitality, now sent and commanded me to repose for a while after the fatigues of my journey, and to dine.

The cuisine was of the Oriental kind,—highly artificial, and, as I thought, very good. I rejoiced too in the wine of the Lebanon.

After dinner the Doctor arrived with Miladi's compliments, and an intimation that she would be happy to receive me if I were so disposed. It had now grown dark, and the rain was falling heavily, so that I got rather wet in following my guide through the open courts that I had to pass in order to reach the presence chamber. At last I was ushered into a small chamber, protected from the draughts of air passing through the doorway by a folding screen ; passing this, I came alongside of a common European sofa. There sat the Lady Prophetess. She rose from her seat very formally—spoke to me a few words of welcome, pointed to a chair—one already placed exactly opposite to her sofa at a couple of yards distance—and remained standing up to the full of her majestic height, perfectly still, and motionless, until I had taken my appointed place : she then resumed her seat—not packing herself up according to the mode of the Orientals, but allowing her feet to rest on the floor or the footstool ; at the moment of seating herself she covered her lap with a mass of loose, white drapery. It occurred to me at the time, that she did this in order to avoid the awkwardness of sitting in manifest trowsers under the eye of an European ; but I can hardly fancy now, that, with her wilful nature, she would have brooked such a compromise as this.

The woman before me had exactly the person of a Prophetess—not, indeed, of the divine Sibyl imagined by Domenichino, so sweetly distracted betwixt Love and Mystery, but of a good, business-like, practical Prophetess, long used to the exercise of her sacred calling. I have been told by those who knew Lady Hester Stanhope in her youth, that any notion of a resemblance betwixt her and the great Chatham must have been fanciful; but at the time of my seeing her, the large commanding features of the gaunt woman, then sixty years old or more, certainly reminded me of the statesman that lay dying[1] in the House of Lords according to Copley's picture: her face was of the most astonishing whiteness[2]; she wore a very large turban made seemingly of pale cashmere shawls, and so disposed as to conceal the hair; her dress, from the chin down to the point at which it was concealed by the drapery on her lap, was a mass of white linen loosely folding—an ecclesiastical sort of affair—more like a surplice than any of those blessed creations which our souls love under the names of ' dress ', and ' frock ', and 'boddice', and 'collar', and ' habit-shirt ', and sweet ' chemisette '.

Such was the outward seeming of the personage that sat before me; and indeed she was almost bound by the fame of her actual achievements, as well as by her sublime pretensions, to look a little differently from the rest of womankind. There had been something of grandeur in her career. After the death of Lady Chatham, which happened in 1803, she lived under the roof of her uncle, the second Pitt, and when he resumed the Government in 1804, she became the

---

[1] Historically ' *fainting* '; the death did not occur until long afterwards.

[2] I am told that in youth she was exceedingly sallow.

dispenser of much patronage, and sole Secretary of
State for the department of Treasury banquets. Not
having seen the Lady until late in her life, when she
was fired with spiritual ambition, I can hardly fancy
that she could have performed her political duties in
the saloons of the Minister with much of feminine
sweetness and patience : I am told, however, that she
managed matters very well indeed ; perhaps it was
better for the lofty-minded leader of the House to
have his reception-rooms guarded by this stately
creature than by a merely clever and managing
woman ; it was fitting that the wholesome awe with
which he filled the minds of the country gentleman,
should be aggravated by the presence of his majestic
niece. But the end was approaching. The sun of
Austerlitz showed the Czar madly sliding his splendid
army, like a weaver's shuttle, from his right hand to
his left, under the very eyes—the deep, gray, watchful eyes of Napoleon; before night came, the coalition
was a vain thing—meet for history ; and the heart of
its great author, when the terrible tidings came to his
ears, was wrung with grief—fatal grief. In the bitterness of his despair, he cried out to his niece, and bid
her ' ROLL UP THE MAP OF EUROPE '; there was
a little more of suffering, and at last, with his swollen
tongue (so they say) still muttering something for
England, he died by the noblest of all sorrows.

Lady Hester, meeting the calamity in her own
fierce way, seems to have scorned the poor island that
had not enough of God's grace to keep the ' heaven-
sent ' Minister alive. I can hardly tell why it should
be, but there is a longing for the East, very commonly
felt by proud people when goaded by sorrow. Lady
Hester Stanhope obeyed this impulse ; for some time,
I believe, she was at Constantinople, and there her
magnificence, as well as her near alliance to the late

Minister, gained her great influence.   Afterwards she
passed into Syria.   The people of that country,
excited by the achievements of Sir Sydney Smith,
had begun to imagine the possibility of their land
being occupied by the English, and many of them
looked upon Lady Hester as a Princess who came to
prepare the way for the expected conquest.   I don't
know it from her own lips, or indeed from any certain
authority, but I have been told that she began her
connection with the Bedouins by making a large
present of money (£500—immense in piastres) to the
Sheik whose authority was recognised in the Desert,
between Damascus and Palmyra.   The prestige
created by the rumours of her high and undefined
rank, as well as of her wealth and corresponding
magnificence, was well sustained by her imperious
character and her dauntless bravery.   Her influence
increased.   I never heard anything satisfactory as to
the real extent or duration of her sway, but I understood that, for a time at least, she certainly exercised
something like sovereignty amongst the wandering
tribes.   And now that her earthly kingdom had
passed away, she strove for spiritual power, and im-
piously dared, as it was said, to boast some mystic
union with the very God of very God!

A couple of black slave girls came at a signal, and
supplied their mistress as well as myself, with lighted
tchibouques, and coffee.

The custom of the East sanctions, and almost
commands, some moments of silence whilst you are
inhaling the first few breaths of the fragrant pipe:
the pause was broken, I think, by my Lady, who
addressed to me some inquiries respecting my mother,
and particularly as to her marriage; but before I had
communicated any great amount of family facts, the
spirit of the Prophetess kindled within her, and

presently (though with all the skill of a woman of the world) she shuffled away the subject of poor dear Somersetshire, and bounded onward into loftier spheres of thought.

My old acquaintance with some of 'the twelve' enabled me to bear my part (of course a very humble one) in a conversation relative to occult science. Milnes once spread a report that every gang of gipsies was found upon inquiry to have come last from a place to the westward, and to be about to make the next move in an eastern direction ; either, therefore, they were to be all gathered together towards the rising of the sun by the mysterious finger of Providence, or else they were to revolve round the globe for ever and ever. Both of these suppositions were highly gratifying, because they were both marvellous ; and though the story on which they were founded plainly sprang from the inventive brain of a poet, no one had ever been so odiously statistical as to attempt a contradiction of it. I now mentioned the story as a report to Lady Hester Stanhope, and asked her if it were true : I could not have touched upon any imaginable subject more deeply interesting to my hearer—more closely akin to her habitual train of thinking ; she immediately threw off all the restraint belonging to an interview with a stranger ; and when she had received a few more similar proofs of my aptness for the marvellous, she went so far as to say that she would adopt me as her 'elève' in occult science.

For hours and hours, this wondrous white woman poured forth her speech, for the most part concerning sacred and profane mysteries ; but every now and then she would stay her lofty flight, and swoop down upon the world again : whenever this happened, I was interested in her conversation.

She adverted more than once to the period of her
lost sway amongst the Arabs, and mentioned some
of the circumstances that aided her in obtaining
influence with the wandering tribes.   The Bedouin,
so often engaged in irregular warfare, strains his
eyes to the horizon in search of a coming enemy just
as habitually as the sailor keeps his 'bright look
out' for a strange sail.   In the absence of telescopes,
a far-reaching sight is highly valued ; and Lady
Hester had this power.   She told me that, on one
occasion, when there was good reason to expect
hostilities, a far-seeing Arab created great excitement
in the camp by declaring that he could distinguish
some moving objects upon the very farthest point
within the reach of his eyes : Lady Hester was
consulted, and she instantly assured her comrades
in arms that there were indeed a number of horses
within sight, but they were without riders : the
assertion proved to be correct, and from that time
forth her superiority over all others in respect of far
sight remained undisputed.

Lady Hester related to me this other anecdote of
her Arab life.   It was when the heroic qualities of
the Englishwoman were just beginning to be felt
amongst the people of the desert, that she was
marching one day, along with the forces of the tribe
to which she had allied herself.   She perceived that
preparations for an engagement were going on ; and
upon her making inquiry as to the cause, the Sheik
at first affected mystery and concealment, but at last
confessed that war had been declared against his
tribe on account of its alliance with the English
Princess, and that they were now unfortunately
about to be attacked by a very superior force : he
made it appear that Lady Hester was the sole cause
of hostility betwixt his tribe and the impending

enemy, and that his sacred duty of protecting
the Englishwoman whom he had admitted as his
guest was the only obstacle which prevented an
amicable settlement of the dispute.   The Sheik
hinted that his tribe was likely to sustain an almost
overwhelming blow, but at the same time declared
that no fear of the consequences, however terrible to
him and his whole people, should induce him to
dream of abandoning his illustrious guest.   The
heroine instantly took her part : it was not for her
to be a source of danger to her friends, but rather to
her enemies ; so she resolved to turn away from the
people, and trust for help to none, save only her
haughty self.   The Sheiks affected to dissuade her
from so rash a course, and fairly told her that
although they (having been freed from her presence)
would be able to make good terms for themselves,
yet that there were no means of allaying the
hostility felt towards her, and that the whole face of
the desert would be swept by the horsemen of her
enemies so carefully, as to make her escape into other
districts almost impossible.   The brave woman was
not to be moved by terrors of this kind ; and bidding
farewell to the tribe which had honoured and
protected her, she turned her horse's head, and rode
straight away, without friend or follower.   Hours
had elapsed, and for some time she had been alone in
the centre of the round horizon, when her quick eye
perceived some horsemen in the distance.   The party
came nearer and nearer ; soon it was plain that they
were making towards her ; and presently some
hundreds of Bedouins, fully armed, galloped up to
her, ferociously shouting, and apparently intending
to take her life at the instant with their pointed
spears.   Her face at the time was covered with the
yashmack, according to Eastern usage ; but at the

moment when the foremost of the horsemen had all
but reached her with their spears, she stood up in
her stirrups—withdrew the yashmack that veiled the
terrors of her countenance—waved her arms slowly
and disdainfully, and cried out with a loud voice,
' Avaunt ! '[1] The horsemen recoiled from her glance,
but not in terror. The threatening yells of the
assailants were suddenly changed for loud shouts of
joy and admiration at the bravery of the stately
Englishwoman, and festive gun-shots were fired on
all sides around her honoured head. The truth was
that the party belonged to the tribe with which she
had allied herself, and that the threatened attack,
as well as the pretended apprehension of an engagement, had been contrived for the mere purpose of
testing her courage. The day ended in a great feast
prepared to do honour to the heroine ; and from
that time her power over the minds of the people
grew rapidly. Lady Hester related this story with
great spirit ; and I recollect that she put up her
yashmack for a moment, in order to give me a better
idea of the effect which she produced by suddenly
revealing the awfulness of her countenance.

With respect to her then present mode of life,
Lady Hester informed me that for her sin she had
subjected herself during many years to severe penance,
and that her self-denial had not been without its
reward. ' Vain and false,' said she, ' is all the
pretended knowledge of the Europeans—their doctors
will tell you that the drinking of milk gives yellow-
ness to the complexion ; milk is my only food, and
you see if my face be not white.' Her abstinence
from food intellectual was carried as far as her

[1] She spoke it, I dare say, in English ; the words would not
be the less effective for being spoken in an unknown tongue.
Lady Hester, I believe, never learnt to speak the Arabic with
a perfect accent.

physical fasting : she never, she said, looked upon a book, nor a newspaper, but trusted alone to the stars for her sublime knowledge ; she usually passed the nights in communing with these heavenly teachers, and lay at rest during the day-time. She spoke with great contempt of the frivolity and benighted ignorance of the modern Europeans ; and mentioned, in proof of this, that they were not only untaught in astrology, but were unacquainted with the common and every-day phenomena produced by magic art : she spoke as if she would make me understand that all sorcerous spells were completely at her command, but that the exercise of such powers would be derogatory to her high rank in the heavenly kingdom. She said that the spell by which the face of an absent person is thrown upon a mirror was within the reach of the humblest and most contemptible magicians, but that the practice of such like arts was unholy, as well as vulgar.

We spoke of the bending twig by which, it is said, precious metals may be discovered. In relation to this, the Prophetess told me a story rather against herself, and inconsistent with the notion of her being perfect in her science ; but I think that she mentioned the facts as having happened before she attained to the great spiritual authority which she now arrogated. She told that vast treasures were known to exist in a situation which she mentioned, if I rightly remember, as being near Suez ; that Napoleon, profanely brave, thrust his arm into the cave containing 'the coveted gold, and that instantly his flesh became palsied : but the youthful hero (for she said he was great in his generation) was not to be thus daunted ; he fell back characteristically upon his brazen resources, and ordered up his artillery ; yet man could not strive with demons, and Napoleon was foiled. In latter

years came Ibrahim Pasha, with heavy guns, and
wicked spells to boot; but the infernal guardians of
the treasure were too strong for him. It was after
this that Lady Hester passed by the spot, and she
described with animated gesture the force and energy
with which the divining twig had suddenly leaped in
her hands: she ordered excavations, and no demons
opposed her enterprise; the vast chest in which the
treasure had been deposited was at length discovered,
but lo! and behold, it was full of pebbles! She said,
however, that the times were approaching, in which
the hidden treasures of the earth would become avail-
able to those who had 'true knowledge'.

Speaking of Ibrahim Pasha, Lady Hester said that
he was a bold, bad man, and was possessed of some
of those common and wicked magical arts upon which
she looked down with so much contempt: she said,
for instance, that Ibrahim's life was charmed against
balls and steel, and that after a battle he loosened
the folds of his shawl, and shook out the bullets
like dust.

It seems that the St. Simonians once made over-
tures to Lady Hester: she told me that the Père
Enfantin (the chief of the sect) had sent her a service
of plate, but that she had declined to receive it. She
delivered a prediction as to the probability of the
St. Simonians finding the 'mystic mother', and this
she did in a way which would amuse you: unfortunately I am not at liberty to mention this part of the
woman's prophecies; why, I cannot tell, but so it is,
that she bound me to eternal secrecy.

Lady Hester told me that since her residence at
Djoun, she had been attacked by an illness so severe
as to render her for a long time perfectly helpless;
all her attendants fled, and left her to perish. Whilst
she lay thus alone and quite unable to rise, robbers

came and carried away her property [1]: she told me
that they actually unroofed a great part of the building, and employed engines with pullies for the purpose
of hoisting out such of her valuables as were too bulky
to pass through doors. It would seem that before
this catastrophe Lady Hester had been rich in the
possession of Eastern luxuries ; for she told me, that
when the chiefs of the Ottoman force took refuge
with her after the fall of Acre, they brought their
wives also in great numbers : to all of these, Lady
Hester, as she said, presented magnificent dresses ;
but her generosity occasioned strife only instead of
gratitude, for every woman who fancied her present
less splendid than that of another, with equal or less
pretension, became absolutely furious. All these audacious guests had now been got rid of; but the Albanian
soldiers who had taken refuge with Lady Hester at
the same time still remained under her protection.

In truth, this half-ruined convent, guarded by the
proud heart of an English gentlewoman, was the only
spot throughout all Syria and Palestine in which the
will of Mehemet Ali and his fierce Lieutenant was not
the law. More than once had the Pasha of Egypt
commanded that Ibrahim should have the Albanians
delivered up to him ; but this white woman of the

---

[1] The proceedings thus described to me, by Lady Hester,
as having taken place during her illness, were afterwards re-
enacted at the time of her death. Since I wrote the words to
which this note is appended, I received from Warburton an
interesting account of the heroine's death, or rather the circumstances attending the discovery of the event ; and I caused it
to be printed in the former editions of this work. I must now
give up the borrowed ornament, and omit my extract from my
friend's letter, for the rightful owner has reprinted it in 'The
Crescent and the Cross.' I know what a sacrifice I am making ;
for in noticing the first edition of this book, reviewers turned
aside from the text to the note, and remarked upon the interesting information which Warburton's letter contained, and the
descriptive force with which it was written.

mountain (grown classical, not by books, but by very pride) answered only with a disdainful invitation to 'come and take them'. Whether it was that Ibrahim was acted upon by any superstitious dread of interfering with the Prophetess (a notion not at all incompatible with his character as an able Oriental commander), or that he feared the ridicule of putting himself in collision with a gentlewoman, he certainly never ventured to attack the sanctuary; and so long as Chatham's grand-daughter breathed a breath of life, there was always this one hillock, and that too in the midst of a most populous district, which stood out, and kept its freedom. Mehemet Ali used to say, I am told, that the Englishwoman had given him more trouble than all the insurgent people of Syria and Palestine.

The Prophetess announced to me that we were upon the eve of a stupendous convulsion which would destroy the then recognised value of all property upon earth; and, declaring that those only who should be in the East at the time of the great change could hope for greatness in the new life that was then close at hand, she advised me, whilst there was yet time, to dispose of my property in poor, frail England, and gain a station in Asia: she told me that, after leaving her, I should go into Egypt, but that in a little while I should return into Syria. I secretly smiled at this last prophecy as 'a bad shot', because I had fully determined, after visiting the Pyramids, to take ship from Alexandria for Greece. But men struggle vainly in the meshes of their destiny! the unbelieved Cassandra was right after all: the plague came, and the necessity of avoiding the quarantine detention, to which I should have been subjected if I had sailed from Alexandria, forced me to alter my route. I went down into Egypt, and stayed there for a time, and then crossed the Desert once more, and came back to the mountains of the Lebanon, exactly as the Prophetess had foretold.

Lady Hester talked to me long and earnestly on the subject of Religion, announcing that the Messiah was yet to come. She strived to impress me with the vanity and falseness of all European creeds, as well as with a sense of her own spiritual greatness. Throughout her conversation upon these high topics, she carefully insinuated, without actually asserting, her heavenly rank.

Amongst other much more marvellous powers, the Lady claimed one which most women have more or less,—namely, that of reading men's characters in their faces. She examined the line of my features very attentively, and told me the result : this, however, I mean to keep hidden.

One favoured subject of discourse was that of 'race': upon this she was very diffuse, and yet rather mysterious. She set great value upon the ancient French [1], not Norman blood (for that she vilified), but professed to despise our English notion of 'an old family'. She had a vast idea of the Cornish miners on account of their race ; and said, if she chose she could give me the means of rousing them to the most tremendous enthusiasm.

Such are the topics on which the Lady mainly conversed ; but very often she would descend to more worldly chat, and then she was no longer the Prophetess, but the sort of woman that you some-

---

[1] In a letter which I afterwards received from Lady Hester, she mentioned incidentally Lord Hardwicke, and said that he was 'the kindest-hearted man existing—a most manly, firm character. He comes from a good breed,—all the Yorkes excellent, with *ancient* French blood in their veins.' The underscoring of the word 'ancient' is by the writer of the letter, who had certainly no great love or veneration for the French of the present day : she did not consider them as descended from her favourite stock.

times see, I am told, in London drawing-rooms,—cool
—decisive in manner—unsparing of enemies—full of
audacious fun, and saying the downright things that
the sheepish society around her is afraid to utter.
I am told that Lady Hester was, in her youth,
a capital mimic; and she showed me that not all the
queenly dulness to which she had condemned herself,
—not all her fasting and solitude,—had destroyed
this terrible power. The first whom she crucified in
my presence was poor Lord Byron. She had seen
him, it appeared, I know not where, soon after his
arrival in the East, and was vastly amused at his
little affectations. He had picked up a few sentences of
the Romaic, and with these he affected to give orders
to his Greek servant in a 'ton d'apameibomenos'
style. I can't tell whether Lady Hester's mimicry of
the bard was at all close, but it was amusing: she
attributed to him a curiously coxcomical lisp.

Another person, whose style of speaking the Lady
took off very amusingly, was one who would scarcely
object to suffer by the side of Lord Byron,—I mean
Lamartine. The peculiarity which attracted her ridicule was an over-refinement of manner. According
to my Lady's imitation of Lamartine (I have never
seen him myself), he had none of the violent grimace
of his countrymen, and not even their usual way of
talking, but rather bore himself mincingly, like the
humbler sort of English dandy.[1]

[1] It is said that deaf people can hear what is said concerning
themselves, and it would seem that those who live without
books or newspapers, know all that is written about them.
Lady Hester Stanhope, though not admitting a book or
newspaper into her fortress, seems to have known the way in
which M. Lamartine mentioned her in his book; for in a letter
which she wrote to me after my return to England, she says,
'although neglected, as Monsieur Le M.' (referring as I believe
to M. Lamartine) 'describes, and without books, yet my head
is organized to supply the want of them, as well as acquired
knowledge.'

Lady Hester seems to have heartily despised every thing approaching to exquisiteness. She told me, by the by (and her opinion upon that subject is worth having), that a downright manner, amounting even to brusqueness, is more effective than any other with the Oriental; and that amongst the English, of all ranks and all classes, there is no man so attractive to the Orientals—no man who can negotiate with them half so effectively, as a good, honest, open-hearted, and positive naval officer of the old school.

I have told you, I think, that Lady Hester could deal fiercely with those she hated: one man above all others (he is now uprooted from society) she blasted with her wrath; you would have thought that, in the scornfulness of her nature, she must have sprung upon her foe with more of fierceness than of skill; but this was not so, for, with all the force and vehemence of her invective, she displayed a sober, patient, and minute attention to the details of vituperation, which contributed to its success a thousand times more than mere violence.

During the hours that this sort of conversation or rather discourse was going on, our tchibouques were from time to time replenished, and the Lady as well as I continued to smoke with little or no intermission till the interview ended. I think that the fragrant fumes of the Latakiah must have helped to keep me on my good behaviour as a patient disciple of the Prophetess.

It was not till after midnight that my visit for the evening came to an end. When I quitted my seat the lady rose, and stood up in the same formal attitude (almost that of a soldier in a state of 'attention') which she had assumed on my entrance; at the same time she pushed the loose drapery from her lap, and let it fall down upon the floor.

The next morning after breakfast I was visited by
my Lady's Secretary—the only European, except the
Doctor, whom she retained in her household. This
Secretary, like the Doctor, was Italian, but he preserved more signs of European dress and European
pretensions than his medical fellow-slave. He spoke
little or no English, though he wrote it pretty well,
having been formerly employed in a mercantile house
connected with England. The poor fellow was in an
unhappy state of mind. In order to make you understand the extent of his spiritual anxieties, I ought to
have told you that the Doctor (who had sunk into the
complete Asiatic, and had condescended accordingly
to the performance of even menial services) had
adopted the common faith of all the neighbouring
people, and had become a firm and happy believer
in the divine power of his mistress. Not so the
Secretary. When I had strolled with them to such
a distance from the building as rendered him safe
from being overheard by human ears, he told me in
a hollow voice, trembling with emotion, that there
were times at which he doubted the divinity of
'Milédi'. I said nothing to encourage the poor
fellow in his frightful state of scepticism, for I saw
that, if indulged, it might end in positive infidelity.
Lady Hester, it seemed, had rather arbitrarily
abridged the amusements of her Secretary; and
especially she had forbidden him from shooting small
birds on the mountain side. This oppression had
aroused in him a spirit of inquiry that might end
fatally—perhaps for himself—perhaps for the 'religion
of the place'.

The Secretary told me that his mistress was strongly
disliked by the surrounding people, and that she
oppressed them a good deal by her exactions. I know
not whether this statement had any truth in it; but

whether it was or was not well founded, it is certain
that in Eastern countries hate and veneration are very
commonly felt for the same object ; and the general
belief in the superhuman power of this wonderful
white lady—her resolute and imperious character, and
above all, perhaps, her fierce Albanians (not backward
to obey an order for the sacking of a village), inspired
sincere respect amongst the surrounding inhabitants.
Now the being 'respected' amongst Orientals is not
an empty or merely honorary distinction, but carries
with it a clear right to take your neighbour's corn,
his cattle, his eggs, and his honey, and almost any
thing that is his, except his wives. This law was
acted upon by the Princess of Djoun, and her establishment was supplied by contributions apportioned
amongst the nearest of the villages.

I understood that the Albanians (restrained, I suppose, by the dread of being delivered up to Ibrahim)
had not given any very troublesome proofs of their
unruly natures. The Secretary told me that their
rations, including a small allowance of coffee and
tobacco, were served out to them with tolerable
regularity.

I asked the Secretary how Lady Hester was off for
horses, and said that I would take a look at the stable.
The man did not raise any opposition to my proposal,
and affected no mystery about the matter, but said
that the only two steeds which then belonged to
Milédi were of a very humble sort. This answer, and
a storm of rain then beginning to descend, prevented
me at the time from undertaking my journey to the
stables ; and I don't know that I ever thought of the
matter afterwards, until my return to England, when
I saw Lamartine's eye-witnessing account of the
strange horse saddled, as he pretends, by the hands of
his Maker !

When I returned to my room (this, as my hostess
told me, was the only one in the whole building that
kept out the rain), Lady Hester sent to say she
would be glad to receive me again. I was rather
surprised at this, for I had understood that she
reposed during the day, and it was now little later
than noon. 'Really', said she, when I had taken my
seat and my pipe, 'we were together for hours last
night, and still I have heard nothing at all of my old
friends; now, *do* tell me something of your dear
mother, and her sister; I never knew your father—
it was after I left Burton Pynsent that your mother
married.' I began to make slow answer; but my
questioner soon went off again to topics more
sublime; so that this second interview, though it
lasted two or three hours, was all occupied by the
same sort of varied discourse as that which I have
been describing.

In the course of the afternoon the captain of an
English man-of-war arrived at Djoun, and Lady
Hester determined to receive him for the same reason
as that which had induced her to allow my visit—
namely, an early intimacy with his family. I and the
new visitor—he was a pleasant, amusing man—dined
together, and we were afterwards invited to the
presence of my Lady, and with her we sat smoking
till midnight. The conversation turned chiefly, I think,
upon magical science. I had determined to be off at
an early hour the next morning, and so at the end of
this interview I bade my Lady farewell. With her
parting words she once more advised me to abandon
Europe, and seek my reward in the East; and she
urged me too to give the like counsels to my father,
and tell him that '*She had said it*'.

Lady Hester's unholy claim to supremacy in the
spiritual kingdom was, no doubt, the suggestion of

fierce and inordinate pride most perilously akin to madness; but I am quite sure that the mind of the woman was too strong to be thoroughly overcome by even this potent feeling. I plainly saw that she was not an unhesitating follower of her own system; and I even fancied that I could distinguish the brief moments during which she contrived to believe in Herself, from those long and less happy intervals in which her own reason was too strong for her.

As for the Lady's faith in Astrology and Magic science, you are not for a moment to suppose that this implied any aberration of intellect. She believed these things in common with those around her; and it could scarcely be otherwise, for she seldom spoke to anybody except crazy old dervishes who at once received her alms and fostered her extravagances; and even when (as on the occasion of my visit) she was brought into contact with a person entertaining different notions, she still remained uncontradicted. This entourage, and the habit of fasting from books and newspapers, were quite enough to make her a facile recipient of any marvellous story.

I think that in England we scarcely acknowledge to ourselves how much we owe to the wise and watchful press which presides over the formation of our opinions, and which brings about this splendid result, namely, that in matters of belief the humblest of us are lifted up to the level of the most sagacious, so that really a simple Cornet in the Blues is no more likely to entertain a foolish belief about ghosts, or witchcraft, or any other supernatural topic, than the Lord High Chancellor, or the Leader of the House of Commons. How different is the intellectual régime of Eastern countries! In Syria, and Palestine, and Egypt, you might as well dispute the efficacy of grass or grain as of Magic. There is no controversy about

the matter.   The effect of this, the unanimous belief
of an ignorant people, upon the mind of a stranger, is
extremely curious, and well worth noticing.   A man
coming freshly from Europe is at first proof against
the nonsense with which he is assailed ; but often it
happens that after a little while the social atmosphere
of Asia will begin to infect him, and, if he has been
unaccustomed to the cunning of fence by which
Reason prepares the means of guarding herself against
fallacy, he will yield himself at last to the faith of
those around him ; and this he will do by sympathy,
it would seem, rather than from conviction.   I have
been much interested in observing that the mere
'practical man', however skilful and shrewd in his
own way, has not the kind of power that will enable
him to resist the gradual impression made upon his
mind by the common opinion of those whom he sees
and hears from day to day.   Even amongst the
English (though their good sense and sound religious
knowledge would be likely to guard them from error)
I have known the calculating merchant, the inquisitive
traveller, and the post-captain, with his bright,
wakeful eye of command—I have known all these
surrender themselves to the *really* magic-like influence
of other people's minds.   Their language at first is
that they are 'staggered'; leading you by that
expression to suppose that they had been witnesses
to some phenomenon which it was very difficult to
account for otherwise than by supernatural causes ;
but when I have questioned further, I have always
found that these 'staggering' wonders were not even
specious enough to be looked upon as good 'tricks'.
A man in England, who gained his whole livelihood
as a conjurer, would soon be starved to death if he
could perform no better miracles than those which
are wrought with so much effect in Syria and Egypt.

Sometimes, no doubt, a magician will make a good hit (Sir John once said a 'good thing'); but all such successes range, of course, under the head of mere 'tentative miracles', as distinguished by the strong-brained Paley.

CHAPTER IX

THE SANCTUARY

I crossed the plain of Esdraelon, and entered amongst the hills of beautiful Galilee. It was at sunset that my path brought me sharply round into the gorge of a little valley, and close upon a grey mass of dwellings that lay happily nestled in the lap of the mountain. There was one only shining point still touched with the light of the sun, who had set for all besides; a brave sign this to 'holy Shereef', and the rest of my Moslem men; for the one glittering summit was the head of a minaret, and the rest of the seeming village that had veiled itself so meekly under the shades of evening was Christian Nazareth!

Within the precincts of the Latin convent there stands the great Catholic church which encloses the Sanctuary—the dwelling of the blessed Virgin.[1] This

---

[1] The Greek Church does not recognize this as the true Sanctuary, and many Protestants look upon all the traditions, by which it is attempted to ascertain the holy places of Palestine, as utterly fabulous. For myself, I do not mean either to affirm or deny the correctness of the opinion which has fixed upon this as the true site, but merely to mention it as a belief entertained without question by my brethren of the Latin Church, whose guest I was at the time. It would be a great aggravation of the trouble of writing about these matters, if I were to stop in the midst of every sentence for the purpose of saying 'so-called', or 'so it is said', and would besides sound very

is a grotto of about ten feet either way, forming
a little chapel or recess, and reached by descending
steps. It is decorated with splendour: on the left
hand a column of granite hangs from the top of the
grotto to within a few feet of the ground; immediately
beneath, another column of the same size rises from
the ground as if to meet the one above; but between
this and the suspended pillar there is an interval of
more than a foot. These fragments once formed the
single column on which the angel leant when he spoke
and told to Mary the mystery of her awful blessedness.
Hard by, near the altar, the holy Virgin was kneeling.

I had been journeying (cheerily indeed, for the
voices of my followers were ever within my hearing,
but yet), as it were, in solitude, for I had no comrade
to whet the edge of my reason, or wake me from my
noonday dreams. I was left all alone to be taught
and swayed by the beautiful circumstances of Palestine travelling—by the clime, and the land, and the
name of the land, with all its mighty import—by the
glittering freshness of the sward, and the abounding
masses of flowers that furnished my sumptuous pathway—by the bracing and fragrant air that seemed
to poise me in my saddle, and to lift me along as
a planet appointed to glide through space.

And the end of my journey was Nazareth—the
home of the blessed Virgin! In the first dawn of my

ungraciously; yet I am anxious to be literally true in all I write.
Now, thus it is that I mean to get over my difficulty. When
ever in this great bundle of papers, or book (if book it is to be),
you see any words about matters of religion which would seem
to involve the assertion of my own opinion, you are to understand me just as if one or other of the qualifying phrases above-
mentioned had been actually inserted in every sentence. My
general direction for you to construe me thus, will render
all that I write as strictly and actually true, as if I had every time
lugged in a formal declaration of the fact that I was merely
expressing the notions of other people.

manhood the old painters of Italy had taught me
their dangerous worship of the beauty that is more
than mortal; but those images all seemed shadowy
now, and floated before me so dimly, the one overcasting the other, that they left me no one sweet idol
on which I could look, and look again, and say, 'Maria
mia'! Yet they left me more than an idol—they
left me (for to them I am wont to trace it) a faint
apprehension of Beauty not compassed with lines and
shadows—they touched me (forgive, proud Marie of
Anjou!) they touched me with a faith in loveliness
transcending mortal shapes.

I came to Nazareth, and was led from the convent
to the Sanctuary. Long fasting will sometimes heat
a man's brain, and draw him away out of the world—
will disturb his judgement, confuse his notions of right
and wrong, and weaken his power of choosing the
right. I had fasted perhaps too long, for I was fevered
with the zeal of an insane devotion to the Heavenly
Queen of Christendom. But I knew the feebleness of
this gentle malady, and knew how easily my watchful
reason, if ever so slightly provoked, would drag me
back to life : let there but come one chilling breath of
the outer world, and all this loving piety would cower,
and fly before the sound of my own bitter laugh.
And so as I went, I trod tenderly, not looking to the
right nor to the left, but bending my eyes to the
ground.

The attending friar served me well—he led me
down quietly, and all but silently, to the Virgin's
home. The mystic air was so burnt with the con-
suming flames of the altar, and so laden with incense,
that my chest laboured strongly and heaved with
luscious pain. There—there with beating heart the
Virgin knelt, and listened : I strived to grasp, and
hold with my riveted eyes some one of the feigned

Madonnas; but of all the heaven-lit faces imagined by men, there was none that would abide with me in this the very Sanctuary.   Impatient of vacancy, I grew madly strong against Nature; and if by some awful spell—some impious rite—I could—Oh! most sweet Religion, that bid me fear God, and be pious, and yet not cease from loving, Religion and gracious Custom commanded me that I fall down loyally, and kiss the rock that blessed Mary pressed.   With a half consciousness—with the semblance of a thrilling hope that I was plunging deep, deep into my first know-ledge of some most holy mystery, or of some new, rapturous, and daring sin, I knelt, and bowed down my face till I met the smooth rock with my lips. One moment—one moment—my heart, or some old Pagan demon within me woke up, and fiercely bounded—my bosom was lifted, and swung—as though I had touched her warm robe.   One moment—one more, and then—the fever had left me.   I rose from my knees.   I felt hopelessly sane.   The mere world reappeared.   My good old Monk was there, dangling his key with listless patience; and as he guided me from the church, and talked of the refectory and the coming repast, I listened to his words with some attention and pleasure.

CHAPTER X

THE MONKS OF PALESTINE

WHENEVER you come back to me from Palestine, we will find some 'golden wine [1]' of Lebanon, that we may celebrate with apt libations the monks of the Holy Land; and though the poor fellows be

[1] Vino d'oro.

theoretically 'dead to the world', we will drink to
every man of them a good long life, and a merry one!
Graceless is the traveller who forgets his obligations
to these saints upon earth—little love has he for
merry Christendom, if he has not rejoiced with great
joy to find, in the very midst of water-drinking
infidels, those lowly monasteries where the blessed
juice of the grape is quaffed in peace. Ay! ay!
We will fill our glasses till they look like cups of
amber, and drink profoundly to our gracious hosts
in Palestine.

Christianity permits and sanctions the drinking of
wine; and of all the holy brethren in Palestine there
are none who hold fast to this gladsome rite so
strenuously as the monks of Damascus; not that they
are more zealous Christians than the rest of their
fellows in the Holy Land, but that they have better
wine. Whilst I was at Damascus, I had my quarters
at the Franciscan convent there; and very soon after
my arrival I asked one of the monks to let me know
something of the spots that deserved to be seen:
I made my inquiry in reference to the associations
with which the city had been hallowed by the
sojourn and adventures of St. Paul. 'There is
nothing in all Damascus', said the good man, 'half
so well worth seeing as our cellars'; and forthwith he
invited me to go, see, and admire the long range of
liquid treasure that he and his brethren had laid up
for themselves on earth. And these, I soon found,
were not as the treasures of the miser that lie in
unprofitable disuse; for day by day, and hour by
hour, the golden juice ascended from the dark
recesses of the cellar to the uppermost brains of the
friars. Dear old fellows! in the midst of that
solemn land, their Christian laughter rang loudly
and merrily—their eyes kept flashing with joyful

fire, and their heavy woollen petticoats could no
more weigh down the springiness of their paces,
than the filmy gauze of a danseuse can clog her
bounding step.

You would be likely enough to fancy that these
monastics are men who have retired to the sacred
sites of Palestine from an enthusiastic longing to
devote themselves to the exercise of religion in the
midst of the very land on which its first seeds were
cast ; and this is partially, at least, the case with the
monks of the Greek Church ; but it is not with
enthusiasts that the Catholic establishments are
filled. The monks of the Latin convents are chiefly
persons of the peasant class, from Italy and Spain,
who have been handed over to these remote asylums
by order of their ecclesiastical superiors, and can no
more account for their being in the Holy Land, than
men of marching regiments can explain why they
are in 'stupid quarters'. I believe that these monks
are for the most part well-conducted men,—punctual
in their ceremonial duties, and altogether humble-
minded Christians. Their humility is not at all
misplaced, for you see at a glance (poor fellows) that
they belong to the 'lag remove' of the human race.
If the taking of the cowl does not imply a complete
renouncement of the world, it is at least (in these
days) a thorough farewell to every kind of useful and
entertaining knowledge ; and accordingly, the low
bestial brow and the animal caste of those almost
Bourbon features show plainly enough that all the
intellectual vanities of life have been really and truly
abandoned. But it is hard to quench altogether the
spirit of inquiry that stirs in the human breast, and
accordingly these monks inquire—they are *always*
inquiring—inquiring for 'news'! Poor fellows!
they could scarcely have yielded themselves to the

sway of any passion more difficult of gratification,
for they have no means of communicating with the
busy world, except through European travellers ; and
these, in consequence, I suppose, of that restlessness
and irritability that generally haunt their wanderings,
seem to have always avoided the bore of giving any
information to their hosts.   As for me, I am more
patient and good-natured ; and when I found that
the kind monks who gathered round me at Nazareth
were longing to know the real truth about the
General Bonaparte who had recoiled from the siege
of Acre, I softened my heart down to the good
humour of Herodotus, and calmly began to ' sing
History ', telling my eager hearers of the French
Empire, and the greatness of its glory, and of
Waterloo, and the fall of Napoleon !   Now my story
of this marvellous ignorance on the part of the poor
monks is one upon which (though depending on my
own testimony) I look ' with considerable suspicion ' :
it is quite true (how silly it would be to *invent*
anything so witless !), and yet I think I could satisfy
the mind of a ' reasonable man ' that it is false.
Many of the older monks must have been in Europe
at the time when the Italy and the Spain, from
which they came, were in the act of taking their
French lessons, or had parted so lately with
their teachers, that not to know of ' the Emperor '
was impossible ; and these men could scarcely,
therefore, have failed to bring with them some
tidings of Napoleon's career.   Yet I say that that
which I have written is true—the one who believes
because I have said it, will be right—(she always
is), whilst poor Mr. ' reasonable man ', who is
convinced by the weight of my argument, will be
completely deceived.

In Spanish politics, however, the monks are better

instructed.   The revenues of the monasteries, which
had been principally supplied by the bounty of their
most Catholic Majesties, have been withheld since
Ferdinand's death ; and the interests of these establishments being thus closely involved in the destinies
of Spain, it is not wonderful that the brethren should
be a little more knowing in Spanish affairs than in
other branches of history.   Besides, a large proportion of the monks were natives of the Peninsula : to
these, I remember, Mysseri's familiarity with the Spanish language and character was a source of immense
delight ; they were always gathering around him, and
it seemed to me that they treasured like gold the few
Castilian words which he deigned to spare them.

The monks do a world of good in their way ; and
there can be no doubting that (previously to the
arrival of Bishop Alexander, with his numerous
young family, and his pretty English nursemaids)
they were the chief Propagandists of Christianity in
Palestine.   My old friends of the Franciscan convent
at Jerusalem, some time since, gave proof of their
goodness by delivering themselves up to the peril of
death for the sake of duty.   When I was their guest,
they were forty, I believe, in number ; and I don't
recollect that there was one of them whom I should
have looked upon as a desirable life-holder of any
property to which I might be entitled in expectancy.
Yet these forty were reduced in a few days to
nineteen : the plague was the messenger that
summoned them to taste of real death, but the
circumstances under which they perished are rather
curious ; and though I have no authority for the
story except an Italian newspaper, I harbour no
doubt of its truth, for the facts were detailed with
minuteness, and strictly corresponded with all that
I knew of the poor fellows to whom they related.

It was about three months after the time of my leaving Jerusalem, that the plague set his spotted foot on the Holy City. The monks felt great alarm: they did not shrink from their duty, but for its performance they chose a plan most sadly well fitted for bringing down upon them the very death which they were striving to ward off. They imagined themselves almost safe so long as they remained within their walls; but then it was quite needful that the Catholic Christians of the place, who had always looked to the convent for the supply of their spiritual wants, should receive the aids of religion in the hour of death. A single monk, therefore, was chosen, either by lot, or by some other fair appeal to Destiny: being thus singled out, he was to go forth into the plague-stricken city, and to perform with exactness his priestly duties: then he was to return, not to the interior of the convent, for fear of infecting his brethren, but to a detached building (which I remember) belonging to the establishment, but at some little distance from the inhabited rooms. He was provided with a bell, and at a certain hour in the morning he was ordered to ring it, *if he could*: but if no sound was heard at the appointed time, then knew his brethren that he was either delirious or dead, and another martyr was sent forth to take his place. In this way twenty-one of the monks were carried off. One cannot well fail to admire the steadiness with which the dismal scheme was carried through; but if there be any truth in the notion that disease may be invited by a frightening imagination, it is difficult to conceive a more dangerous plan than that which was chosen by these poor fellows. The anxiety with which they must have expected each day the sound of the bell—the silence that reigned instead of it,—

and then the drawing of the lots (the odds against death being one point lower than yesterday), and the going forth of the newly-doomed man—all this must have widened the gulf that opens to the shades below. When his victim had already suffered so much of mental torture, it was but easy work for big, bullying pestilence to follow a forlorn monk from the beds of the dying, and wrench away his life from him, as he lay all alone in an out-house.

In most, I believe in all, of the Holy Land convents, there are two personages so strangely raised above their brethren in all that dignifies humanity, that their bearing the same habit, their dwelling under the same roof, their worshipping the same God (consistent as all this is with the spirit of their religion), yet strikes the mind with a sense of wondrous incongruity: the men I speak of are the 'Padre Superiore' and the 'Padre Missionario'. The former is the supreme and absolute governor of the establishment over which he is appointed to rule; the latter is entrusted with the more active of the spiritual duties attaching to the Pilgrim Church. He is the shepherd of the good Catholic flock, whose pasture is prepared in the midst of Mussulmans and schismatics—he keeps the light of the true faith ever vividly before their eyes— reproves their vices—supports them in their good resolves—consoles them in their afflictions, and teaches them to hate the Greek Church. Such are his labours; and you may conceive that great tact must be needed for conducting with success the spiritual interests of the Church under circumstances so odd as those which surround it in Palestine.

But the position of the Padre Superiore is still more delicate: he is almost unceasingly in treaty with the powers that be, and the worldly prosperity of the whole establishment is in great measure dependent upon the extent of diplomatic skill which he can employ in its favour. I know not from what class of churchmen these personages are chosen, for there is a mystery attending their origin and the circumstance of their being stationed in these convents, which Rome does not suffer to be penetrated. I have heard it said that they are men of great note, and, perhaps, of too high ambition in the Catholic Hierarchy, who, having fallen under the grave censure of the Church, are banished for fixed periods to these distant monasteries. I believe that the term during which they are condemned to remain in the Holy Land is from eight to twelve years. By the natives of the country, as well as by the rest of the brethren, they are looked upon as superior beings; and rightly too, for nature seems to have crowned them in her own true way.

The chief of the Jerusalem convent was a noble creature; his worldly and spiritual authority seemed to have surrounded him, as it were, with a kind of ' Court ', and the manly gracefulness of his bearing did honour to the throne he filled. There were no lords of the bedchamber, and no gold sticks, and stones in waiting, yet everybody who approached him looked as though he were being ' presented '— every interview which he granted wore the air of an ' audience '; the brethren, as often as they came near, bowed low, and kissed his hand; and if he went out, the Catholics of the place, that hovered about the convent, would crowd around him with devout affection, and almost scramble for the blessing which his touch could give. He bore his honours all serenely, as though calmly conscious of his power to ' bind, and to loose '.

CHAPTER XI

GALILEE

NEITHER old 'Sacred [1]' himself, nor any of his
helpers, knew the road which I meant to take from
Nazareth to the Sea of Galilee, and from thence to
Jerusalem, so I was forced to add another to my
party by hiring a guide. The associations of
Nazareth, as well as my kind feeling towards the
hospitable monks, whose guest I had been, inclined
me to set at nought the advice which I had received
against employing Christians. I accordingly engaged
a lithe, active young Nazarene, who was recommended
to me by the monks, and who affected to be familiar
with the line of country through which I intended
to pass. My disregard of the popular prejudices
against Christians was not justified in this particular
instance by the result of my choice. This you will
see by and by.

I passed by Cana, and the house of the marriage
feast prolonged by miraculous wine; I came to the
field in which our Saviour had rebuked the Scotch
Sabbath-keepers of that period, by suffering his
disciples to pluck corn on the Lord's day; I rode
over the ground where the fainting multitude had
been fed, and they showed me some massive fragments—the relics (they said) of that wondrous
banquet, now turned into stone. The petrifaction
was most complete.

I ascended the height where our Lord was standing
when he wrought the miracle. The hill rose lofty
enough to show me the fairness of the land on all

[1] Shereef.

sides; but I have an ancient love for the mere
features of a lake, and so, forgetting all else when
I reached the summit, I looked away eagerly to the
eastward. There she lay, the Sea of Galilee. Less
stern than Wastwater—less fair than gentle Winder-
mere—she had still the winning ways of an English
lake : she caught from the smiling heavens unceasing
light and changeful phases of beauty ; and with all
this brightness on her face, she yet clung fondly to
the dull he-looking mountain at her side, as though
she would

> Sooth him with her finer fancies,
> Touch him with her lighter thought.[1]

If one might judge of men's real thoughts by their
writings, it would seem that there are people who
can visit an interesting locality, and follow up
continuously the exact train of thought that ought
to be suggested by the historical associations of the
place. A person of this sort can go to Athens, and
think of nothing later than the age of Pericles—can
live with the Scipios as long as he stays in Rome.
I am not thus docile : it is only by snatches, and
for few moments together, that I can really associate
a place with its proper history.

‘ There at Tiberias, and along this western shore
towards the North, and upon the bosom too of the
lake, our Saviour and his disciples——’ Away flew
those recollections, and my mind strained eastward,
because that that farthest shore was the end of the
world that belongs to man the dweller—the beginning
of the other and veiled world that is held by the
strange race, whose life (like the pastime of Satan) is
a ‘ going to and fro upon the face of the earth ’.

---

[1] Tennyson.

From those grey hills right away to the gates of
Bagdad stretched forth the mysterious 'Desert'—
not a pale, void, sandy tract, but a land abounding
in rich pastures—a land without cities or towns,
without any 'respectable' people, or any 'respectable'
things, yet yielding its eighty thousand cavalry to
the beck of a few old men. But once more—'Tiberias
—the plain of Gennesareth—the very earth on which
I stood—that the deep, low tones of the Saviour's
voice should have gone forth into Eternity from out
of the midst of these hills and these valleys!'—Ay,
ay, but yet again the calm face of the lake was
uplifted, and smiled upon my eyes with such familiar
gaze that the 'deep low tones' were hushed—the
listening multitudes all passed away, and instead
there came to me a loving thought from over the
seas in England—a thought more sweet than Gospel
to a wilful mortal like this.

I went to Tiberias, and soon got afloat upon the
water. In the evening I took up my quarters in the
Catholic church, and, the building being large
enough, the whole of my people were admitted to
the benefit of the same shelter. With portmanteaus,
and carpet bags, and books, and maps, and fragrant
tea, Mysseri soon made me a home on the southern
side of the church. One of old Shereef's helpers was
an enthusiastic Catholic, and was greatly delighted
at having so sacred a lodging. He lit up the altar
with a number of tapers, and when his preparations
were complete, he began to perform strange orisons;
his lips muttered the prayers of the Latin Church,
but he bowed himself down, and laid his forehead
to the stones beneath him, after the manner of a
Mussulman. The universal aptness of a religious
system for all stages of civilization, and for all sorts
and conditions of men, well befits its claim of divine

origin. She is of all nations, and of all times, that wonderful Church of Rome!

Tiberias is one of the four holy cities[1], according to the Talmud; and it is from this place, or the immediate neighbourhood of it, that the Messiah is to arise.

Except at Jerusalem, never think of attempting to sleep in a 'holy city'. Old Jews from all parts of the world go to lay their bones upon the sacred soil; and since these people never return to their homes, it follows that any domestic vermin they may bring with them are likely to become permanently resident, so that the population is continually increasing. No recent census had been taken when I was at Tiberias; but I know that the congregation of fleas which attended at my church alone must have been something enormous. It was a carnal, self-seeking congregation, wholly inattentive to the service which was going on, and devoted to the one object of having my blood. The fleas of all nations were there. The smug, steady, importunate flea from Holywell Street—the pert, jumping 'puce' from hungry France—the wary, watchful 'pulce' with his poisoned stiletto—the vengeful 'pulga' of Castile with his ugly knife—the German 'floh' with his knife and fork, insatiate, not rising from table —whole swarms from all the Russias, and Asiatic hordes unnumbered—all these were there, and all rejoiced in one great international feast. I could no more defend myself against my enemies, than if I had been 'pain à discretion' in the hands of a French communist. After passing a night like this, you are glad to gather up the remains of your body long, long before morning dawns. Your skin

[1] The other three cities held holy by Jews are Jerusalem, Hebron, and Safet.

is scorched—your temples throb—your lips feel
withered and dried—your burning eye-balls are
screwed inwards against the brain. You have no
hope but only in the saddle, and the freshness of the
morning air.

CHAPTER XII

MY FIRST BIVOUAC

THE course of the Jordan is from the north to the
south, and in that direction, with very little of devious
winding, it carries the shining waters of Galilee
straight down into the solitudes of the Dead Sea.
Speaking roughly, the river in that meridian is
a boundary between the people living under roofs,
and the tented tribes that wander on the farther
side. And so, as I went down in my way from
Tiberias towards Jerusalem, along the western bank
of the stream, my thinking all propended to the
ancient world of herdsmen and warriors, that lay so
close over my bridle arm.

If a man, and an Englishman, be not born of his
mother with a Chiffney-bit in his mouth, there comes
to him a time for loathing the wearisome ways of
society—a time for not liking tamed people—a time
for not sitting in pews—a time for impugning the
foregone opinions of men, and haughtily dividing
truth from falsehood—a time, in short, for question-
ing, scoffing, and railing—for speaking lightly of the
very opera, and all our most cherished institutions.
It is from nineteen to two or three and twenty,
perhaps, that this war of the man against men is
like to be waged most sullenly. You are yet in this
smiling England, but you find yourself bending your

way to the dark sides of her mountains,—climbing
the dizzy crags,—exulting in the fellowship of mists
and clouds, and watching the storms how they
gather, or proving the mettle of your mare upon the
broad and dreary downs, because that you feel
congenially with the yet unparcelled earth. A little
while you are free, and unlabelled, like the ground
that you compass; but Civilization is watching to
throw her lasso; you will be surely enclosed, and
sooner or later brought down to a state of mere
usefulness—your grey hills will be curiously sliced
into acres, and roods, and perches, and you, for all
you sit so wilful in your saddle, you will be caught
—you will be taken up from travel, as a colt from
grass, to be trained, and tried, and matched, and
run. This in time; but first come continental tours,
and the moody longing for eastern travel: the downs
and the moors of England can hold you no longer;
with larger stride you burst away from these slips
and patches of free land—you thread your path
through the crowds of Europe, and at last, on the
banks of Jordan, you joyfully know that you are
upon the very frontier of all accustomed respecta-
bilities. There, on the other side of the river (you
can swim it with one arm), there reigns the people
that will be like to put you to death, for *not* being
a vagrant, for *not* being a robber, for *not* being
armed and houseless. There is comfort in that
—health, comfort, and strength to one who is aching
from very weariness of that poor, dear, middle-aged,
deserving, accomplished, pedantic, and pains-taking
governess, Europe.

I had ridden for some hours along the right bank
of Jordan, when I came to the Djesr el Medjamè (an
old Roman bridge, I believe), which crossed the river.
My Nazarene guide was riding ahead of the party,

and now, to my surprise and delight, he turned left-
wards, and led on over the bridge. I knew that the
true road to Jerusalem must be mainly by the right
bank of Jordan; but I supposed that my guide was
crossing the bridge at this spot in order to avoid
some bend in the river, and that he knew of a ford
lower down by which we should regain the western
bank. I made no question about the road, for I was
but too glad to set my horse's hoofs upon the land of
the wandering tribes. None of my people, except the
Nazarene, knew the country. On we went through
rich pastures upon the eastern side of the water.
I looked for the expected bend of the river, but, far
as I could see, it kept a straight southerly course.
I still left my guide unquestioned.

The Jordan is not a perfectly accurate boundary
betwixt roofs and tents, for, soon after passing the
bridge, I came upon a cluster of huts. Some time
afterwards, the guide, upon being closely questioned
by my servants, confessed that the village which we
had left behind was the last that we should see, but
he declared that he knew a spot at which we should
find an encampment of friendly Bedouins, who would
receive me with all hospitality. I had long determined
not to leave the East without seeing something of the
wandering tribes, but I had looked forward to this as
a pleasure to be found in the Desert between El Arish
and Egypt—I had no idea that the Bedouins on the
East of Jordan were accessible. My delight was so
great at the near prospect of bread and salt in the
tent of an Arab warrior, that I wilfully allowed my
guide to go on, and mislead me. I saw that he was
taking me out of the straight route towards Jerusalem, and was drawing me into the midst of the
Bedouins, but the idea of his betraying me seemed
(I know not why) so utterly absurd that I could not

entertain it for a moment. I fancied it possible that
the fellow had taken me out of my route in order to
attempt some little mercantile enterprise with the
tribe for which he was seeking, and I was glad of the
opportunity which I might thus gain of coming in
contact with the wanderers.

Not long after passing the village a horseman met
us. It appeared that some of the cavalry of Ibrahim
Pasha had crossed the river, for the sake of the rich
pastures on the eastern bank, and that this man was
one of the troopers. He stopped, and saluted. He
was obviously surprised at meeting an unarmed, or
half-armed, cavalcade, and at last he fairly told us
that we were on the wrong side of the river, and
that, if we went on, we must lay our account with
falling amongst robbers. All this while, and throughout the day, my Nazarene kept well ahead of the
party, and was constantly up in his stirrups, straining
forward, and searching the distance for some objects
which still remained unseen.

For the rest of the day we saw no human being;
we pushed on eagerly, in the hope of coming up with
the Bedouins before nightfall. Night came, and we
still went on in our way, till about ten o'clock. Then
the thorough darkness of the night, and the weariness
of our beasts (they had already done two good days'
journey in one), forced us to determine upon coming
to a stand-still. Upon the heights to the eastward
we saw lights; these shone from caves on the moun-
tain-side, inhabited, as the Nazarene told us, by
rascals of a low sort—not real Bedouins—men
whom we might frighten into harmlessness, but
from whom there was no willing hospitality to be
expected.

We heard at a little distance the brawling of
a rivulet, and on the banks of this it was determined

to establish our bivouac; we soon found the stream,
and following its course for a few yards came to a spot
which was thought to be fit for our purpose.   It was
a sharply cold night in February, and, when I dis-
mounted, I found myself standing upon some wet,
rank herbage that promised ill for the comfort of our
resting place.   I had bad hopes of a fire, for the
pitchy darkness of the night was a great obstacle to
any successful search for fuel, and, besides, the boughs
of trees or bushes would be so full of sap, in this
early spring, that they would not easily burn.   However, we were not likely to submit to a dark and cold
bivouac without an effort, and my fellows groped
forward through the darkness, till, after advancing
a few paces, they were happily stopped by a complete
barrier of dead prickly bushes.   Before our swords
could be drawn to reap this welcome harvest, it was
found to our surprise that the fuel was already hewn,
and strewed along the ground in a thick mass.   A
spot for the fire was found with some difficulty, for
the earth was moist, and the grass high and rank.
At last there was a clicking of flint and steel, and
presently there stood out from darkness one of the
tawney faces of my muleteers, bent down to near
the ground, and suddenly lit up by the glowing
of the spark, which he courted with careful breath.
Before long there was a particle of dry fibre or leaf
that kindled to a tiny flame; then another was lit
from that, and then another.   Then small, crisp twigs,
little bigger than bodkins, were laid athwart the
glowing fire.   The swelling cheeks of the muleteer,
laid level with the earth, blew tenderly at first, then
more boldly, and the young flame was daintily nursed
and fed, and fed more plentifully till it gained good
strength.   At last a whole armful of dry bushes was
piled up over the fire, and presently, with a loud,

cheery cracking and crackling, a royal tall blaze
shot up from the earth, and showed me once more
the shapes and faces of my men, and the dim outlines of the horses and mules that stood grazing
hard by.

My servants busied themselves in unpacking the
baggage, as though we had arrived at an hotel—
Shereef and his helpers unsaddled their cattle. We
had left Tiberias without the slightest idea that we
were to make our way to Jerusalem along the desolate
side of the Jordan, and my servants (generally pro-
vident in those matters) had brought with them only,
I think, some unleavened bread, and a rocky fragment
of goat's milk cheese. These treasures were produced.
Tea and the contrivances for making it were always
a standing part of my baggage. My men gathered
in circle round the fire. The Nazarene was in a false
position, from having misled us so strangely, and he
would have shrunk back, poor devil, into the cold and
outer darkness, but I made him draw near, and share
the luxuries of the night. My quilt and my pelisse.
were spread, and the rest of my people had all their
capotes, or pelisses, or robes of some sort, which
furnished their couches. The men gathered in circle,
some kneeling, some sitting, some lying reclined
around our common hearth. Sometimes on one,
sometimes on another, the flickering light would glare
more fiercely. Sometimes it was the good Shereef
that seemed the foremost, as he sat with venerable
beard, the image of manly piety—unknowing of all
geography, unknowing where he was, or whither he
might go, but trusting in the goodness of God, and
the clenching power of fate, and the good star of the
Englishman. Sometimes, like marble, the classic
face of the Greek Mysseri would catch the sudden
light, and then again, by turns, the ever-perturbed

Dthemetri, with his odd Chinaman's eye, and bristling, terrier-like moustache, shone forth illustrious.

I always liked the men who attended me on these Eastern travels, for they were all of them brave, cheery-hearted fellows, and, although their following my career brought upon them a pretty large share of those toils and hardships which are so much more amusing to gentlemen than to servants, yet not one of them ever uttered or hinted a syllable of complaint, or even affected to put on an air of resignation. I always liked them, but never perhaps so much as when they were thus grouped together under the light of the bivouac fire. I felt towards them as my comrades, rather than as my servants, and took delight in breaking bread with them, and merrily passing the cup.

The love of tea is a glad source of fellow-feeling between the Englishman and the Asiatic; in Persia it is drunk by all, and, although it is a luxury that is rarely within the reach of the Osmanlees, there are few of them who do not know and love the blessed 'tchäi'. Our camp-kettle, filled from the brook, hummed doubtfully for a while, then busily bubbled under the sidelong glare of the flames—cups clinked and rattled—the fragrant steam ascended; and soon this little circlet in the wilderness grew warm and genial as my lady's drawing-room.

And after this there came the tchibouque—great comforter of those that are hungry and way-worn. And it has this virtue—it helps to destroy the *gêne* and awkwardness which one sometimes feels at being in company with one's dependants: for, whilst the amber is at your lips, there is nothing ungracious in your remaining silent, or speaking pithily in short inter-whiff sentences. And for us that night there was pleasant and plentiful matter of talk; for the

where we should be on the morrow, and the where-
withal we should be fed—whether by some ford we
should regain the western bank of Jordan, or find
bread and salt under the tents of a wandering tribe,
or whether we should fall into the hands of the Philistines, and so come to see Death—the last, and greatest
of all 'the fine sights' that there be—these were
questionings not dull nor wearisome to us, for we
were all concerned in the answers. And it was not
an all-imagined morrow that we probed with our
sharp guesses; for the lights of those low Philistines
—the men of the caves—still shone on the rock
above, and we knew by their yells that the fire of our
bivouac had shown us.

At length we thought it well to seek for sleep.
Our plans were laid for keeping up a good watch
through the night. My quilt, and my pelisse, and my
cloak were spread out so that I might lie spokewise,
with my feet towards the central fire. I wrapped my
limbs daintily round, and gave myself orders to sleep
like a veteran soldier. But my attempt to sleep upon
the earth that God gave me was more new and
strange than I had fancied it. I had grown used to
the scene which was before me whilst I was sitting,
or reclining, by the side of the fire, but now that
I laid myself down at full length, it was the deep
black mystery of the heavens that hung over my
eyes—not an earthly thing in the way from my own
very forehead right up to the end of all space. I grew
proud of my boundless bed-chamber. I might have
'found sermons' in all this greatness (if I had I
should surely have slept), but such was not then my
way. If this cherished Self of mine had built the
Universe, I should have dwelt with delight on 'the
wonders of creation'. As it was, I felt rather the
vain-glory of my promotion, from out of mere rooms

and houses, into the midst of that grand, dark, infinite palace.

And then, too, my head, far from the fire, was in cold latitudes, and it seemed to me strange that I should be lying so still and passive, whilst the sharp night-breeze walked free over my cheek, and the cold damp clung to my hair, as though my face grew in the earth, and must bear with the footsteps of the wind and the falling of the dew, as meekly as the grass of the field. And so, when, from time to time, the watch quietly and gently kept up the languishing fire, he seldom, I think, was unseen to my restless eyes. Yet, at last, when they called me, and said that the morn would soon be dawning, I rose from a state of half-oblivion, not much unlike to sleep, though sharply qualified by a sort of vegetable's consciousness of having been growing still colder and colder, for many and many an hour.

CHAPTER XIII

THE DEAD SEA

The gray light of the morning showed us, for the first time, the ground we had chosen for our resting place. We found that we had bivouacked upon a little patch of barley, plainly belonging to the men of the caves. The dead bushes which we found so happily placed in readiness for our fire, had been strewn as a fence for the protection of the little crop. This was the only cultivated spot of ground which we had seen for many a league, and I was rather sorry to find that our night fire, and our cattle, had spread so much ruin upon this poor solitary slip of corn land.

yellow, and naked, walled up in her tomb for ever the
dead and damned Gomorrah. There was no fly that
hummed in the forbidden air, but, instead, a deep
stillness—no grass grew from the earth—no weed
peered through the void sand, but, in mockery of all
life, there were trees borne down by Jordan in some
ancient flood, and these, grotesquely planted upon the
forlorn shore, spread out their grim skeleton arms all
scorched, and charred to blackness, by the heats of
the long, silent years.

I now struck off towards the debouchure of the
river ; but I found that the country, though seemingly
quite flat, was intersected by deep ravines, which did
not show themselves until nearly approached. For
some time my progress was much obstructed ; but at
last I came across a track leading towards the river,
and which might, as I hoped, bring me to a ford.
I found, in fact, when I came to the river's side, that
the track reappeared upon the opposite bank, plainly
showing that the stream had been fordable at this
place. Now, however, in consequence of the late
rains, the river was quite impracticable for baggage
horses. A body of waters, about equal to the Thames
at Eton, but confined to a narrower channel, poured
down in a current so swift and heavy, that the idea
of passing with laden baggage horses was utterly
forbidden. I could have swum across myself, and
I might, perhaps, have succeeded in swimming a horse
over. But this would have been useless, because in
such case I must have abandoned not only my
baggage, but all my attendants, for none of them
were able to swim, and, without that resource, it
would have been madness for them to rely upon the
swimming of their beasts across such a powerful
stream. I still hoped, however, that there might be
a chance of passing the river at the point of its actual

junction with the Dead Sea, and I therefore went on in that direction.

Night came upon us whilst labouring across gullies and sandy mounds, and we were obliged to come to a stand-still, quite suddenly, upon the very edge of a precipitous descent. Every step towards the Dead Sea had brought us into a country more and more dreary; and this sand-hill, which we were forced to choose for our resting-place, was dismal enough. A few slender blades of grass, which here and there singly pierced the sand, mocked bitterly the hunger of our jaded beasts, and, with our small remaining fragment of goat's milk rock by way of supper, we were not much better off than our horses; we wanted, too, the great requisite of a cheery bivouac—fire. Moreover, the spot on which we had been so suddenly brought to a stand-still was relatively high, and unsheltered, and the night wind blew swiftly and cold.

The next morning I reached the debouchure of the Jordan, where I had hoped to find a bar of sand that might render its passage possible. The river, however, rolled its eddying waters fast down to the 'sea', in a strong, deep stream that shut out all hope of crossing.

It now seemed necessary either to construct a raft of some kind, or else to retrace my steps, and remount the banks of the Jordan. I had once happened to give some attention to the subject of military bridges —a branch of military science which includes the construction of rafts and contrivances of the like sort, and I should have been very proud, indeed, if I could have carried my people and my baggage across by dint of any idea gathered from Sir Howard Douglas or Robinson Crusoe. But we were all faint and languid from want of food, and, besides, there were

no materials.   Higher up the river there were bushes
and river plants, but nothing like timber, and the
cord with which my baggage was tied to the pack-
saddles amounted altogether to a very small quantity
—not nearly enough to haul any sort of craft across
the stream.

And now it was, if I remember rightly, that
Dthemetri submitted to me a plan for putting to
death the Nazarene, whose misguidance had been the
cause of our difficulties.   There was something fascinating in this suggestion ; for the slaying of the guide
was, of course, easy enough, and would look like an
act of what politicians call 'vigour'.   If it were only
to become known to my friends in England that I had
calmly killed a fellow-creature for taking me out of
my way, I might remain perfectly quiet and tranquil
for all the rest of my days, quite free from the danger
of being considered 'slow'; I might ever after live
on upon my reputation, like 'single-speech Hamilton'
in the last century, or 'single-sin ——' in this,
without being obliged to take the trouble of doing
any more harm in the world.   This was a great
temptation to an indolent person ; but the motive was
not strengthened by any sincere feeling of anger with
the Nazarene.   Whilst the question of his life and
death was debated, he was riding in front of our
party, and there was something in the anxious writh-
ing of his supple limbs, that seemed to express a sense
of his false position, and struck me as highly comic.
I had no crotchet at that time against the punish-
ment of death, but I was unused to blood, and the
proposed victim looked so thoroughly capable of
enjoying life (if he could only get to the other side
of the river), that I thought it would be hard for
him to die, merely in order to give me a character
for energy.   Acting on the result of these considera-

tions, and reserving to myself a free and unfettered discretion to have the poor villain shot at any future moment, I magnanimously decided that, for the present, he should live, and not die.

I bathed in the Dead Sea. The ground covered by the water sloped so gradually, that I was not only forced to 'sneak in', but to walk through the water nearly a quarter of a mile, before I could get out of my depth. When at last I was able to attempt to dive, the salts held in solution made my eyes smart so sharply, that the pain I thus suffered, joined with the weakness occasioned by want of food, made me giddy and faint for some moments; but I soon grew better. I knew beforehand the impossibility of sinking in this buoyant water; but I was surprised to find that I could not swim at my accustomed pace: my legs and feet were lifted so high and dry out of the lake, that my stroke was baffled, and I found myself kicking against the thin air, instead of the dense fluid upon which I was swimming. The water is perfectly bright and clear; its taste detestable. After finishing my attempts at swimming and diving, I took some time in regaining the shore, and, before I began to dress, I found that the sun had already evaporated the water which clung to me, and that my skin was thickly encrusted with salts.

CHAPTER XIV

THE BLACK TENTS

My steps were reluctantly turned towards the north. I had ridden some way, and still it seemed that all life was fenced and barred out from the desolate ground over which I was journeying. On the west there flowed the impassable Jordan; on the east stood an endless range of barren mountains; and on the south lay that desert sea that knew not the plashing of an oar; greatly, therefore, was I surprised, when suddenly there broke upon my ear the long, ludicrous, persevering bray of a donkey. I was riding at this time some few hundred yards ahead of all my party, except the Nazarene (who, by a wise instinct, kept closer to me than to Dthemetri), and I instantly went forward in the direction of the sound, for I fancied that where there were donkeys, there too most surely would be men. The ground on all sides of me seemed thoroughly void and lifeless, but at last I got down into a hollow, and presently a sudden turn brought me within thirty yards of an Arab encampment. The low black tents which I had so long lusted to see were right before me, and they were all teeming with live Arabs—men, women, and children.

I wished to have let my people behind know where I was, but I recollected that they would be able to trace me by the prints of my horse's hoofs in the sand, and, having to do with Asiatics, I felt the danger of the slightest movement which might be looked upon as a sign of irresolution. Therefore, without looking behind me—without looking to the right or to the left, I rode straight up towards the foremost tent. Before it was strewed a semicircular fence of dead boughs; through this, and about opposite to the front of the tent, there was a narrow opening. As I advanced, some twenty or thirty of the most uncouth-looking fellows imaginable came forward to meet me. In their appearance they showed nothing of the Bedouin blood; they were of many colours, from dingy brown to jet black, and some of these last had much of the negro look about them. They were tall, powerful fellows, but repulsively ugly. They wore nothing but the Arab shirts, confined at the waist by leather belts.

I advanced to the gap left in the fence, and at once alighted from my horse. The chief greeted me after his fashion by alternately touching first my hand and then his own forehead, as if he were conveying the virtue of the touch like a spark of electricity.   Presently I found myself seated upon a sheepskin spread for me under the sacred shade of Arabian canvas. The tent was of a long, narrow, oblong form, and contained a quantity of men, women, and children, so closely huddled together, that there was scarcely one of them who was not in actual contact with his neighbour. The moment I had taken my seat, the chief repeated his salutations in the most enthusiastic manner, and then the people having gathered densely about me, got hold of my unresisting hand, and passed it round like a claret jug for the benefit of everybody.   The women soon brought me a wooden bowl full of buttermilk, and welcome indeed came the gift to my hungry and thirsty soul.

After some time, my people, as I had expected, came up ; and when poor Dthemetri saw me on my sheep-skin, 'the life and soul' of this ragamuffin party, he was so astounded that he even failed to check his cry of horror ; he plainly thought that now, at last, the Lord had delivered me (interpreter and all) into the hands of the lowest Philistines.

Mysseri carried a tobacco-pouch slung at his belt, and as soon as its contents were known, the whole population of the tent began begging like spaniels for bits of the beloved weed.   I concluded, from the abject manner of these people, that they could not possibly be thorough-bred Bedouins, and I saw, too, that they must be in the very last stage of misery, for poor indeed is the man · in these climes who cannot command a pipeful of tobacco. I began to think that I had fallen amongst thorough savages, and it seemed likely enough that they would gain their very first knowledge of civilization by seizing and studying the contents of my dearest portmanteaus, but still my impression was that they would hardly venture upon such an attempt ; I observed, indeed, that they did not offer me the bread and salt (the pledges of peace amongst wandering tribes), but I fancied that they refrained from this act of hospitality, not in consequence of any hostile determination, but in order that the notion of robbing me might remain for the present an 'open question'. I afterwards found that the poor fellows had no bread to offer. They were literally 'out at grass': it is true that they had a scanty supply of milk from goats, but they were living almost entirely upon certain grass stems which were just in season at that time of the year. These, if not highly nourishing, are pleasant enough to the taste, and their acid juices come gratefully to thirsty lips.

CHAPTER XV

PASSAGE OF THE JORDAN

AND now Dthemetri began to enter into a negotiation with my hosts for a passage over the river. I never interfered with my worthy Dragoman upon these occasions, because from my entire ignorance of the Arabic, I should have been quite unable to exercise any real control over his words, and it would have been silly to break the stream of his

eloquence to no purpose. I have reason to fear,
however, that he lied transcendently, and especially
in representing me as the bosom friend of Ibrahim
Pasha.   The mention of that name produced
immense agitation and excitement, and the Sheik
explained to Dthemetri the grounds of the infinite
respect which he and his tribe entertained for the
Pasha. Only a few weeks before, Ibrahim had
craftily sent a body of troops across the Jordan.
The force went warily round to the foot of the
mountains on the East, so as to cut off the retreat
of this tribe, and then surrounded them as they
lay encamped in the vale ; their camels, and indeed
all their possessions worth taking, were carried off
by the soldiery, and moreover the then Sheik,
together with every tenth man of the tribe, was
brought out and shot.   You would think that this
conduct on the part of the Pasha might not procure
for his ' friend ' a very gracious reception amongst
the people whom he had thus despoiled and
decimated ; but the Asiatic seems to be animated
with a feeling of profound respect, almost bordering
upon affection, for those who have done him any
bold and violent wrong ; and there is always, too, so
much of vague and undefined apprehension mixed
up with his really well-founded alarms, that I can
see no limit to the yielding and bending of his mind
when it is worked upon by the idea of power.

After some discussion the Arabs agreed, as
I thought, to conduct me to a ford, and we moved
on towards the river followed by seventeen of the
most able-bodied of the tribe under the guidance of
several gray-bearded elders, and Sheik Ali Djourban
at the head of the whole detachment.   Upon leaving
the encampment a sort of ceremony was performed
for the purpose, it seemed, of ensuring, if possible,

a happy result for the undertaking. There was an uplifting of arms, and a repeating of words, that sounded like formulae, but there were no prostrations, and I did not understand that the ceremony was of a religious character. The tented Arabs are looked upon as very bad Mahometans.

We arrived upon the banks of the river—not at a ford, but at a deep and rapid part of the stream ; and I now understood that it was the plan of these men, if they helped me at all, to transport me across the river by some species of raft. But a reaction had taken place in the opinions of many, and a violent dispute arose, upon a motion which seemed to have been made by some honourable member, with a view to robbery. The fellows all gathered together in circle at a little distance from my party, and there disputed with great vehemence and fury for nearly two hours. I can't give a correct report of the debate, for it was held in a barbarous dialect of the Arabic unknown to my Dragoman. I recollect I sincerely felt at the time, that the arguments in favour of robbing me must have been almost unanswerable, and I gave great credit to the speakers on my side for the ingenuity and sophistry which they must have shown in maintaining the fight so well.

During the discussion I remained lying in front of my baggage, for this had been already taken from the pack-saddles, and placed upon the ground. I was so languid from want of food that I had scarcely animation enough to feel as deeply interested as you would suppose in the result of the discussion. I thought, however, that the pleasantest toys to play with during this interval were my pistols, and now and then, when I listlessly visited my loaded barrels with the swivel ramrods, or drew a sweet musical click from my English firelocks, it seemed to me that I exercised a slight and gentle influence on the debate. Thanks to Ibrahim Pasha's terrible visitation, the men of the tribe were wholly unarmed, and my advantage in this respect might have counterbalanced in some measure the superiority of numbers.

Mysseri (not interpreting in Arabic) had no duty to perform, and he seemed to be faint and listless as myself. Shereef looked perfectly resigned to any fate. But Dthemetri (faithful terrier !) was bristling with zeal and watchfulness : he could not understand the debate, for it was carried on at a distance too great to be easily heard, even if the language had been familiar ; but he was always on the alert, and now and then conferring with men who had straggled out of the assembly. At last he found an opportunity of making an offer which at once produced immense sensation ; he proposed on my behalf that the tribe should bear themselves loyally towards me, and take my people and my baggage in safety to the other bank of the river, and that I on my part should give such a ' teskeri ', or written certificate of their good conduct, as might avail them hereafter in the hour of their direst need. This proposal was received and instantly accepted by all the men of the tribe there present with the utmost enthusiasm. I was to give the men too a ' baksheish', that is, a present of money usually made upon the conclusion of any sort of treaty, but, although the people of the tribe were so miserably poor, they seemed to look upon the pecuniary part of the arrangement as a matter quite trivial in comparison with the ' teskeri '. Indeed the sum which Dthemetri promised them was extremely small, and no attempt was made to extort any further reward.

The Council broke up, and most of the men rushed madly towards me, overwhelming me with vehement gratulations, and kissing my hands and my boots.

The Arabs then earnestly began their attempt to effect the passage of the river. They had brought with them a great number of skins used for carrying water in the desert; these they filled with air, and fastened several of them to small boughs cut from the banks of the river. In this way they constructed a raft not more than about four or five feet square, but rendered buoyant by the inflated skins. Upon this a portion of my baggage was placed, and was firmly tied to it by the cords used on my pack-saddles. The little raft, with its weighty cargo, was then gently lifted into the water, and I had the satisfaction to see that it floated well.

Twelve of the Arabs now stripped, and tied inflated skins to their loins. Six of the men went down into the river, got in front of the little raft, and pulled it off a few feet from the bank. The other six then dashed into the stream with loud shouts, and swam along after the raft, pushing it from behind. Off went the craft in capital style at first, for the stream was easy on the eastern side, but I saw that the tug was to come, for the main torrent swept round in a bend near the western bank of the river.

The old men with their long gray grisly beards stood shouting and cheering, praying and commanding. At length the raft entered upon the difficult part of its course; the whirling stream seized and twisted it about, and then bore it rapidly downwards; the swimmers flagged, and seemed to be beaten in the struggle. But now the old men on the bank, with their rigid arms uplifted straight, sent forth a cry, and a shout that tore the wide air, and then to make their urging yet more strong, they shrieked out the dreadful syllables ''brahim Pasha!' The swimmers, one moment before so blown and so weary, found lungs to answer the cry, and shouted back the name of their great destroyer, they dashed on through the torrent, and bore the raft in safety to the western bank.

Afterwards the swimmers returned with the raft, and attached to it the rest of my baggage. I took my seat upon the top of the cargo, and the raft thus laden passed the river in the same way and with the same struggle as before. The skins, however, not being perfectly air tight, had lost a great part of their buoyancy, so that I, as well as the luggage that passed on this last voyage, got wet in the waters of Jordan. The raft could not be trusted for another trip, and the rest of my people passed the river in a different, and (for them) much safer way. Inflated skins were fastened to their loins, and thus supported, they were tugged across by Arabs swimming on either side of them. The horses and mules were thrown into the water, and forced to swim over. The poor beasts had a hard struggle for their lives in that swift stream, and I thought that one of the horses would have been drowned, for he was too weak to gain a footing on the western bank, and the stream bore him down. At last, however, he swam back to the side from which he had come. Before night all had passed the river except this one horse and old Shereef. He, poor fellow, was shivering on the eastern bank, for his dread of the passage was so great that he delayed it as long as he could, and at last it became so dark that he was obliged to wait till the morning.

I lay that night on the bank of the river. The Arabs at a little distance from me contrived to kindle

a fire, and sat all round in a circle. They were
made most savagely happy by the tobacco with
which I supplied them, and they soon determined
that the whole night should be one smoking festival.
The poor fellows had only a cracked bowl, without
any tube at all, but this morsel of a pipe they
handed round from one to the other, allowing to
each a fixed number of whiffs. In that way they
passed the whole night.

The next morning old Shereef was brought across.
It was strange to see this solemn old Mussulman,
with his shaven head and his sacred beard, sprawling
and puffing upon the surface of the water. When
at last he reached the bank, the people told him that
by his baptism in Jordan he had surely become
a mere Christian. Poor Shereef! the holy man! the
descendant of the Prophet!—he was sadly hurt by
the taunt, and the more so as he seemed to feel that
there was some foundation for it, and that he really
might have absorbed some Christian errors.

When all was ready for departure, I wrote the
'Teskeri' in French, and delivered it to Sheik Ali
Djourban, together with the promised 'baksheish'.
He was exceedingly grateful, and I parted in a very
friendly way from this ragged tribe.

In two or three hours I gained Rihah, a village
said to occupy the site of ancient Jericho. There
was one building there which I observed with some
emotion, for although it may not have been actually
standing in the days of Jericho, it contained at this
day a most interesting collection of—modern loaves.

Some hours after sunset I reached the convent of
Santa Saba, and there remained for the night.

CHAPTER XVI

TERRA SANTA

THE enthusiasm that had glowed, or seemed to glow, within me, for one blessed moment, when I knelt by the shrine of the Virgin at Nazareth, was not rekindled at Jerusalem. In the stead of the solemn gloom and the deep stillness rightfully belonging to the Holy City, there was the hum and the bustle of active life. It was the 'height of the season'. The Easter ceremonies drew near; the pilgrims were flocking in from all quarters, and, although their objects were partly at least of a religious character, yet their 'arrivals' brought as much stir and liveliness to the city, as if they had come up to marry their daughters.

The votaries who every year crowd to the Holy Sepulchre are chiefly of the Greek and Armenian Churches. They are not drawn into Palestine by a mere sentimental longing to stand upon the ground trodden by our Saviour, but rather they perform the pilgrimage as a plain duty strongly inculcated by their religion. A very great proportion of those who belong to the Greek Church contrive at some time or other in the course of their lives to achieve the enterprise. Many in their infancy and childhood are brought to the holy sites by their parents, but those who have not had this advantage will often make it the main object of their lives to save money enough for this holy undertaking.

The pilgrims begin to arrive in Palestine some weeks before the Easter festival of the Greek Church. They come from Egypt, from all parts of Syria, from Armenia and Asia Minor, from Stamboul, from

Roumelia, from the provinces of the Danube, and
from all the Russias.   Most of these people bring
with them some articles of merchandise, but I myself
believe (notwithstanding the common taunt against
pilgrims) that they do this rather as a mode of
paying the expenses of their journey, than from
a spirit of mercenary speculation. They generally
travel in families, for the women are of course more
ardent than their husbands in undertaking these
pious enterprises, and they take care to bring with
them all their children, however young.   They do
this because the efficacy of the rites is quite independent of the age of the votary, and people whose
careful mothers have obtained for them the benefit
of the pilgrimage in early life, are saved from the
expense and trouble of undertaking the journey at
a later age.

The superior veneration so often excited by objects
that are distant and unknown shows—not perhaps
the wrongheadedness of a man, but rather the
transcendent power of his Imagination. However
this may be, and whether it is by mere obstinacy
that they force their way through intervening
distance, or whether they come by the winged
strength of Fancy, quite certainly the pilgrims who
flock to Palestine from remote homes are the people
most eager in the enterprise, and in number too they
bear a very high proportion to the whole mass.

The great bulk of the pilgrims make their way by
sea to the Port of Jaffa. A number of families will
charter a vessel amongst them, all bringing their
own provisions: these are of the simplest and
cheapest kind. On board every vessel thus freighted,
there is, I believe, a priest, who helps the people in
their religious exercises, and tries (and fails) to
maintain something like order and harmony. The

vessels employed in the service are usually Greek brigs or brigantines, and schooners, and the number of passengers stowed in them is almost always horribly excessive. The voyages are sadly protracted, not only by the land-seeking, storm-flying habits of the Greek seamen, but also by the endless schemes and speculations, for ever tempting them to touch at the nearest port. The voyage, too, must be made during winter, in order that Jerusalem may be reached some weeks before the Greek Easter.

When the pilgrims have landed at Jaffa, they hire camels, horses, mules, or donkeys, and make their way as well as they can to the Holy City. The space fronting the church of the Holy Sepulchre soon becomes a kind of bazaar, or rather perhaps reminds you of an English fair. On this spot the pilgrims display their merchandise, and there, too, the trading residents of the place offer their goods for sale. I have never, I think, seen elsewhere in Asia so much commercial animation as upon this square of ground by the church door: the 'money changers' seemed to be almost as brisk and lively as if they had been *within* the temple.

When I entered the church, I found a Babel of worshippers. Greek, Roman, and Armenian priests were performing their different rites in various nooks and corners, and crowds of disciples were rushing about in all directions,—some laughing and talking, some begging, but most of them going round in a regular and methodical way to kiss the sanctified spots, and speak the appointed syllables, and lay down the accustomed coin. If this kissing of the shrines had seemed as though it were done at the bidding of Enthusiasm, or of any poor sentiment even feebly approaching to it, the sight would have been less odd to English eyes; but as it was, I felt

shocked at the sight of grown men thus steadily and
carefully embracing the sticks and the stones—not
from love or from zeal (else God forbid that I should
have blamed), but from a calm sense of duty: they
seemed to be not 'working out', but *transacting* the
great business of Salvation.

Dthemetri, however (he generally came with me
when I went out, in order to do duty as interpreter),
really had in him some enthusiasm ; he was a zealous
and almost fanatical member of the Greek Church,
and had long since performed the pilgrimage ; so
now great indeed was the pride and delight with
which he guided me from one holy spot to another.
Every now and then, when he came to an unoccupied
shrine, he fell down on his knees and performed
devotion. He was almost distracted by the tempta-
tions that surrounded him : there were so many
stones absolutely requiring to be kissed, that he
rushed about happily puzzled, and sweetly teazed,
like ' Jack among the maidens '.

A Protestant, familiar with the Holy Scriptures,
but ignorant of tradition and the geography of
modern Jerusalem, finds himself a good deal ' mazed '
when he first looks for the sacred sites. The Holy
Sepulchre is not in a field without the walls, but in
the midst, and in the best part, of the town, under
the roof of the great church which I have been
talking about. It is a handsome tomb of oblong
form, partly subterranean, and partly above ground,
and closed in on all sides except the one by which it
is entered. You descend into the interior by a few
steps, and there find an altar with burning tapers.
This is the spot held in greater sanctity than any
other in Jerusalem. When you have seen enough of
it, you feel perhaps weary of the busy crowd, and
inclined for a gallop ; you ask your Dragoman

whether there will be time before sunset to send for
horses and take a ride to Mount Calvary. Mount
Calvary, Signor ?—eccolo ! it is *upstairs—on the first
floor*. In effect, you ascend, if I remember rightly,
just thirteen steps, and then you are shown the now
golden sockets in which the crosses of our Lord and
the two thieves were fixed. All this is startling, but
the truth is that the city, having gathered round
the Sepulchre (the main point of interest), has
gradually crept northward, and thus in great
measure are occasioned the many geographical sur-
prises that puzzle the 'Bible Christian'.

The church of the Holy Sepulchre comprises very
compendiously almost all the spots associated with
the closing career of our Lord. Just there, on your
right, he stood and wept ;—by the pillar on your
left he was scourged ;—on the spot just before you
he was crowned with the crown of thorns ;—up there
he was crucified, and down here he was buried. A
locality is assigned to every the minutest event
connected with the recorded history of our Saviour ;
even the spot where the cock crew when Peter denied
his Master is ascertained, and surrounded by the
walls of an Armenian convent. Many Protestants
are wont to treat these traditions contemptuously,
and those who distinguish themselves from their
brethren by the appellation of 'Bible Christians' are
almost fierce in their denunciation of these supposed
errors.

It is admitted, I believe, by everybody that the
formal sanctification of these spots was the act of
the Empress Helena, the mother of Constantine, but
I think it is fair to suppose that she was guided by
a careful regard to the then prevailing traditions.
Now the nature of the ground upon which Jerusalem
stands is such that the localities belonging to the

events there enacted might have been more easily and permanently ascertained by tradition, than those of any city that I know of. Jerusalem, whether ancient or modern, was built upon and surrounded by sharp, salient rocks, intersected by deep ravines. Up to the time of the siege Mount Calvary, of course, must have been well enough known to the people of Jerusalem; the destruction of the mere buildings could not have obliterated from any man's memory the names of those steep rocks and narrow ravines in the midst of which the city had stood. It seems to me therefore highly probable that in fixing the site of Calvary the Empress was rightly guided. Recollect, too, that the voice of tradition at Jerusalem is quite unanimous, and that Romans, Greeks, Armenians, and Jews, all hating each other sincerely, concur in assigning the same localities to the events told in the Gospel. I concede, however, that the attempt of the Empress to ascertain the sites of the minor events cannot be safely relied upon. With respect, for instance, to the certainty of the spot where the cock crew, I am far from being convinced.

Supposing that the Empress acted arbitrarily in fixing the holy sites, it would seem that she followed the Gospel of St. John, and that the geography sanctioned by her can be more easily reconciled with that history than with the accounts of the other Evangelists.

The authority exercised by the Mussulman Government in relation to the holy sites, is in one view somewhat humbling to the Christians, for it is almost as an arbitrator between the contending sects (this always, of course, for the sake of pecuniary advantage) that the Mussulman lends his contemptuous aid: he not only grants, but enforces toleration. All persons of whatever religion are allowed to go as they will into every part of the church of the Holy Sepulchre, but in order to prevent indecent contests, and also from motives arising out of money payments, the Turkish Government assigns the peculiar care of each sacred spot to one of the ecclesiastic bodies. Since this guardianship carries with it the receipt of all the coins deposited by the pilgrims upon the sacred shrines, it is strenuously fought for by all the rival Churches, and the artifices of intrigue are busily exerted at Stamboul, in order to procure the issue or revocation of the firmans, by which the coveted privilege is granted. In this strife the Greek Church has of late years signally triumphed, and the most famous of the shrines are committed to the care of their priesthood. They possess the golden socket in which stood the cross of our Lord, whilst the Latins are obliged to content themselves with the apertures in which were inserted the crosses of the two thieves. They are naturally discontented with that poor privilege, and sorrowfully look back to the days of their former glory—the days when Napoleon was Emperor, and Sebastiani ambassador at the Porte.

Although the pilgrims perform their devotions at the several shrines with so little apparent enthusiasm, they are driven to the verge of madness by the miracle displayed before them on Easter Saturday. Then it is that the heaven-sent fire issues from the Holy Sepulchre. The pilgrims assemble in the great church, and already, long before the wonder is worked, they are wrought by anticipation of God's sign, as well as by their struggles for room and breathing space, to a most frightful state of excitement. At length the Chief Priest of the Greeks, accompanied (of all people in the world) by the Turkish Governor, enters the tomb. After this, there is a long pause, but at last, and suddenly, from out of the small apertures on either side of the Sepulchre, there issue long, shining flames. The pilgrims now rush forward, madly struggling to light their tapers at the holy fire. This is the dangerous moment, and many lives are often lost.

The year before that of my going to Jerusalem, Ibrahim Pasha, from some whim or motive of policy, chose to witness the miracle. The vast church was of course thronged, as it always is on that awful day. It seems that the appearance of the fire was delayed for a very long time, and that the growing frenzy of the people was heightened by suspense. Many, too, had already sunk under the effect of the heat and the stifling atmosphere, when at last the fire flashed from the Sepulchre. Then a terrible struggle ensued— many sunk, and were crushed. Ibrahim had taken his station in one of the galleries, but now, feeling perhaps his brave blood warmed by the sight and sound of such strife, he took upon himself to quiet the people by his personal presence, and descended into the body of the church with only a few guards. He had forced his way into the midst of the dense crowd, when unhappily he fainted away; his guards shrieked out, and the event instantly became known. A body of soldiers recklessly forced their way through the crowd, trampling over every obstacle that they might save the life of their general. Nearly two hundred people were killed in the struggle.

The following year, however, the Government took better measures for the prevention of these calamities. I was not present at the ceremony, having gone away from Jerusalem some time before, but I afterwards returned into Palestine, and I then learned that the day had passed off without any disturbance of a fatal kind. It is, however, almost too much to expect that

so many ministers of peace can assemble without
finding some occasion for strife, and in that year a
tribe of wild Bedouins became the subject of discord.
These men, it seems, led an Arab life in some of the
desert tracks bordering on the neighbourhood of
Jerusalem, but were not connected with any of the
great ruling tribes. Some whim or notion of policy
had induced them to embrace Christianity; but they
were grossly ignorant of the rudiments of their
adopted faith; and having no priest with them in
their desert, they had as little knowledge of religious
ceremonies as of religion itself: they were not even
capable of conducting themselves in a place of
worship with ordinary decorum, but would interrupt
the service with scandalous cries and warlike shouts.
Such is the account the Latins give of them, but
I have never heard the other side of the question.
These wild fellows, notwithstanding their entire
ignorance of all religion, are yet claimed by the
Greeks, not only as proselytes who have embraced
Christianity generally, but as converts to the
particular doctrines and practice of their Church.
The people thus alleged to have concurred with the
Greeks in rejecting the great Roman Catholic schism
are never, I believe, within the walls of a church, or
even of any building at all, except upon this occasion
of Easter; and, as they then never fail to find a row
of some kind going on by the side of the Sepulchre,
they fancy, it seems, that the ceremonies there
enacted are funeral games, of a martial character,
held in honour of a deceased chieftain, and that a
Christian festival is a peculiar kind of battle, fought
between walls, and without cavalry. It does not
appear, however, that these men are guilty of any
ferocious acts, or that they attempt to commit
depredations. The charge against them is merely

that by their way of applauding the performance—
by their horrible cries and frightful gestures—they
destroy the solemnity of divine service ; and upon
this ground the Franciscans obtained a firman for
the exclusion of such tumultuous worshippers. The
Greeks, however, did not choose to lose the aid of
their wild converts merely because they were a little
backward in their religious education, and they
therefore persuaded them to defy the firman by
entering the city *en masse*, and overawing their
enemies. The Franciscans, as well as the Government authorities, were obliged to give way, and the
Arabs triumphantly marched into the church. The
festival, however, must have seemed to them rather
flat ; for although there may have been some
' casualties' in the way of eyes black, and noses
bloody, and women ' missing', there was no return
of ' killed'.

Formerly the Latin Catholics concurred in acknow-
ledging (but not, I hope, in working) the annual
miracle of the heavenly fire ; but they have for many
years withdrawn their countenance from this exhibition, and they now repudiate it as a trick of the
Greek Church. Thus, of course, the violence of
feeling with which the rival Churches meet at the
Holy Sepulchre on Easter Saturday is greatly
increased, and a disturbance of some kind is certain.
In the year I speak of, though no lives were lost,
there was, as it seems, a tough struggle in the church.
I was amused at hearing of a taunt that was thrown
that day upon an English traveller : he had taken
his station in a convenient part of the church, and
was no doubt displaying that peculiar air of serenity
and gratification with which an English gentleman
usually looks on at a row, when one of the Franciscans
came by, all reeking from the fight, and was so dis-

gusted at the coolness and placid contentment of the
Englishman, that he forgot his monkish humility, as
well as the duties of hospitality (the Englishman was
a guest at the convent), and plainly said, 'You sleep
under our roof—you eat our bread—you drink our
wine, and then, when Easter Saturday comes, you
don't fight for us'!

Yet these rival Churches go on quietly enough till
their blood is up. The terms on which they live
remind one of the peculiar relation subsisting at
Cambridge between 'town and gown'!

The contests, waged by the priests and friars,
certainly do not originate with the lay-pilgrims, for
the great body of these are quiet and inoffensive
people. It is true, however, that their pious
enterprise is believed by them to operate as a counter-
poise for a multitude of sins, whether past or future,
and perhaps they exert themselves in after-life to
restore the balance of good and evil. The Turks
have a maxim, which, like most cynical apothegms,
carries with it the buzzing trumpet of falsehood, as
well as the small, fine 'sting of truth'. 'If your
friend has made the pilgrimage once, distrust him;
if he has made the pilgrimage twice, cut him dead!'
The caution is said to be as applicable to the
visitants of Jerusalem as to those of Mecca; but
I cannot help believing that the frailties of all the
Hadjis [1], whether Christian or Mahometan, are
greatly exaggerated. I certainly regarded the
pilgrims to Palestine as a well-disposed, orderly
body of people, not strongly enthusiastic, but desirous to comply with the ordinances of their religion,
and to attain the great end of salvation as quietly
and economically as possible.

[1] Hadji—a pilgrim.

When the solemnities of Easter are concluded, the
pilgrims move off in a body to complete their good
work by visiting the sacred scenes in the neighbourhood of Jerusalem, including the Wilderness of John
the Baptist, Bethlehem, and above all the Jordan,
for to bathe in those sacred waters is one of the
chief objects of the expedition.   All the pilgrims—
men, women, and children—are submerged *en chemise*,
and the saturated linen is carefully wrapped up, and
preserved as a burial dress that shall inure for salvation in the realms of death.

I saw the burial of a pilgrim; he was a Greek,
miserably poor and very old.   He had just crawled
into the Holy City, and had reached at once the
goal of his pious journey and the end of his sufferings
upon earth.   There was no coffin, nor wrapper, and
as I looked full upon the face of the dead, I saw
how deeply it was rutted with the ruts of age and
misery.   The priest, strong and portly, fresh, fat, and
alive with the life of the animal kingdom—unpaid,
or ill paid for his work—would scarcely deign to
mutter out his forms, but hurried over the words
with shocking haste.   Presently he called out
impatiently, ' Yalla ! Goor ! ' (Come ! look sharp !)
and then the dead Greek was seized ; his limbs
yielded inertly to the rude men that handled them,
and down he went into his grave, so roughly bundled
in, that his neck was twisted by the fall,—so twisted,
that if the sharp malady of life were still upon him,
the old man would have shrieked, and groaned, and
the lines of his face would have quivered with pain.
The lines of his face were not moved, and the old
man lay still and heedless—so well cured of that
tedious life-ache, that nothing could hurt him now.
His clay was *itself again*—cool, firm, and tough.
The pilgrim had found great rest.   I threw the

accustomed handful of the holy soil upon his patient
face, and then, and in less than a minute, the earth
closed coldly round him.

I did not say ' Alas ! ' —(nobody ever does that
I know of, though the word is so frequently written).
I thought the old man had got rather well out of
the scrape of being alive and poor.

The destruction of the mere buildings in such
a place as Jerusalem would not involve the permanent
dispersion of the inhabitants, for the rocky neighbourhood in which the town is situate abounds in caves,
and these would give an easy refuge to the people,
until they gain an opportunity of rebuilding their
dwellings. Therefore I could not help looking upon
the Jews of Jerusalem as being in some sort the
representatives, if not the actual descendants, of the
men who crucified our Saviour. Supposing this to
be the case, I felt that there would be some interest
in knowing how the events of the Gospel History
were regarded by the Israelites of modern Jerusalem.
The result of my inquiry upon this subject was, so
far as it went, entirely favourable to the truth of
Christianity. I understood that *the performance of
the miracles was not doubted by any of the Jews in
the place*; all of them concurred in attributing the
works of our Lord to the influence of magic, but
they were divided as to the species of enchantment
from which the power proceeded : the great mass of
the Jewish people believe, I fancy, that the miracles
had been wrought by aid of the powers of darkness,
but many, and those the more enlightened, would
call Jesus ' the good Magician '. To Europeans,
repudiating the notion of all magic, good or bad,
the opinion of the Jews as to the agency by which
the miracles were worked is a matter of no importance, but the circumstance of their admitting that

those miracles *were in fact performed*, is certainly curious, and perhaps not quite immaterial.

If you stay in the Holy City long enough to fall into anything like regular habits of amusement and occupation, and to become, in short, for the time ' a man about town ' at Jerusalem, you will necessarily lose the enthusiasm which you may have felt when you trod the sacred soil for the first time, and it will then seem almost strange to you to find yourself so entirely surrounded in all your daily pursuits by the signs and sounds of religion. Your Hotel is a monastery—your rooms are cells—the landlord is a stately abbot, and the waiters are hooded monks. If you walk out of the town you find yourself on the Mount of Olives, or in the Valley of Jehoshaphat, or on the Hill of Evil Counsel. If you mount your horse and extend your rambles, you will be guided to the Wilderness of St. John, or the birth-place of our Saviour. Your club is the great church of the Holy Sepulchre, where everybody meets everybody every day. If you lounge through the town, your Pall Mall is the Via Dolorosa, and the object of your hopeless affections is some maid or matron all forlorn, and sadly shrouded in her pilgrim's robe. If you would hear music, it must be the chanting of friars. If you look at pictures, you see Virgins with mis-foreshortened arms, or devils out of drawing, or angels tumbling up the skies in impious perspective. If you would make any purchases, you must go again to the church doors; and when you inquire for the manufactures of the place, you find that they consist of double-blessed beads, and sanctified shells. These last are the favourite tokens which the pilgrims carry off with them. The shell is graven, or rather scratched on the white side with a rude drawing of the Blessed Virgin, or of the Crucifixion, or some

other scriptural subject; having passed this stage it
goes into the hands of a priest; by him it is subjected
to some process for rendering it efficacious against the
schemes of our ghostly enemy: the manufacture is
then complete, and is deemed to be fit for use.

The village of Bethlehem lies prettily couched on
the slope of a hill. The sanctuary is a subterranean
grotto, and is committed to the joint-guardianship
of the Romans, Greeks, and Armenians: these vie
with each other in adorning it. Beneath an altar
gorgeously decorated and lit with everlasting fires,
there stands the low slab of stone which marks the
holy site of the Nativity; and near to this is a hollow
scooped out of the living rock. Here the infant
Jesus was laid. Near the spot of the Nativity is the
rock against which the Blessed Virgin was leaning
when she presented her babe to the adoring shepherds.

Many of those Protestants who are accustomed to
despise tradition, consider that this sanctuary is
altogether unscriptural—that a grotto is not a
stable, and that mangers are made of wood. It
is perfectly true, however, that the many grottos and
caves which are found among the rocks of Judea
were formerly used for the reception of cattle; they
are so used at this day. I have myself seen grottos
appropriated to this purpose.

You know what a sad and sombre decorum it is
that outwardly reigns through the lands oppressed
by Moslem sway. The Mahometans make beauty
their prisoner, and enforce such a stern and gloomy
morality, or at all events such a frightfully close
semblance of it, that far and long the wearied
traveller may go without catching one glimpse of
outward happiness. By a strange chance in these
latter days, it happened that, alone of all the places
in the land, this Bethlehem, the native village of our

Lord, escaped the moral yoke of the Mussulmans,
and heard again, after ages of dull oppression, the
cheering clatter of social freedom, and the voices of
laughing girls. It was after an insurrection which
had been raised against the authority of Mehemet
Ali, that Bethlehem was freed from the hateful laws
of Asiatic decorum. The Mussulmans of the village
had taken an active part in the movement, and when
Ibrahim had quelled it, his wrath was still so hot
that he put to death every one of the few Mahometans
of Bethlehem who had not already fled. The effect
produced upon the Christian inhabitants, by the
sudden removal of this restraint, was immense. The
village smiled once more. It is true that such sweet
freedom could not long endure. Even if the population of the place should continue to be entirely
Christian, the sad decorum of the Mussulmans, or
rather of the Asiatics, would sooner or later be
restored by the force of opinion and custom. But
for a while the sunshine would last; and when I was
at Bethlehem, though long after the flight of the
Mussulmans, the cloud of Moslem propriety had not
yet come back to cast its cold shadow upon life.
When you reach that gladsome village, pray Heaven
there still may be heard there the voice of free
innocent girls. It will sound so dearly welcome!

To a Christian and thorough-bred Englishman,
not even the licentiousness generally accompanying
it can compensate for the oppressiveness of that
horrible outward decorum which turns the cities and
the palaces of Asia into deserts and gaols. So, I say,
when you see and hear them, those romping girls of
Bethlehem will gladden your very soul. Distant at
first, and then nearer and nearer the timid flock will
gather round you with their large burning eyes
gravely fixed against yours, so that they see into

your brain ; and if you imagine evil against them
they will know of your ill thought before it is yet
well born, and will fly and be gone in a moment.
But presently, if you will only look virtuous enough
to prevent alarm, and vicious enough to avoid
looking silly, the blithe maidens will draw nearer
and nearer to you ; and soon there will be one,
the bravest of the sisters, who will venture right
up to your side, and touch the hem of your
coat in playful defiance of the danger, and then
the rest will follow the daring of their youthful
leader, and gather round you, and hold a shrill
controversy on the wondrous formation that you call
a hat, and the cunning of the hands that clothed
you with cloth so fine ; and then, growing more
profound in their researches, they will pass from the
study of your mere dress, to a serious contemplation
of your stately height, and your nut-brown hair,
and the ruddy glow of your English cheeks. And
if they catch a glimpse of your ungloved fingers,
then again will they make the air ring with their
sweet screams of delight and amazement, as they
compare the fairness of your hand with the hues
of your sunburnt face, or with their own warmer
tints. Instantly the ringleader of the gentle rioters
imagines a new sin : with tremulous boldness she
touches—then grasps your hand, and smoothes it
gently betwixt her own, and prys curiously into its
make and colour, as though it were silk of Damascus,
or shawl of Cashmere. And when they see you, even
then, still sage, and gentle, the joyous girls will
suddenly, and screamingly, and all at once, explain
to each other that you are surely quite harmless and
innocent—a lion that makes no spring—a bear that
never hugs ; and upon this faith, one after the other,
they will take your passive hand, and strive to

explain it, and make it a theme and a controversy.
But the one—the fairest, and the sweetest of all, is
yet the most timid: she shrinks from the daring
deeds of her playmates, and seeks shelter behind their
sleeves, and strives to screen her glowing consciousness
from the eyes that look upon her. But her laughing
sisters will have none of this cowardice; they vow
that the fair one *shall* be their complice—*shall* share
their dangers—*shall* touch the hand of the stranger;
they seize her small wrist, and drag her forward by
force, and at last, whilst yet she strives to turn away,
and to cover up her whole soul under the folds of down-
cast eyelids, they vanquish her utmost strength, they
vanquish her utmost modesty, and marry her hand
to yours. The quick pulse springs from her fingers,
and throbs like a whisper upon your listening palm.
For an instant her large timid eyes are upon you—
in an instant they are shrouded again, and there
comes a blush so burning, that the frightened girls
stay their shrill laughter, as though they had played
too perilously, and harmed their gentle sister. A
moment, and all with a sudden intelligence turn
away, and fly like deer; yet soon again like deer
they wheel round and return, and stand, and gaze
upon the danger, until they grow brave once more.

'I regret to observe that the removal of the moral
restraint imposed by the presence of the Mahometan
inhabitants has led to a certain degree of boisterous,
though innocent levity, in the bearing of the
Christians, and more especially in the demeanour of
those who belong to the younger portion of the
female population; but I feel assured that a more
thorough knowledge of the principles of their own
pure religion will speedily restore these young people
to habits of propriety, even more strict than those
which were imposed upon them by the authority of

their Mahometan brethren.' Bah! thus you might
chant, if you choose; but loving the truth, you will
not so disown sweet Bethlehem—you will not disown
nor dissemble your right good hearty delight, when
you find, as though in a desert, this gushing spring of
fresh and joyous girlhood.

CHAPTER XVII

THE DESERT

GAZA stands upon the verge of the Desert, and
bears towards it the same kind of relation as a sea-
port bears to the sea. It is there that you *charter*
your camels ('the ships of the Desert'), and lay in
your stores for the voyage.

These preparations kept me in the town for some
days. Disliking restraint, I declined making myself
the guest of the Governor (as it is usual and proper
to do), but took up my quarters at the Caravanserai,
or 'Khan', as they call it in that part of Asia.

Dthemetri had to make the arrangements for my
journey, and in order to arm himself with sufficient
authority for doing all that was required, he found
it necessary to put himself in communication with
the Governor. The result of this diplomatic inter-
course was that the Governor with his train of
attendants came to me one day at my Caravanserai,
and formally complained that Dthemetri had grossly
insulted him. I was shocked at this, for the man
had been always attentive and civil to me, and I was
disgusted at the idea of his being rewarded with
insult. Dthemetri was present when the complaint
was made, and I angrily asked him whether it was
true that he had really insulted the Governor, and

what the deuce he meant by it. This I asked with
the full certainty that Dthemetri, as a matter of
course, would deny the charge—would swear that a
'wrong construction had been put upon his words,
and that nothing was further from his thoughts,'
&c., &c., after the manner of the Parliamentary
people; but to my surprise he very plainly answered
that he certainly *had* insulted the Governor, and that
rather grossly, but, he said, it was quite necessary to
do this in order to 'strike terror and inspire respect'.
'Terror and respect! What on earth do you mean
by that nonsense?'—'Yes, but without striking
terror and inspiring respect, he (Dthemetri) would
never be able to force on the arrangements for my
journey, and Vossignoria would be kept at Gaza for
a month!' This would have been awkward; and
certainly I could not deny that poor Dthemetri had
succeeded in his odd plan of inspiring respect, for at
the very time that this explanation was going on in
Italian, the Governor seemed more than ever, and
more anxiously, disposed to overwhelm me with
assurances of good will and proffers of his best
services. All this kindness or promise of kindness
I naturally received with courtesy—a courtesy that
greatly perturbed Dthemetri, for he evidently feared
that my civility would undo all the good that his
insults had achieved.

You will find, I think, that one of the greatest
drawbacks to the pleasure of travelling in Asia is
the being obliged more or less to make your way by
bullying. It is true that your own lips are not soiled
by the utterance of all the mean words that are spoken
for you, and that you don't even know of the sham
threats, and the false promises, and the vain-glorious
boasts, put forth by your dragoman; but now and
then there happens some incident of the sort which

I have just been mentioning, which forces you to believe, or suspect, that your dragoman is habitually fighting your battles for you in a way that you can hardly bear to think of.

A Caravanserai is not ill adapted to the purposes for which it is meant : it forms the four sides of a large quadrangular court. The ground-floor is used for warehouses, the first floor for guests, and the open court for the temporary reception of the camels, as well as for the loading and unloading of their burthens and the transaction of mercantile business generally. The apartments used for the guests are small cells opening into a kind of corridor which runs through the inner sides of the court.

Whilst I lay near the opening of my cell, looking down into the court below, there arrived from the Desert a caravan—that is, a large assemblage of travellers : it consisted chiefly of Moldavian pilgrims, who, to make their good work even more than complete, had begun by visiting the shrine of the Virgin in Egypt, and were now going on to Jerusalem. They had been overtaken in the Desert by a gale of wind, which so drove the sand, and raised up such mountains before them, that their journey had been terribly perplexed and obstructed, and their provisions (including water, the most precious of all) had been exhausted long before they reached the end of their toilsome march. They were sadly way-worn. The arrival of the caravan drew many and various groups into the court. There was the Moldavian pilgrim with his sable dress, and cap of fur, and heavy masses of bushy hair—the Turk with his various and brilliant garments—the Arab superbly stalking under his striped blanket that hung like royalty upon his stately form—the jetty Ethiopian in his slavish frock—the sleek, smooth-faced scribe with his comely pelisse, and his silver ink-box stuck in like a dagger at his girdle.   And mingled with these were the camels —some standing, some kneeling and being unladen, some twisting round their long necks, and gently stealing the straw from out of their own pack-saddles.

In a couple of days I was ready to start.   The way of providing for the passage of the desert is this : there is an agent in the town who keeps himself in communication with some of the desert Arabs that are hovering within a day's journey of the place ; a party of these, upon being guaranteed against seizure or other ill treatment at the hands of the governor, come into the town, bringing with them the number of camels which you require, and then they stipulate for a certain sum to take you to the place of your destination in a given time.   The agreement thus made by them includes a safe-conduct through their country, as well as the hire of the camels.   According to the contract made with me, I was to reach Cairo within ten days from the commencement of the journey.   I had four camels, one for my baggage, one for each of my servants, and one for myself. Four Arabs, the owners of the camels, came with me on foot.   My stores were a small soldier's tent, two bags of dried bread brought from the convent at Jerusalem, and a couple of bottles of wine from the same source, two goatskins filled with water, tea, sugar, a cold tongue, and (of all things in the world) a jar of Irish butter which Mysseri had purchased from some merchant.   There was also a small sack of charcoal, for the greater part of the desert through which we were to pass is void of fuel.

The camel kneels to receive her load, and for a while she will allow the packing to go on with silent resignation, but when she begins to suspect that her master is putting more than a just burthen upon her poor hump, she turns round her supple neck, and looks sadly upon the increasing load, and then gently remonstrates against the wrong with the sigh of a patient wife. If sighs will not move you, she can weep. You soon learn to pity, and soon to love her for the sake of her gentle and womanish ways.

You cannot, of course, put an English or any other riding saddle upon the back of the camel, but your quilt or carpet, or whatever you carry for the purpose of lying on at night, is folded and fastened on to the pack-saddle upon the top of the hump, and on this you ride, or rather sit. You sit as a man sits on a chair when he sits astride. I made an improvement on this plan : I had my English stirrups strapped on to the cross bars of the pack-saddle ; and thus, by gaining rest for my dangling legs, and gaining, too, the power of varying my position more easily than I could otherwise have done, I added very much to my comfort.

The camel, like the elephant, is one of the old-fashioned sort of animals that still walk along upon the (now nearly exploded) plan of the ancient beasts that lived before the flood : she moves forward both her near legs at the same time, and then awkwardly swings round her off-shoulder and haunch, so as to repeat the manœuvre on that side ; her pace therefore is an odd, disjointed, and disjoining sort of movement that is rather disagreeable at first, but you soon grow reconciled to it. The height to which you are raised is of great advantage to you in passing the burning sands of the desert, for the air at such a distance from the ground is much cooler and more lively than that which circulates beneath.

For several miles beyond Gaza the land, freshened by the rains of the last week, was covered with rich verdure, and thickly jewelled with meadow flowers so

bright and fragrant that I began to grow almost
uneasy—to fancy that the very desert was receding
before me, and that the long-desired adventure of
passing its ' burning sands ' was to end in a mere ride
across a field.   But as I advanced, the true character
of the country began to display itself with sufficient
clearness to dispel my apprehensions, and before the
close of my first day's journey I had the gratification
of finding that I was surrounded on all sides by a
tract of real sand, and had nothing at all to complain
of, except that there peeped forth at intervals a few
isolated blades of grass, and many of those stunted
shrubs which are the accustomed food of the camel.

Before sunset I came up with an encampment of
Arabs (the encampment from which my camels had
been brought), and my tent was pitched amongst
theirs.   I was now amongst the true Bedouins.
Almost every man of this race closely resembles his
brethren ; almost every man has large and finely
formed features, but his face is so thoroughly stripped
of flesh, and the white folds from his head-gear fall
down by his haggard cheeks so much in the burial
fashion, that he looks quite sad and ghastly ; his
large dark orbs roll slowly and solemnly over the
white of his deep-set eyes ; his countenance shows
painful thought and long suffering—the suffering of
one fallen from a high estate.   His gait is strangely
majestic, and he marches along with his simple
blanket, as though he were wearing the purple.   His
common talk is a series of piercing screams and cries [1]
very painful to hear.

The Bedouin women are not treasured up like the
wives and daughters of other Orientals, and indeed

---

[1] Milnes cleverly goes to the French for the exact word
which conveys the impression produced by the voice of the
Arabs, and calls them ' un peuple *criard* '.

they seemed almost entirely free from the restraints
imposed by jealousy. The feint which they made of
concealing their faces from me was always slight:
when they first saw me, they used to hold up a part
of their drapery with one hand across their faces, but
they seldom persevered very steadily in subjecting
me to this privation. They were sadly plain. The
awful haggardness that gave something of character
to the faces of the men was sheer ugliness in the poor
women. It is a great shame, but the truth is that
except when we refer to the beautiful devotion of the
mother to her child, all the fine things we say and
think about women apply only to those who are
tolerably good-looking or graceful. These Arab
women were not within the scope of the privilege, and
indeed were altogether much too plain and clumsy
for this vain and lovesome world. They may have
been good women enough, so far as relates to the
exercise of the minor virtues, but they had so grossly
neglected the prime duty of looking pretty in this
transitory life that I could not at all forgive them;
they seemed to feel the weight of their guilt, and to
be truly and humbly penitent. I had the complete
command of their affections, for at any moment I
could make their young hearts bound, and their old
hearts jump, by offering a handful of tobacco, yet,
believe me, it was not in the first *soirée* that my store
of Latakaea was exhausted!

The Bedouin women have no religion; this is
partly the cause of their clumsiness. Perhaps, if
from Christian girls they would learn how to pray,
their souls might become more gentle, and their limbs
be clothed with grace.

You who are going into their country have a direct
personal interest in knowing something about 'Arab
hospitality'; but the deuce of it is, that the poor

fellows with whom I have happened to pitch my tent
were scarcely ever in a condition to exercise that
magnanimous virtue with much éclat; indeed Mysseri's
canteen generally enabled me to outdo my hosts in
the matter of entertainment. They were always
courteous, however, and were never backward in
offering me the 'youart', a kind of whey, which is
the principal delicacy to be found amongst the
wandering tribes.

Practically, I think, Childe Harold would have
found it a dreadful bore to make 'the desert his
dwelling-place', for at all events if he adopted the
life of the Arabs, he would have tasted no solitude.
The tents are partitioned, not so as to divide the
Childe, and the 'fair spirit' who is his 'minister',
from the rest of the world, but so as to separate the
twenty or thirty brown men that sit screaming in
the one compartment from the fifty or sixty brown
women and children that scream and squeak in the
other. If you adopt the Arab life for the sake of
seclusion, you will be horribly disappointed, for you
will find yourself in perpetual contact with a mass
of hot fellow-creatures. It is true that all who are
inmates of the same tent are related to each other,
but I am not quite sure that that circumstance adds
much to the charm of such a life.

In passing the Desert you will find your Arabs
wanting to start and to rest at all sorts of odd times;
they like, for instance, to be off at one in the morning,
and to rest during the whole of the afternoon. You
must not give way to their wishes in this respect: I
tried their plan once, and found it very harassing and
unwholesome. An ordinary tent can give you very
little protection against heat, for the fire strikes
fiercely through single canvass, and you soon find
that whilst you lie crouching, and striving to hide

yourself from the blazing face of the sun, his power is harder to bear than it is where you boldly defy him from the airy heights of your camel.

It had been arranged with my Arabs that they were to bring with them all the food which they would want for themselves during the passage of the Desert, but as we rested at the end of the first day's journey by the side of an Arab encampment, my camel-men found all that they required for that night in the tents of their own brethren. On the evening of the second day, however, just before we encamped for the night, my four Arabs came to Dthemetri, and formally announced that they had not brought with them one atom of food, and that they looked entirely to my supplies for their daily bread. This was awkward intelligence. We were now just two days deep in the Desert, and I had brought with me no more bread than might be reasonably required for myself and my European attendants. I believed at the moment (for it seemed likely enough) that the men had really mistaken the terms of the arrangement, and feeling that the bore of being put upon half rations would be a less evil (and even to myself a less inconvenience) than the starvation of my Arabs, I at once told Dthemetri to assure them that my bread should be equally shared with all. Dthemetri, however, did not approve of this concession; he assured me quite positively that the Arabs thoroughly understood the agreement, and that if they were now without food, they had wilfully brought themselves into this strait for the wretched purpose of bettering their bargain by the value of a few paras' worth of bread. This suggestion made me look at the affair in a new light. I should have been glad enough to put up with the slight privation to which my concession would subject me, and could have borne to witness

the semi-starvation of poor Dthemetri with a fine
philosophical calm, but it seemed to me that the
scheme, if scheme it were, had something of audacity
in it, and was well enough calculated to try the extent
of my softness. I knew the danger of allowing such
a trial to result in a conclusion that I was one who
might be easily managed; and therefore after
thoroughly satisfying myself from Dthemetri's clear
and repeated assertions that the Arabs had really
understood the arrangement, I determined that they
should not now violate it by taking advantage of my
position in the midst of their big desert; so I desired
Dthemetri to tell them that they should touch no
bread of mine. We stopped, and the tent was
pitched; the Arabs came to me, and prayed loudly
for bread; I refused them.

'Then we die!'

'God's will be done.'

I gave the Arabs to understand that I regretted
their perishing by hunger, but that I should bear this
calmly, like any other misfortune not my own—that,
in short, I was happily resigned to *their* fate. The
men would have talked a great deal, but they were
under the disadvantage of addressing me through a
hostile interpreter. They looked hard upon my face,
but they found no hope there, so at last they retired,
as they pretended, to lay them down and die.

In about ten minutes from this time I found that
the Arabs were busily cooking their bread! Their
pretence of having brought no food was false, and
was only invented for the purpose of saving it.
They had a good bag of meal, which they had contrived to stow away under the baggage, upon one of
the camels, in such a way as to escape notice. In
Europe the detection of a scheme like this would have
occasioned a disagreeable feeling between the master

and the delinquent, but you would no more recoil
from an Oriental on account of a matter of this sort,
than in England you would reject a horse that had
tried and failed to throw you. Indeed I felt quite
good-humouredly towards my Arabs because they
had so woefully failed in their wretched attempt, and
because, as it turned out, I had done what was right;
they too, poor fellows, evidently began to like me
immensely, on account of the hard-heartedness which
had enabled me to baffle their scheme.

The Arabs adhere to those ancestral principles of
bread-baking which have been sanctioned by the
experience of ages. The very first baker of bread
that ever lived must have done his work exactly as
the Arab does at this day. He takes some meal,
and holds it out in the hollow of his hands whilst
his comrade pours over it a few drops of water;
he then mashes up the moistened flour into a paste,
pulls the lump of dough so made into small pieces,
and thrusts them into the embers. His way of
baking exactly resembles the craft or mystery of
roasting chesnuts, as practised by children; there
is the same prudence and circumspection in choosing a good berth for the morsel—the same enterprise and self-sacrificing valour in pulling it out with
the fingers.

The manner of my daily march was this. At about
an hour before dawn, I rose, and made the most of
about a pint of water which I allowed myself for
washing. Then I breakfasted upon tea and bread.
As soon as the beasts were loaded, I mounted my
camel and pressed forward. My poor Arabs being
on foot would sometimes moan with fatigue, and pray
for rest, but I was anxious to enable them to perform
their contract for bringing me to Cairo within the
stipulated time, and I did not therefore allow a halt

until the evening came. About mid-day, or soon
after, Mysseri used to bring up his camel alongside of
mine and supply me with a piece of the dried bread
softened in water, and also (as long as it lasted) with
a piece of the tongue. After this there came into my
hand (how well I remember it!) the little tin cup
half filled with wine and water.

As long as you are journeying in the interior of
the Desert you have no particular point to make for
as your resting place. The endless sands yield nothing
but small stunted shrubs; even these fail after the
first two or three days, and from that time you pass
over broad plains—you pass over newly reared hills
—you pass through valleys dug out by the last week's
storm, and the hills and the valleys are sand, sand,
sand, still sand, and only sand, and sand, and sand
again. The earth is so samely, that your eyes turn
towards heaven—towards heaven, I mean, in sense
of sky. You look to the Sun, for he is your task-
master, and by him you know the measure of the
work that you have done, and the measure of the
work that remains for you to do. He comes when
you strike your tent in the early morning, and then,
for the first hour of the day, as you move forward on
your camel, he stands at your near side, and makes
you know that the whole day's toil is before you;
then for a while, and a long while, you see him no
more, for you are veiled and shrouded, and dare not
look upon the greatness of his glory, but you know
where he strides over head, by the touch of his flaming
sword. No words are spoken, but your Arabs moan,
your camels sigh, your skin glows, your shoulders
ache, and for sights you see the pattern and the web
of the silk that veils your eyes, and the glare of the
outer light. Time labours on—your skin glows, your
shoulders ache, your Arabs moan, your camels sigh,

and you see the same pattern in the silk, and the same glare of light beyond; but conquering Time marches on, and by and by the descending sun has compassed the heaven, and now softly touches your right arm, and throws your lank shadow over the sand right along on the way for Persia. Then again you look upon his face, for his power is all veiled in his beauty, and the redness of flames has become the redness of roses; the fair, wavy cloud that fled in the morning now comes to his sight once more—comes blushing, yet still comes on—comes burning with blushes, yet comes and clings to his side.

Then begins your season of rest. The world about you is all your own, and there, where you will, you pitch your solitary tent; there is no living thing to dispute your choice. When at last the spot had been fixed upon and we came to a halt, one of the Arabs would touch the chest of my camel, and utter at the same time a peculiar gurgling sound. The beast instantly understood and obeyed the sign, and slowly sunk under me, till she brought her body to a level with the ground: then gladly enough I alighted. The rest of the camels were unloaded and turned loose to browse upon the shrubs of the Desert, where shrubs there were, or where these failed, to wait for the small quantity of food that was allowed them out of our stores.

My servants, helped by the Arabs, busied themselves in pitching the tent and kindling the fire. Whilst this was doing, I used to walk away towards the East, confiding in the print of my foot as a guide for my return. Apart from the cheering voices of my attendants, I could better know and feel the loneliness of the Desert. The influence of such scenes, however, was not of a softening kind, but filled me rather with a sort of childish exultation in the self-sufficiency

which enabled me to stand thus alone in the wideness
of Asia—a short-lived pride, for wherever man wan-
ders, he still remains tethered by the chain that links
him to his kind; and so when the night closed round
me, I began to return—to return as it were to my
own gate. Reaching at last some high ground, I
could see, and see with delight, the fire of our small
encampment; and when, at last, I regained the spot,
it seemed a very home that had sprung up for me in
the midst of these solitudes. My Arabs were busy
with their bread,—Mysseri rattling tea-cups,—the
little kettle with her odd, oldmaidish looks sat hum-
ming away old songs about England, and two or
three yards from the fire my tent stood prim and
tight with open portal, and with welcoming look—
a look like 'the own arm chair' of our Lyrist's
'sweet Lady Anne'.

Sometimes in the earlier part of my journey the
night breeze blew coldly; when that happened, the
dry sand was heaped up outside round the skirts of
the tent, and so the Wind that everywhere else could
sweep as he listed along those dreary plains, was
forced to turn aside in his course, and make way as
he ought for the Englishman. Then within my tent
there were heaps of luxuries—dining-rooms, dressing-
rooms, libraries, bed-rooms, drawing-rooms, oratories,
all crowded into the space of a hearth-rug. The first
night, I remember, with my books and maps about
me, I wanted a light. They brought me a taper,
and immediately from out of the silent Desert there
rushed in a flood of life, unseen before. Monsters of
moths of all shapes and hues, that never before
perhaps had looked upon the shining of a flame, now
madly thronged into my tent, and dashed through
the fire of the candle till they fairly extinguished it
with their burning limbs. Those who had failed in

attaining this martyrdom suddenly became serious, and clung despondingly to the canvas.

By and by there was brought to me the fragrant tea, and big masses of scorched and scorching toast, and the butter that had come all the way to me in this Desert of Asia, from out of that poor, dear, starving Ireland. I feasted like a king,—like four kings,—like a boy in the fourth form.

When the cold, sullen morning dawned, and my people began to load the camels, I always felt loath to give back to the waste this little spot of ground that had glowed for a while with the cheerfulness of a human dwelling. One by one the cloaks, the saddles, the baggage, the hundred things that strewed the ground and made it look so familiar—all these were taken away, and laid upon the camels. A speck in the broad tracts of Asia remained still impressed with the mark of patent portmanteaus and the heels of London boots; the embers of the fire lay black and cold upon the sand; and these were the signs we left.

My tent was spared to the last, but when all else was ready for the start, then came its fall; the pegs were drawn, the canvas shivered, and in less than a minute there was nothing that remained of my genial home but only a pole and a bundle. The encroaching Englishman was off, and instant upon the fall of the canvas, like an owner who had waited and watched, the Genius of the Desert stalked in.

To servants, as I suppose to any other Europeans not much accustomed to amuse themselves by fancy or memory, it often happens that after a few days' journeying, the loneliness of the Desert will become frightfully oppressive. Upon my poor fellows the access of melancholy came heavy, and all at once, as a blow from above; they bent their necks, and bore it as best they could, but their joy was great on the fifth day, when we came to an Oasis, called Gatieh, for here we found encamped a caravan (that is, an assemblage of travellers) from Cairo. The Orientals living in cities never pass the Desert except in this way. Many will wait for weeks, and even for months, until a sufficient number of persons can be found ready to undertake the journey at the same time— until the flock of sheep is big enough to fancy itself a match for wolves. They could not, I think, really secure themselves against any serious danger by this contrivance; for though they have arms, they are so little accustomed to use them, and so utterly un-organized, that they never could make good their resistance to robbers of the slightest respectability. It is not of the Bedouins that such travellers are afraid, for the safe-conduct granted by the Chief of the ruling tribe is never, I believe, violated; but it is said that there are deserters and scamps of various sorts who hover about the skirts of the Desert, par-ticularly on the Cairo side, and are anxious to succeed to the property of any poor devils whom they may find more weak and defenceless than themselves.

These people from Cairo professed to be amazed at the ludicrous disproportion between their numerical forces and mine. They could not understand, and they wanted to know, by what strange privilege it is that an Englishman with a brace of pistols and a couple of servants rides safely across the Desert, whilst they, the natives of the neighbouring cities, are forced to travel in troops, or rather in herds. One of them got a few minutes of private conversation with Dthemetri, and ventured to ask him anxiously whether the English did not travel under the protection of Evil Demons. I had previously known (from Methley, I think, who had travelled in Persia) that this notion, so conducive to the safety of our countrymen, is generally prevalent amongst Orientals. It owes its origin partly to the strong wilfulness of the English Gentleman (a quality which, not being backed by any visible authority either civil or military, seems perfectly superhuman to the soft Asiatic), but partly too to the magic of the Banking system, by force of which the wealthy traveller will make all his journeys without carrying a handful of coin, and yet, when he arrives at a city, will rain down showers of gold. The theory is that the English traveller has committed some sin against God and his conscience, and that for this the Evil Spirit has hold of him, and drives him from his home like a victim of the old Grecian Furies, and forces him to travel over countries far and strange, and most chiefly over Deserts and desolate places, and to stand upon the sites of cities that once were, and are now no more, and to grope among the tombs of dead men. Often enough there is something of truth in this notion; often enough the wandering Englishman is guilty (if guilt it be) of some pride or ambition, big or small, imperial or parochial, which being offended has made the lone places more tolerable than ball-rooms to him a sinner.

I can understand the sort of amazement of the Orientals at the scantiness of the retinue with which an Englishman passes the Desert, for I was somewhat struck myself when I saw one of my countrymen making his way across the wilderness in this simple style. At first there was a mere moving speck in the horizon; my party, of course, became all alive with excitement, and there were many surmises; soon it appeared that three laden camels were approaching, and that two of them carried riders; in a little while we saw that one of the riders wore the European dress, and at last the travellers were pronounced to be an English gentleman and his servant; by their side there were a couple of Arabs on foot; and this, if I rightly remember, was the whole party.

You,—you love sailing,—in returning from a cruise to the English coast you see often enough a fisherman's humble boat far away from all shores, with an ugly, black sky above, and an angry sea beneath,—you watch the grisly old man at the helm carrying his craft with strange skill through the turmoil of waters, and the boy, supple-limbed, yet weather-worn already, and with steady eyes that look through the blast,— you see him understanding commandments from the jerk of his father's white eye-brow,—now belaying, and now letting go,—now scrunching himself down into mere ballast, or baling out Death with a pipkin. Familiar enough is the sight, and yet when I see it, I always stare anew, and with a kind of Titanic exultation, because that a poor boat with the brain of a man, and the hands of a boy on board, can match herself so bravely against black Heaven and Ocean: well, so when you have travelled for days and days over an Eastern Desert without meeting the likeness of a human being, and then at last see an English shooting-jacket, and a single servant come listlessly slouching along from out of the forward horizon, you stare at the wide unproportion between this slender company, and the boundless plains of sand through which they are keeping their way.

This Englishman, as I afterwards found, was a military man returning to his country from India, and crossing the Desert at this part in order to go through Palestine. As for me, I had come pretty straight from England, and so here we met in the wilderness at about half way from our respective starting points. As we approached each other, it became with me a question whether we should speak. I thought it likely that the stranger would accost

me, and in the event of his doing so, I was quite
ready to be as sociable and chatty as I could be
according to my nature; but still I could not think
of anything particular that I had to say to him. Of
course among civilized people, the not having anything to say is no excuse at all for not speaking;
but I was shy, and indolent, and I felt no great wish
to stop, and talk like a morning visitor, in the midst
of those broad solitudes. The traveller, perhaps,
felt as I did, for, except that we lifted our hands to
our caps, and waved our arms in courtesy, we passed
each other quite as distantly as if we had passed in
Pall Mall. Our attendants, however, were not to be
cheated of the delight that they felt in speaking to
new listeners, and hearing fresh voices once more.
The masters, therefore, had no sooner passed each
other, than their respective servants quietly stopped
and entered into conversation. As soon as my camel
found that her companions were not following her,
she caught the social feeling and refused to go on.
I felt the absurdity of the situation, and determined
to accost the stranger, if only to avoid the awkwardness of remaining stuck fast in the Desert whilst our
servants were amusing themselves. When with this
intent I turned round my camel, I found that the
gallant officer had passed me by about thirty or
forty yards, and was exactly in the same predicament
as myself. I put my now willing camel in motion
and rode up towards the stranger: seeing this he
followed my example, and came forward to meet me.
He was the first to speak: too courteous to address
me as if he admitted the possibility of my wishing
to accost him from any feeling of mere sociability or
civilian-like love of vain talk, he at once attributed
my advances to a laudable wish of acquiring statistical
information, and accordingly when we got within

speaking distance, he said, 'I dare say you wish to know how the Plague is going on at Cairo?' and then he went on to say he regretted that his information did not enable him to give me in numbers a perfectly accurate statement of the daily deaths. He afterwards talked pleasantly enough upon other and less ghastly subjects. I thought him manly and intelligent — a worthy one of the few thousand strong Englishmen to whom the Empire of India is committed.

The night after the meeting with the people of the caravan, Dthemetri, alarmed by their warnings, took upon himself to keep watch all night in the tent: no robbers came, except a jackal that poked his nose into my tent from some motive of rational curiosity. Dthemetri did not shoot him, for fear of waking me. These brutes swarm in every part of Syria; and there were many of them even in the midst of those void sands which would seem to give such poor promise of food. I can hardly tell what prey they could be hoping for, unless it were that they might find now and then the carcase of some camel that had died on the journey. They do not marshal themselves into great packs like the wild dogs of Eastern cities, but follow their prey in families like the place-hunters of Europe. Their voices are frightfully like to the shouts and cries of human beings: if you lie awake in your tent at night, you are almost continually hearing some hungry family as it sweeps along in full cry; you hear the exulting scream with which the sagacious dam first winds the carrion, and the shrill response of the unanimous cubs as they snuff the tainted air—'Wha! wha! —wha! wha!—wha! wha!—whose gift is it in, mamma?'

Once during this passage my Arabs lost their way

among the hills of loose sand that surrounded us,
but after a while we were lucky enough to recover
our right line of march. The same day we fell in
with a Sheik, the head of a family, that actually
dwells at no great distance from this part of the
desert during nine months of the year. The man
carried a matchlock, and of this he was inordinately
proud on account of the supposed novelty and ingenuity of the contrivance. We stopped, and sat
down and rested awhile, for the sake of a little talk.
There was much that I should have liked to ask
this man, but he could not understand Dthemetri's
language, and the process of getting at his knowledge
by double interpretation through my Arabs was
tedious. I discovered, however (and my Arabs knew
of that fact), that this man and his family lived
habitually for nine months of the year without
touching or seeing either bread or water. The
stunted shrub growing at intervals through the sand
in this part of the desert enables the camel mares to
yield a little milk, and this furnishes the sole food
and drink of their owner and his people. During
the other three months (the hottest I suppose), even
this resource fails, and then the Sheik and his people
are forced to pass into another district. You would
ask me why the man should not remain always in
that district which supplies him with water during
three months of the year, but I don't know enough
of Arab politics to answer the question. The Sheik
was not a good specimen of the effect produced by
his way of living : he was very small, very spare, and
sadly shrivelled—a poor over-roasted snipe—a mere
cinder of a man. I made him sit down by my
side, and gave him a piece of bread and a cup of
water from out of my goat-skins. This was not very
tempting drink to look at, for it had become turbid,

and was deeply reddened by some colouring matter contained in the skins, but it kept its sweetness, and tasted like a strong decoction of Russian leather. The Sheik sipped this drop by drop with ineffable relish, and rolled his eyes solemnly round between every draught, as though the drink were the drink of the Prophet, and had come from the seventh heaven.

An inquiry about distances led to the discovery that this Sheik had never heard of the division of time into hours.

About this part of my journey I saw the likeness of a fresh-water lake: I saw, as it seemed, a broad sheet of calm water stretching far and fair towards the south—stretching deep into winding creeks, and hemmed in by jutting promontories, and shelving smooth off towards the shallow side: on its bosom the reflected fire of the sun lay playing and seeming to float as though upon deep still waters.

Though I knew of the cheat, it was not till the spongy foot of my camel had almost trodden in the seeming lake, that I could undeceive my eyes, for the shore-line was quite true and natural. I soon saw the cause of the phantasm. A sheet of water, heavily impregnated with salts, had gathered together in a vast hollow between the sand hills, and when dried up by evaporation had left a white saline deposit; this exactly marked the space which the waters had covered, and so traced out a good shore-line. The minute crystals of the salt, by their way of sparkling in the sun, were made to seem like the dazzled face of a lake that is calm and smooth.

The pace of the camel is irksome, and makes your shoulders and loins ache from the peculiar way in which you are obliged to suit yourself to the movements of the beast; but one soon, of course, becomes

inured to the work, and after my first two days this
way of travelling became so familiar to me that (poor
sleeper as I am) I now and then slumbered for some
moments together on the back of my camel. On the
fifth day of my journey the air above lay dead, and
all the whole earth that I could reach with my utmost
sight and keenest listening was still and lifeless, as
some dispeopled and forgotten world that rolls round
and round in the heavens through wasted floods of
light. The sun, growing fiercer and fiercer, shone
down more mightily now than ever on me he shone
before, and as I drooped my head under his fire, and
closed my eyes against the glare that surrounded
me, I slowly fell asleep—for how many minutes or
moments, I cannot tell; but after a while I was
gently awakened by a peal of church bells—my native
bells—the innocent bells of Marlen, that never before
sent forth their music beyond the Blaygon hills!
My first idea naturally was that I still remained fast
under the power of a dream. I roused myself, and
drew aside the silk that covered my eyes, and plunged
my bare face into the light. Then at least I was
well enough awakened; but still those old Marlen
bells rang on, not ringing for joy, but properly,
prosily, steadily, merrily ringing 'for church'. After
a while the sound died away slowly. It happened
that neither I nor any of my party had a watch by
which to measure the exact time of its lasting, but it
seemed to me that about ten minutes had passed
before the bells ceased. I attributed the effect to the
great heat of the sun, the perfect dryness of the clear
air through which I moved, and the deep stillness of
all around me. It seemed to me that these causes,
by occasioning a great tension, and consequent sus-
ceptibility of the hearing organs, had rendered them
liable to tingle under the passing touch of some mere

memory that must have swept across my brain in a moment of sleep. Since my return to England it has been told me that like sounds have been heard at sea, and that the sailor, becalmed under a vertical sun in the midst of the wide ocean, has listened in trembling wonder to the chime of his own village bells.

During my travels I kept a journal—a journal sadly meagre and intermittent, but one which enabled me to find out the day of the month and the week according to the European calendar; referring to this, I found that the day was Sunday, and, roughly allowing for the difference of longitude, I concluded that at the moment of my hearing that strange peal, the church-going bells of Marlen must have been actually calling the prim congregation of the parish to morning prayer. The coincidence amused me faintly, but I could not allow myself a hope that the effect I had experienced was anything other than an illusion—an illusion liable to be explained (as every illusion is in these days) by some of the philosophers who guess at Nature's riddles. It would have been sweeter to believe that my kneeling mother, by some pious enchantment, had asked and found this spell to rouse me from my scandalous forgetfulness of God's holy day,—but my fancy was too weak to carry a faith like that. Indeed, the vale through which the bells of Marlen send their song is a highly respectable vale, and its people (save one, two, or three) are wholly unaddicted to the practice of magical arts.

After the fifth day of my journey, I no longer travelled over shifting hills, but came upon a dead level—a dead level bed of sand, quite hard, and studded with small shining pebbles.

The heat grew fierce; there was no valley nor hollow, no hill, no mound, no shadow of hill nor of mound by which I could mark the way I was making.

Hour by hour I advanced, and saw no change—I was still the very centre of a round horizon ; hour by hour I advanced, and still there was the same, and the same, and the same—the same circle of flaming sky —the same circle of sand still glaring with light and fire. Over all the heaven above—over all the earth beneath there was no visible power that could baulk the fierce will of the Sun ; 'he rejoiced as a strong man to run a race ; his going forth was from the end of the heaven, and his circuit unto the ends of it : and there was nothing hid from the heat thereof.' From pole to pole, and from the East to the West, he brandished his fiery sceptre as though he had usurped all Heaven and Earth. As he bid the soft Persian in ancient times, so now, and fiercely too, he bid me bow down and worship him ; so now in his pride he seemed to command me, and say 'Thou shalt have none other gods but me.' I was all alone before him. There were these two pitted together, and face to face,—the mighty Sun for one, and for the other—this poor, pale, solitary Self of mine that I always carry about with me.

But on the eighth day, and before I had yet turned away from Jehovah for the glittering god of the Persians, there appeared a dark line upon the edge of the forward horizon, and soon the line deepened into a delicate fringe that sparkled here and there as though it were sown with diamonds. There then before me were the gardens and the minarets of Egypt, and the mighty works of the Nile, and I (the eternal Ego that I am !)—I had lived to see, and I saw them.

When evening came I was still within the confines of the Desert, and my tent was pitched as usual, but one of my Arabs stalked away rapidly towards the West without telling me of the errand on which he

was bent.   After a while he returned : he had toiled
on a graceful service ; he had travelled all the way on
to the border of the living world, and brought me
back for a token an ear of rice, full, fresh, and green.

The next day I entered upon Egypt, and floated
along (for the delight was as the delight of bathing)
through green wavy fields of rice, and pastures fresh
and plentiful, and dived into the cold verdure of
groves and gardens, and quenched my hot eyes in
shade, as though in a bed of deep waters.

CHAPTER XVIII

CAIRO AND THE PLAGUE [1]

CAIRO and Plague !   During the whole time of my
stay the Plague was so master of the city, and stared
so plain in every street and every alley, that I can't
now affect to dissociate the two ideas.

[1] There is some semblance of bravado in my manner of
talking about the Plague.   I have been more careful to describe
the terrors of other people than my own.   The truth is, that
during the whole period of my stay at Cairo I remained
thoroughly impressed with a sense of my danger.   I may
almost say that I lived under perpetual apprehension, for even
in sleep, as I fancy, there remained with me some faint notion
of the peril with which I was encompassed.   But Fear does not
necessarily damp the spirits ; on the contrary, it will often
operate as an excitement giving rise to unusual animation ; and
thus it affected me.   If I had not been surrounded at this time
by new faces, new scenes, and new sounds, the effect produced
upon my mind by one unceasing cause of alarm may have been
very different.   As it was, the eagerness with which I pursued
my rambles among the wonders of Egypt was sharpened and
increased by the sting of the fear of death.   Thus my account
of the matter plainly conveys an impression that I remained at
Cairo without losing my cheerfulness and buoyancy of spirits.
And this is the truth, but it is also true, as I have freely confessed, that my sense of danger during the whole period was
lively and continuous.

When, coming from the Desert, I rode through a village lying near to the city on the eastern side, there approached me with busy face and earnest gestures a personage in the Turkish dress; his long flowing beard gave him rather a majestic look, but his briskness of manner and his visible anxiety to accost me seemed strange in an Oriental. The man in fact was French or of French origin, and his object was to warn me of the Plague, and prevent me from entering the city.

Arrêtez-vous, Monsieur, je vous en prie—arrêtez-vous; il ne faut pas entrer dans la ville; la Peste y règne partout.

Oui, je sais [1], mais——

Mais, Monsieur, je dis la Peste—la Peste; c'est de LA PESTE qu'il est question.

Oui, je sais, mais—

Mais, Monsieur, je dis encore LA PESTE—LA PESTE. Je vous conjure de ne pas entrer dans la ville—vous seriez dans une ville empestée.

Oui, je sais, mais—

Mais, Monsieur, je dois donc vous avertir tout bonnement que si vous entrez dans la ville, vous serez —enfin vous serez COMPROMIS! [2]

Oui, je sais, mais——

The Frenchman was at last convinced that it was vain to reason with a mere Englishman who could not understand what it was to be 'compromised'. I thanked him most sincerely for his kindly meant warning. In hot countries it is very unusual indeed

---

[1] Anglicè for 'je le sais'. These answers of mine as given above are not meant as specimens of mere French, but of that fine terse nervous *Continental English* with which I and my compatriots make our way through Europe.

[2] The import of the word 'compromised', when used in reference to contagion, is explained in page 8.

for a man to go out in the glare of the sun and give free advice to a stranger.

When I arrived at Cairo I summoned Osman Effendi, who was, as I knew, the owner of several houses, and would be able to provide me with apartments; he had no difficulty in doing this, for there was not one European traveller in Cairo besides myself. Poor Osman! he met me with a sorrowful countenance, for the fear of the Plague sat heavily on his soul; he seemed as if he felt that he was doing wrong in lending me a resting-place, and he betrayed such a listlessness about temporal matters as one might look for in a man who believed that his days were numbered. He caught me, too, soon after my arrival, coming out from the public baths[1], and from that time forward he was sadly afraid of me, for upon the subject of contagion he held European opinions.

Osman's history is a curious one. He was a Scotchman born, and when very young, being then a drummer-boy, he landed in Egypt with Fraser's force. He was taken prisoner, and according to Mahometan custom, the alternative of Death or the Koran was offered to him; he did not choose Death, and therefore went through the ceremonies necessary for turning him into a good Mahometan. But what amused me most in his history was this—that very soon after having embraced Islam, he was obliged in practice to become curious and discriminating in his new faith —to make war upon Mahometan dissenters, and follow the orthodox standard of the Prophet in fierce cam-

---

[1] It is said that when a Mussulman finds himself attacked by the Plague he goes and takes a bath. The couches on which the bathers recline would carry infection according to the notions of the Europeans. Whenever, therefore, I took the bath at Cairo (except the first time of my doing so), I avoided that part of the luxury which consists in being ‘put up to dry’ upon a kind of bed.

paigns against the Wahabees, the Unitarians of the Mussulman world. The Wahabees were crushed, and Osman, returning home in triumph from his holy wars, began to flourish in the world; he acquired property, and became effendi, or gentleman. At the time of my visit to Cairo he seemed to be much respected by his brother Mahometans, and gave pledge of his sincere alienation from Christianity by keeping a couple of wives. He affected the same sort of reserve in mentioning them as is generally shown by Orientals. He invited me, indeed, to see his Hareem, but he made both his wives bundle out before I was admitted; he felt, as it seemed to me, that neither of them would bear criticism, and I think that this idea, rather than any motive of sincere jealousy, induced him to keep them out of sight. The rooms of the hareem reminded me of an English nursery, rather than of a Mahometan paradise. One is apt to judge of a woman before one sees her by the air of elegance or coarseness with which she surrounds her home: I judged Osman's wives by this test, and condemned them both. But the strangest feature in Osman's character was his inextinguishable nationality. In vain they had brought him over the seas in early boyhood—in vain had he suffered captivity, conversion, circumcision—in vain they had passed him through fire in their Arabian campaigns—they could not cut away or burn out poor Osman's inborn love of all that was Scotch; in vain men called him Effendi—in vain he swept along in eastern robes— in vain the rival wives adorned his hareem; the joy of his heart still plainly lay in this, that he had three shelves of books, and that the books were thorough-bred Scotch—the Edinburgh this, the Edinburgh that, and above all, I recollect he prided himself upon the 'Edinburgh Cabinet Library'.

The fear of the Plague is its forerunner. It is likely enough that at the time of my seeing poor Osman the deadly taint was beginning to creep through his veins, but it was not till after I had left Cairo that he was visibly stricken. He died.

As soon as I had seen all that interested me in Cairo and its neighbourhood, I wished to make my escape from a city that lay under the terrible curse of the Plague, but Mysseri fell ill in consequence, I believe, of the hardships which he had been suffering in my service; after a while he recovered sufficiently to undertake a journey, but then there was some difficulty in procuring beasts of burthen, and it was not till the nineteenth day of my sojourn that I quitted the city.

During all this time the power of the Plague was rapidly increasing. When I first arrived, it was said that the daily number of 'accidents' by Plague out of a population of about 200,000 did not exceed four or five hundred, but before I went away the deaths were reckoned at twelve hundred a day. I had no means of knowing whether the numbers (given out, as I believe they were, by officials) were at all correct, but I could not help knowing that from day to day the number of the dead was increasing. My quarters were in one of the chief thoroughfares of the city, and as the funerals in Cairo take place between day-break and noon (a time during which I generally stayed in my rooms), I could form some opinion as to the briskness of the Plague. I don't mean that I got up every morning with the sun. It was not so, but the funerals of most people in decent circumstances at Cairo are attended by singers and howlers, and the performances of these people woke me in the early morning and prevented me from remaining in ignorance of what was going on in the street below.

These funerals were very simply conducted. The bier was a shallow wooden tray carried upon a light and weak wooden frame. The tray had in general no lid, but the body was more or less hidden from view by a shawl or scarf. The whole was borne upon the shoulders of men, and hurried forward at a great pace. Two or three singers generally preceded the bier; the howlers (these are paid for their vocal labours) followed after; and last of all came such of the dead man's friends and relations as could keep up with such a rapid procession; these, especially the women, would get terribly blown, and would straggle back into the rear; many were fairly 'beaten off'. I never observed any appearance of mourning in the mourners; the pace was too severe for any solemn affectation of grief.

When first I arrived at Cairo the funerals that daily passed under my windows were many, but still there were frequent and long intervals without a single howl. Every day, however (except one, when I fancied that I observed a diminution of funerals), these intervals became less frequent and shorter, and at last, the passing of the howlers from morn to noon was almost incessant. I believe that about one half of the whole people was carried off by this visitation. The Orientals, however, have more quiet fortitude than Europeans under afflictions of this sort, and they never allow the Plague to interfere with their religious usages. I rode one day round the great burial-ground. The tombs are strewed over a great expanse among the vast mountains of rubbish (the accumulations of many centuries) which surround the city. The ground, unlike the Turkish 'cities of the dead', which are made so beautiful by their dark cypresses, has nothing to sweeten melancholy —nothing to mitigate the hatefulness of death.

Carnivorous beasts and birds possess the place by
night, and now in the fair morning it was all alive
with fresh comers—alive with dead. Yet at this
very time when the Plague was raging so furiously,
and on this very ground which resounded so mourn--
fully with the howls of arriving funerals, preparations
were going on for the religious festival called the
Kourban Bairam. Tents were pitched, and *swings
hung for the amusement of children* — a ghastly
holiday ! but the Mahometans take a pride, and
a just pride, in following their ancient customs
undisturbed by the shadow of death.

I did not hear whilst I was at Cairo that any
prayer for a remission of the Plague had been offered
up in the mosques. I believe that, however frightful
the ravages of the disease may be, the Mahometans
refrain from approaching Heaven with their com-
plaints until the Plague has endured for a long space,
and then at last they pray God—not that the Plague
may cease, but that it may go to another city !

A good Mussulman seems to take pride in repudiating the European notion that the will of God can
be eluded by shunning the touch of a sleeve. When
I went to see the Pyramids of Sakkara, I was the
guest of a noble old fellow—an Osmanlee (how sweet
it was to hear his soft rolling language, after suffering
as I had suffered of late from the shrieking tongue
of the Arabs !). This man was aware of the European
ideas about contagion, and his first care therefore was
to assure me that not a single instance of Plague had
occurred in his village ; he then inquired as to the
progress of the Plague at Cairo. I had but a bad
account to give. Up to this time my host had carefully refrained from touching me, out of respect to
the European theory of contagion, but as soon as it
was made plain that he, and not I, would be the

person endangered by contact, he gently laid his hand
upon my arm in order to make me feel sure that the
circumstance of my coming from an infected city did
not occasion him the least uneasiness.   In that touch
there was true hospitality.

Very different is the faith and the practice of the
Europeans, or rather I mean of the Europeans settled
in the East, and commonly called Levantines.   When
I came to the end of my journey over the desert I
had been so long alone that the prospect of speaking
to somebody at Cairo seemed almost a new excitement.   I felt a sort of consciousness that I had a
little of the wild beast about me, but I was quite in
the humour to be charmingly tame and to be quite
engaging in my manners, if I should have an opportunity of holding communion with any of the human
race whilst at Cairo.   I knew no one in the place,
and had no letters of introduction, but I carried
letters of credit ; and it often happens in places
remote from England that those 'advices' operate
as a sort of introduction, and obtain for the bearer
(if disposed to receive them) such ordinary civilities
as it may be in the power of the banker to offer.

Very soon after my arrival I found out the abode
of the Levantine to whom my credentials were
addressed.   At his door several persons (all Arabs)
were hanging about and keeping guard.   It was not
till after some delay and the interchange of some
communications with those in the interior of the
citadel that I was admitted.   At length, however,
I was conducted through the court, and up a flight of
stairs, and finally into the apartment where business
was transacted.   The room was divided by a good
substantial fence of iron bars, and behind these
defences the banker had his station.   The truth was
that from fear of the Plague he had adopted the

course usually taken by European residents, and had shut himself up 'in strict quarantine',—that is to say, that he had, as he hoped, cut himself off from all communication with infecting substances. The Europeans long resident in the East, without any, or with scarcely any exception, are firmly convinced that the Plague is propagated by contact, and by contact only—that if they can but avoid the touch of an infecting substance, they are safe, and that if they cannot, they die. This belief induces them to adopt the contrivance of putting themselves in that state of siege which they call 'Quarantine'. It is a part of their faith that metals and hempen rope, and also, I fancy, one or two other substances, will not carry the infection : and they likewise believe that the germ of pestilence lying in an infected substance may be destroyed by submersion in water, or by the action of smoke. They, therefore, guard the doors of their houses with the utmost care against intrusion, and condemn themselves with all the members of their family, including European servants, to a strict imprisonment within the walls of their dwelling. Their native attendants are not allowed to enter at all, but they make the necessary purchases of pro- visions : these are hauled up through one of the windows by means of a rope, and are afterwards soaked in water.

I knew nothing of these mysteries, and was not therefore prepared for the sort of reception I met with. I advanced to the iron fence, and putting my letter between the bars, politely proffered it to Mr. Banker. Mr. Banker received me with a sad and dejected look, and not 'with open arms', or with any arms at all, but with—a pair of tongs ! I placed my letter between the iron fingers : these instantly picked it up as it were a viper, and conveyed it away

to be scorched and purified by fire and smoke. I
was disgusted at this reception, and at the idea that
any thing of mine could carry infection to the poor
wretch who stood on the other side of the bars—pale
and trembling, and already meet for Death. I looked
with something of the Mahometan's feeling upon
these little contrivances for eluding Fate : and in this
instance at least they were vain : a little while and
the poor money-changer who had strived to guard
the days of his life (as though they were coins) with
bolts and bars of iron—he was seized by the Plague,
and he died.

To people entertaining such opinions as these
respecting the fatal effect of contact, the narrow and
crowded streets of Cairo were terrible as the easy
slope that leads to Avernus. The roaring Ocean and
the beetling crags owe something of their sublimity
to this—that if they be tempted, they can take the
warm life of a man. To the contagionist, filled as
he is with the dread of final causes, having no faith
in Destiny, nor in the fixed will of God, and with
none of the devil-may-care indifference which might
stand him instead of creeds—to such one, every rag
that shivers in the breeze of a plague-stricken city has
this sort of sublimity. If by any terrible ordinance
he be forced to venture forth, he sees Death dangling
from every sleeve ; and as he creeps forward, he poises
his shuddering limbs between the imminent jacket
that is stabbing at his right elbow, and the murderous
pelisse, that threatens to mow him clean down as it
sweeps along on his left. But most of all he dreads
that which most of all he should love—the touch of
a woman's dress ; for mothers and wives hurrying
forth on kindly errands from the bedsides of the
dying go slouching along through the streets more
wilfully and less courteously than the men. For a

while it may be that the caution of the poor Levantine
may enable him to avoid contact, but sooner or later
perhaps the dreaded chance arrives : that bundle of
linen, with the dark tearful eyes at the top of it that
labours along with the voluptuous clumsiness of Grisi
—she has touched the poor Levantine with the hem
of her sleeve! From that dread moment, his peace
is gone ; his mind, for ever hanging upon the fatal
touch, invites the blow which he fears ; he watches
for the symptoms of plague so carefully that sooner
or later they come in truth. The parched mouth is
a sign—his mouth *is* parched ; the throbbing brain
—his brain *does* throb ; the rapid pulse—he touches
his own wrist (for he dares not ask counsel of any
man, lest he be deserted), he touches his wrist, and
feels how his frighted blood goes galloping out of his
heart. There is nothing but the fatal swelling that
is wanting to make his sad conviction complete ;
immediately he has an odd feel under the arm—no
pain, but a little straining of the skin ; he would to
God it were his fancy that were strong enough to give
him that sensation : this is the worst of all. It now
seems to him that he could be happy and contented
with his parched mouth, and his throbbing brain,
and his rapid pulse, if only he could know that there
were no swelling under the left arm ; but dares he
try ?—in a moment of calmness and deliberation he
dares not, but when for a while he has writhed under
the torture of suspense, a sudden strength of will
drives him to seek and know his fate ; he touches the
gland, and finds the skin sane and sound, but under
the cuticle there lies a small lump like a pistol bullet,
that moves as he pushes it. Oh! but is this for all
certainty, is this the sentence of death ? Feel the
gland of the other arm : there is not the same lump
exactly, yet something a little like it : have not some

people glands naturally enlarged?—would to Heaven
he were one! So he does for himself the work of
the Plague, and when the Angel of Death thus
courted does indeed and in truth come, he has only
to finish that which has been so well begun; he
passes his fiery hand over the brain of the victim,
and lets him rave for a season, but all chance-wise, of
people and things once dear, or of people and things
indifferent. Once more the poor fellow is back at
his home in fair Provence, and sees the sun-dial that
stood in his childhood's garden—sees part of his
mother, and the long-since-forgotten face of that
little dear sister—(he sees her, he says, on a Sunday
morning, for all the church bells are ringing;) he
looks up and down through the universe and owns it
well piled with bales upon bales of cotton and cotton
eternal—so much so, that he feels—he knows—he
swears he could make that winning hazard, if the
billiard table would not slant upwards, and if the cue
were a cue worth playing with; but it is not—it's a
cue that won't move—his own arm won't move—in
short, there's the devil to pay in the brain of the
poor Levantine, and, perhaps, the next night but one
he becomes the 'life and the soul' of some squalling
jackal family who fish him out by the foot from his
shallow and sandy grave.

Better fate was mine: by some happy perverseness
(occasioned perhaps by my disgust at the notion of
being received with a pair of tongs) I took it into my
pleasant head that all the European notions about
contagion were thoroughly unfounded,—that the
Plague might be providential, or 'epidemic' (as they
phrase it), but was not contagious, and that I could
not be killed by the touch of a woman's sleeve, nor
yet by her blessed breath. I therefore determined
that the Plague should not alter my habits and

amusements in any one respect. Though I came to
this resolve from impulse, I think that I took the
course which was in effect the most prudent, for the
cheerfulness of spirits which I was thus enabled to
retain discouraged the yellow-winged Angel, and
prevented him from taking a shot at me. I, however,
so far respected the opinion of the Europeans that
I avoided touching when I could do so without
privation or inconvenience. This endeavour furnished me with a sort of amusement as I passed
through the streets. The usual mode of moving
from place to place in the city of Cairo is upon
donkeys; of these great number are always in
readiness with donkey-boys attached. I had two
who constantly (until one of them died of the
Plague) waited at my door upon the chance of being
wanted. I found this way of moving about exceedingly pleasant, and never attempted any other.
I had only to mount my beast, and tell my donkey-boy
the point for which I was bound, and instantly
I began to glide on at a capital pace. The streets
of Cairo are not paved in any way, but strewed with
a dry sandy soil so deadening to sound, that the
foot-fall of my donkey could scarcely be heard.
There is no trottoir, and as you ride through the
streets, you mingle with the people on foot: those
who are in your way upon being warned by the
shouts of the donkey-boy move very slightly aside so
as to leave you a narrow lane for your passage.
Through this you move at a gallop, gliding on
delightfully in the very midst of crowds without
being inconvenienced or stopped for a moment; it
seems to you that it is not the donkey, but the
donkey-boy who wafts you along with his shouts
through pleasant groups and air that comes thick
with the fragrance of burial spice. 'Eh! Sheik, Eh!

Bint,—reggalek,—shumalek, &c., &c.,—O old man,
O virgin, get out of the way on the right—O virgin,
O old man get out of the way on the left,—this
Englishman comes, he comes, he comes!' The
narrow alley which these shouts cleared for my
passage made it possible, though difficult, to go on
for a long way without touching a single person, and
my endeavours to avoid such contact were a sort of
game for me in my loneliness. If I got through
a street without being touched, I won; if I was
touched, I lost,—lost a deuce of a stake according to
the theory of the Europeans, but that I deemed to
be all nonsense,—I only lost that game, and would
certainly win the next.

There is not much in the way of public buildings
to admire at Cairo, but I saw one handsome mosque,
and to this an instructive history is attached. A
Hindostanee merchant, having amassed an immense
fortune, settled in Cairo, and soon found that his
riches in the then state of the political world gave
him vast power in the city—power, however, the
exercise of which was much restrained by the
counteracting influence of other wealthy men. With
a view to extinguish every attempt at rivalry, the
Hindostanee merchant built this magnificent mosque
at his own expense; when the work was complete, he
invited all the leading men of the city to join him
in prayer within the walls of the newly-built temple,
and he then caused to be massacred all those who
were sufficiently influential to cause him any jealousy
or uneasiness,—in short, all 'the respectable men' of
the place; after this he possessed undisputed power
in the city, and was greatly revered,—he is revered
to this day. It struck me that there was a touching
simplicity in the mode which this man so successfully
adopted for gaining the confidence and good will

of his fellow-citizens. There seems to be some improbability in the story (though not nearly so gross as it might appear to an European ignorant of the East, for witness Mehemet Ali's destruction of the Mamelukes, a closely similar act, and attended with the like brilliant success [1]) ; but even if the story be false as a mere fact, it is perfectly true as an illustration,—it is a true exposition of the means by which the respect and affection of Orientals may be conciliated.

I ascended one day to the citadel, and gained from its ramparts a superb view of the town. The fanciful and elaborate gilt work of the many minarets gives a light, a florid grace to the city as seen from this height; but before you can look for many seconds at such things, your eyes are drawn westward—drawn westward and over the Nile till they rest upon the massive enormities of the Ghizeh pyramids.

I saw within the fortress many yoke of men all haggard and woe-begone, and a kennel of very fine lions well fed and flourishing; I say *yoke* of men, for the poor fellows were working together in bonds; I say a *kennel* of lions, for the beasts were not enclosed in cages, but simply chained up like dogs.

I went round the Bazaars : it seemed to me that pipes and arms were cheaper here than at Constantinople, and I should advise you therefore, if you reach both places, to prefer the market of Cairo. In the open slave-market I saw about fifty girls exposed for sale, but all of them black or 'invisible' brown. A slave agent took me to some rooms in the upper story of the building, and also into several obscure houses in the neighbourhood with a view to show me some white women. The owners raised

[1] Mehemet Ali invited the Mamelukes to a feast, and murdered them whilst preparing to enter the banqueting hall.

various objections to the display of their ware, and well they might, for I had not the least notion of purchasing : some refused on account of the illegality of selling to unbelievers,[1] and others declared that all transactions of this sort were completely out of the question as long as the Plague was raging. I only succeeded in seeing one white slave who was for sale, but on this treasure the owner affected to set an immense value, and raised my expectations to a high pitch by saying that the girl was Circassian and was 'fair as the full moon'. There was a good deal of delay, but at last I was led into a long dreary room, and there, after marching timidly forward for a few paces, I descried at the farther end that mass of white linen which indicates an Eastern woman. She was bid to uncover her face, and I presently saw that, though very far from being good looking, according to my notion of beauty, she had not been inaptly described by the man who compared her to the full moon, for her large face was perfectly round, and perfectly white. Though very young, she was nevertheless extremely fat. She gave me the idea of having been got up for sale,—of having been fattened, and whitened by medicines or by some peculiar diet. I was firmly determined not to see any more of her than the face. She was perhaps disgusted at this my virtuous resolve, as well as with my personal appearance,—perhaps she saw my distaste and disappointment ; perhaps she wished to gain favour with her owner by showing her attachment to his faith : at all events she holloed out very lustily and very decidedly that 'she would not be bought by the Infidel'.

Whilst I remained at Cairo, I thought it worth while to see something of the Magicians, because

---

[1] It is not strictly lawful to sell *white* slaves to a Christian.

I considered that these men were in some sort the descendants of those who contended so stoutly against the superior power of Aaron.   I therefore sent for an old man who was held to be the chief of the Magicians, and desired him to show me the wonders of his art.   The old man looked and dressed his character exceedingly well; the vast turban, the flowing beard, and the ample robes were all that one could wish in the way of appearance. The first experiment (a very stale one) which he attempted to perform for me was that of showing the forms and faces of my absent friends, not to me, but to a boy brought in from the streets for the purpose, and said to be chosen at random.   A mangale (pan of burning charcoal) was brought into my room, and the Magician bending over it, sprinkled upon the fire some substances consisting, I suppose, of spices or sweetly burning woods; for immediately a fragrant smoke arose that curled around the bending form of the Wizard, the while that he pronounced his first incantations.   When these were over, the boy was made to sit down, and a common green shade was bound over his brow; then the Wizard took ink, and, still continuing his incantations, wrote certain mysterious figures upon the boy's palm and directed him to rivet his attention to these marks without looking aside for an instant.   Again the incantations proceeded, and after a while the boy, being seemingly a little agitated, was asked whether he saw anything on the palm of his hand.   He declared that he saw, and he described it rather minutely, a kind of military procession with royal flags, and warlike banners flying.   I was then called upon to name the absent person whose form was to be made visible.   I named Keate.   You were not at Eton, and I must tell you, therefore, what manner of

man it was that I named, though I think you must
have some idea of him already, for wherever from
utmost Canada to Bundelcund—wherever there was
the white-washed wall of an officer's room or of any
other apartment in which English gentlemen are
forced to kick their heels, there, likely enough (in the
days of his reign) the head of Keate would be seen,
scratched, or drawn with those various degrees of skill
which one observes in the representation of Saints.
Anybody without the least notion of drawing could
still draw a speaking, nay scolding likeness of Keate.
If you had no pencil, you could draw him well enough
with a poker, or the leg of a chair, or the smoke of a
candle. He was little more (if more at all) than five
feet in height, and was not very great in girth, but
within this space was concentrated the pluck of ten
battalions. He had a really noble voice, and this he
could modulate with great skill, but he had also the
power of quacking like an angry duck, and he almost
always adopted this mode of communication in order
to inspire respect. He was a capital scholar, but his
ingenuous learning had *not* 'softened his manners',
and *had* 'permitted them to be fierce.'—tremendously
fierce ; he had such a complete command over his
temper—I mean, over his *good* temper, that he scarcely
ever allowed it to appear : you could not put him out
of humour—that is, out of the *ill*-humour which he
thought to be fitting for a head master. His red,
shaggy eyebrows were so prominent, that he habitually
used them as arms and hands for the purpose of
pointing out any object towards which he wished to
direct attention ; the rest of his features were equally
striking in their way, and were all and all his own.
He wore a fancy dress, partly resembling the costume
of Napoleon, and partly that of a widow woman. I
could not have named anybody more decidedly

differing in appearance from the rest of the human race.

'Whom do you name?'—'I name John Keate.'—'Now what do you see?' said the Wizard to the boy.—'I see,' answered the boy, 'I see a fair girl with golden hair, blue eyes, pallid face, rosy lips.' *There* was a shot! I shouted out my laughter with profane exultation, and the Wizard, perceiving the grossness of his failure, declared that the boy must have known sin (for none but the innocent can see truth), and accordingly kicked him down stairs.

One or two other boys were tried, but none could 'see truth'.

Notwithstanding the failure of these experiments, I wished to see what sort of mummery my Magician would practise if I called upon him to show me some performances of a higher order than those already attempted. I therefore made a treaty with him, in virtue of which he was to descend with me into the tombs near the Pyramids, and there evoke the Devil. The negotiation lasted some time, for Dthemetri, as in duty bound, tried to beat down the Wizard as much as he could, and the Wizard on his part manfully stuck up for his price, declaring that to raise the Devil was really no joke, and insinuating that to do so was an awesome crime. I let Dthemetri have his way in the negotiation, but I felt in reality very indifferent about the sum to be paid, and for this reason, namely, that the payment (except a very small present which I might make, or not, as I chose) was to be *contingent on success*. At length the bargain was finished, and it was arranged that, after a few days to be allowed for preparation, the Wizard should raise the Devil for two pounds ten, play or pay—no Devil, no piastres.

The Wizard failed to keep his appointment. I sent

to know why the deuce he had not come to raise the
Devil. The truth was that my Mahomet had gone
to the mountain. The Plague had seized him, and
he died.

Although the Plague was now spreading quick and
terrible havoc around him, I did not see very plainly
any corresponding change in the looks of the streets
until the seventh day after my arrival: I then first
observed that the city was *silenced*. There were no
outward signs of despair nor of violent terror, but
many of the voices that had swelled the busy hum of
men were already hushed in death, and the survivors,
so used to scream and screech in their earnestness
whenever they bought or sold, now showed an unwonted indifference about the affairs of this world:
it was less worth while for men to haggle and haggle,
and crack the sky with noisy bargains, when the
Great Commander was there, who could 'pay all their
debts with the roll of his drum'.

At this time I was informed that of 25,000 people
at Alexandria, 12,000 had died already; the Destroyer
had come rather later to Cairo, but there was nothing
of weariness in his strides. The deaths came faster
than ever they befell in the Plague of London; but
the calmness of Orientals under such visitations, and
their habit of using biers for interment instead of
burying coffins along with the bodies, rendered it
practicable to dispose of the dead in the usual way,
without shocking the people by any unaccustomed
spectacle of horror. There was no tumbling of
bodies into carts, as in the Plague of Florence, and
the Plague of London; every man, according to his
station, was properly buried, and that in the accustomed way, except that he went to his grave at a
pace more than usually rapid.

The funerals pouring through the streets were not

the only public evidence of deaths.   In Cairo this
custom prevails:—at the instant of a man's death
(if his property is sufficient to justify the expense)
professional howlers are employed.   I believe that
these persons are brought near to the dying man,
when his end appears to be approaching, and the
moment that life is gone, they lift up their voices,
and send forth a loud wail from the chamber of
Death.   Thus I knew when my near neighbours died :
sometimes the howls were near ; sometimes more
distant.   Once I was awakened in the night by the
wail of death in the next house, and another time by
a like howl from the house opposite ; and there were
two or three minutes, I recollect, during which the
howl seemed to be actually *running* along the street.

I happened to be rather teazed at this time by a
sore throat, and I thought it would be well to get it
cured, if I could, before I again started on my travels.
I therefore inquired for a Frank doctor, and was
informed that the only one then at Cairo was a
Bolognese Refugee, a very young practitioner, and so
poor that he had not been able to take flight, as the
other medical men had done.   At such a time as this
it was out of the question to *send* for an European
physician ; a person thus summoned would be sure
to suppose that the patient was ill of the Plague, and
would decline to come.   I therefore rode to the young
Doctor's residence, ascended a flight or two of stairs,
and knocked at his door.   No one came immediately,
but after some little delay the Medico himself opened
the door and admitted me.   I, of course, made him
understand that I had come to consult him, but
before entering upon my throat grievance, I accepted
a chair, and exchanged a sentence or two of common-
place conversation.   Now, the natural common-place
of the city at this season was of a gloomy sort—

'Come va la peste?' (how goes the plague?), and this was precisely the question I put. A deep sigh, and the words 'Sette cento per giorno, Signor' (seven hundred a day), pronounced in a tone of the deepest sadness and dejection, were the answer I received. The day was not oppressively hot, yet I saw that the Doctor was transpiring profusely, and even the outside surface of the thick shawl dressing-gown in which he had wrapped himself appeared to be moist. He was a handsome, pleasant-looking young fellow, but the deep melancholy of his tone did not tempt me to prolong the conversation, and without farther delay, I requested that my throat might be looked at. The Medico held my chin in the usual way, and examined my throat; he then wrote me a prescription, and almost immediately afterwards I bid him farewell; but as he conducted me towards the door, I observed an expression of strange and unhappy watchfulness in his rolling eyes. It was not the next day, but the next day but one, if I rightly remember, that I sent to request another interview with my Doctor. In due time Dthemetri, my messenger, returned, looking sadly aghast. He had 'met the Medico', for so he phrased it, 'coming out from his house—in a bier!'

It was, of course, plain that when the poor Bolognese stood looking down my throat and almost mingling his breath with mine, he was already stricken of the Plague. I suppose that his violent sweat must have been owing to some medicine administered by himself in the faint hope of a cure. The peculiar rolling of his eyes which I had remarked is, I believe, to experi-enced observers a pretty sure test of the Plague. A Russian acquaintance of mine, speaking from the information of men who had made the Turkish cam-paigns of 1828 and 1829, told me that by this sign

the officers of Sabalkansky's force were able to make
out the plague-stricken soldiers with a good deal of
certainty.

It so happened that most of the people with whom
I had anything to do, during my stay at Cairo, were
seized with Plague; and all these died. Since I had
been for a long time *en route* before I reached Egypt,
and was about to start again for another long journey
over the Desert, there were of course many little
matters touching my wardrobe and my travelling
equipments which required to be attended to whilst
I remained in the city. It happened so many times
that Dthemetri's orders in respect to these matters
were frustrated by the deaths of the tradespeople and
others whom he employed, that at last I became quite
accustomed to the peculiar manner of the man when
he prepared to announce a new death to me. The
poor fellow naturally supposed that I should feel some
uneasiness at hearing of the 'accidents' continually
happening to persons employed by me, and he therefore communicated their deaths as though they were
the deaths of friends; he would cast down his eyes,
and look like a man abashed, and then gently, and
with a mournful gesture, allow the words 'Morto,
Signor', to come through his lips. I don't know how
many of such instances occurred, but they were several,
and besides these (as I told you before), my banker,
my doctor, my landlord, and my magician, all died
of the Plague. A lad who acted as a helper in the
house I occupied lost a brother and a sister within a
few hours. Out of my two established donkey-boys
one died. I did not hear of any instance in which
a plague-stricken patient had recovered.

Going out one morning, I met unexpectedly the
scorching breath of the Khamseen wind, and fearing
that I should faint under the infliction, I returned to

my rooms.   Reflecting, however, that I might have
to encounter this wind in the desert, where there would
be no possibility of avoiding it, I thought it would be
better to brave it once more in the city, and to try
whether I could really bear it or not.   I, therefore,
mounted my ass, and rode to old Cairo and along
the gardens by the banks of the Nile.   The wind was
hot to the touch as though it came from a furnace;
it blew strongly, but yet with such perfect steadiness,
that the trees bending under its force remained fixed
in the same curves without perceptibly waving; the
whole sky was obscured by a veil of yellowish gray
that shut out the face of the sun.   The streets were
utterly silent, being indeed almost entirely deserted,
and not without cause, for the scorching blast, whilst
it fevers the blood, closes up the pores of the skin,
and is terribly distressing therefore to every animal
that encounters it.   I returned to my rooms dread-
fully ill.   My head ached with a burning pain, and
my pulse bounded quick and fitfully, but perhaps
(as in the instance of the poor Levantine whose death
I was mentioning) the fear and excitement I felt in
trying my own wrist may have made my blood flutter
the faster.

    It is a thoroughly well believed theory that, during
the continuance of the Plague, you can't be ill of any
other febrile malady; an unpleasant privilege that!
for ill I was, and ill of fever; and I anxiously wished
that the ailment might turn out to be anything rather
than Plague.   I had some right to surmise that my
illness might have been merely the effect of the hot
wind; and this notion was encouraged by the elasticity
of my spirits, and by a strong forefeeling that much
of my destined life in this world was yet to come, and
yet to be fulfilled.   That was my instinctive belief;
but when I carefully weighed the probabilities on the

one side, and on the other, I could not help seeing
that the strength of argument was all against me.
There was a strong antecedent likelihood in *favour* of
my being struck by the same blow as the rest of the
people who had been dying around me.   Besides, it
occurred to me that, after all, the universal opinion
of the Europeans upon a medical question, such as
that of contagion, might probably be correct; and *if
it were*, I was so thoroughly 'compromised', especially
by the touch and breath of the dying Medico, that I
had no right to expect any other fate than that which
now seemed to have overtaken me.   Balancing then
as well as I could all the considerations suggested by
hope and fear, I slowly and reluctantly came to the
conclusion that, according to all merely reasonable
probability, the Plague had come upon me.

You might suppose that this conviction would have
induced me to write a few farewell lines to those who
were dearest, and that having done that, I should
have turned my thoughts towards the world to come.
Such, however, was not the case; I believe that the
prospect of death often brings with it strong anxieties
about matters of comparatively trivial import, and
certainly with me the whole energy of the mind was
directed towards the one petty object of concealing
my illness until the latest possible moment—until the
delirious stage.   I did not believe that either Mysseri,
or Dthemetri, who had served me so faithfully in all
trials, would have deserted me (as most Europeans
are wont to do) when they knew that I was stricken
by Plague; but I shrank from the idea of putting
them to this test, and I dreaded the consternation
which the knowledge of my illness would be sure to
occasion.

I was very ill indeed at the moment when my dinner
was served, and my soul sickened at the sight of the

food, but I had luckily the habit of dispensing with the attendance of servants during my meal, and as soon as I was left alone, I made a melancholy calculation of the quantity of food I should have eaten if I had been in my usual health, and filled my plates accordingly, and gave myself salt, and so on, as though I were going to dine; I then transferred the viands to a piece of the omnipresent *Times* newspaper, and hid them away in a cupboard, for it was not yet night, and I dared not to throw the food into the street until darkness came. I did not at all relish this process of fictitious dining, but at length the cloth was removed, and I gladly reclined on my divan (I would not lie down), with the *Arabian Nights* in my hand.

I had a feeling that tea would be a capital thing for me, but I would not order it until the usual hour. When at last the time came, I drank deep draughts from the fragrant cup. The effect was almost instantaneous. A plenteous sweat burst through my skin, and watered my clothes through and through. I kept myself thickly covered. The hot tormenting weight which had been loading my brains was slowly heaved away. The fever was extinguished. I felt a new buoyancy of spirits, and an unusual activity of mind. I went into my bed under a load of thick covering, and when the morning came, and I asked myself how I was, I answered, 'perfectly well'.

I was very anxious to procure, if possible, some medical advice for Mysseri, whose illness prevented my departure. Every one of the European practising doctors, of whom there had been many, had either died or fled; it was said, however, that there was an Englishman in the medical service of the Pasha who quietly remained at his post, but that he never engaged in private practice. I determined to try if

I could obtain assistance in this quarter. I did not
venture at first, and at such a time as this, to ask
him to visit a servant who was prostrate on the bed
of sickness; but thinking that I might thus gain an
opportunity of persuading him to attend Mysseri,
I wrote a note mentioning my own affair of the sore
throat, and asking for the benefit of his medical
advice; he instantly followed back my messenger,
and was at once shown up into my room. I entreated
him to stand off, telling him fairly how deeply I was
'compromised', and especially by my contact with
a person actually ill, and since dead of Plague. The
generous fellow, with a good-humoured laugh at the
terrors of the contagionists, marched straight up to
me, and forcibly seized my hand, and shook it with
manly violence. I felt grateful indeed, and swelled
with fresh pride of race, because that my countryman
could carry himself so nobly. He soon cured Mysseri,
as well as me, and all this he did from no other
motives than the pleasure of doing a kindness, and
the delight of braving a danger.

At length the great difficulty [1] I had had in procuring beasts for my departure was overcome, and now,
too, I was to have the new excitement of travelling on
dromedaries. With two of these beasts, and three
camels, I gladly wound my way from out of the pest-
stricken city. As I passed through the streets, I
observed a grave elder, stretching forth his arms, and
lifting up his voice in a speech which seemed to have
some reference to me. Requiring an interpretation,
I found that the man had said, 'The Pasha seeks
camels, and he finds them not—the Englishman says,
"let camels be brought", and behold—there they are.'

---

[1] The difficulty was occasioned by the immense exertions
which the Pasha was making to collect camels for military
purposes.

I no sooner breathed the free, wholesome air of the desert, than I felt that a great burthen which I had been scarcely conscious of bearing was lifted away from my mind. For nearly three weeks I had lived under peril of death; the peril ceased, and not till then did I know how much alarm and anxiety I had really been suffering.

CHAPTER XIX

THE PYRAMIDS

I WENT to see and to explore the Pyramids.

Familiar to one from the days of early childhood are the forms of the Egyptian Pyramids, and now, as I approached them from the banks of the Nile, I had no print, no picture before me, and yet the old shapes were there; there was no change: they were just as I had always known them. I straightened myself in my stirrups, and strived to persuade my understanding that this was real Egypt, and that those angles which stood up between me and the West were of harder stuff, and more ancient than the paper pyramids of the green portfolio. Yet it was not till I came to the base of the great Pyramid, that reality began to weigh upon my mind. Strange to say, the bigness of the distinct blocks of stone was the first sign by which I attained to feel the immensity of the whole pile. When I came, and trod, and touched with my hands, and climbed, in order that by climbing I might come to the top of one single stone, then, and almost suddenly, a cold sense and understanding of the Pyramid's enormity came down overcasting my brain.

Now try to endure this homely, sick-nursish illustration of the effect produced upon one's mind by the mere vastness of the great Pyramid. When I was very young (between the ages, I believe, of three and five years old), being then of delicate health, I was often in time of night the victim of a strange kind of mental oppression. I lay in my bed perfectly conscious, and with open eyes, but without power to speak, or to move, and all the while my brain was oppressed to distraction by the presence of a single and abstract idea,—the idea of solid Immensity. It seemed to me in my agonies, that the horror of this visitation arose from its coming upon me without form or shape—that the close presence of the direst monster ever bred in Hell would have been a thousand times more tolerable than that simple idea of solid size; my aching mind was fixed and riveted down upon the mere quality of vastness, vastness, vastness; and was not permitted to invest with it any particular object. If I could have done so, the torment would have ceased. When at last I was roused from this state of suffering, I could not of course in those days (knowing no verbal metaphysics, and no metaphysics at all, except by the dreadful experience of an abstract idea) I could not of course find words to describe the nature of my sensations, and even now I cannot explain why it is that the forced contemplation of a mere quality, distinct from matter, should be so terrible. Well, now my eyes saw and knew, and my hands and my feet informed my understanding, that there was nothing at all abstract about the great Pyramid,—it was a big triangle, sufficiently concrete, easy to see, and rough to the touch; it could not, of course, affect me with the peculiar sensation I have been talking of, but yet there was something akin to that old night-mare agony in the terrible completeness with which a mere mass of masonry could fill and load my mind.

And Time too; the remoteness of its origin, no
less than the enormity of its proportions, screens an
Egyptian Pyramid from the easy and familiar contact
of our modern minds; at its base the common Earth
ends, and all above is a world,—one not created of
God,—not seeming to be made by men's hands, but
rather the sheer giant-work of some old dismal age
weighing down this younger planet.

Fine sayings! but the truth seems to be, after all,
that the Pyramids are quite of this world; that they
were piled up into the air for the realization of some
kingly crotchets about immortality,—some priestly
longing for burial fees; and that as for the building
—they were built like coral rocks by swarms of
insects,—by swarms of poor Egyptians, who were
not only the abject tools and slaves of power, but
who also ate onions for the reward of their immortal labours! [1] The Pyramids are quite of this
world.

I of course ascended to the summit of the great
Pyramid, and also explored its chambers, but these
I need not describe. The first time that I went to the
Pyramids of Ghizeh, there were a number of Arabs
hanging about in its neighbourhood, and wanting to
receive presents on various pretences: their Sheik was
with them. There was also present an ill-looking
fellow in soldier's uniform. This man on my departure claimed a reward, on the ground that he had
maintained order and decorum amongst the Arabs.
His claim was not considered valid by my Dragoman,
and was rejected accordingly. My donkey-boys
afterwards said they had overheard this fellow propose
to the Sheik to put me to death whilst I was in the

---

[1] Herodotus, in an after age, stood by with his note-book,
and got, as he thought, the exact returns of all the rations
served out.

interior of the great Pyramid, and to share with him
the booty. Fancy a struggle for life in one of those
burial chambers, with acres and acres of solid masonry
between oneself and the daylight! I felt exceedingly
glad that I had not made the rascal a present.

I visited the very ancient Pyramids of Aboucir and
Sakkara. There are many of these, differing the one
from the other in shape as well as size; and it struck
me that, taken together, they might be looked upon
as showing the progress and perfection (such as it is)
of Pyramidical Architecture. One of the Pyramids
at Sakkara is almost a rival for the full-grown monster
at Ghizeh; others are scarcely more than vast heaps
of brick and stone; and these last suggested to me
the idea that, after all, the Pyramid is nothing more
nor less than a variety of the sepulchral mound so
common in most countries (including I believe
Hindostan, from whence the Egyptians are supposed
to have come). Men accustomed to raise these
structures for their dead kings or conquerors, would
carry the usage with them in their migrations; but
arriving in Egypt, and seeing the impossibility of
finding earth sufficiently tenacious for a mound, they
would approximate as nearly as might be to their
ancient custom by raising up a round heap of stones,
in short, conical pyramids. Of these there are several
at Sakkara, and the materials of some are thrown
together without any order or regularity. The tran-
sition from this simple form to that of the square
angular pyramid was easy and natural, and it seemed
to me that the gradations through which the style
passed from infancy up to its mature enormity could
plainly be traced at Sakkara.

CHAPTER XX

THE SPHYNX

AND near the Pyramids, more wondrous, and more awful than all else in the land of Egypt, there sits the lonely Sphynx. Comely the creature is, but the comeliness is not of this world; the once worshipped beast is a deformity and a monster to this generation, and yet you can see that those lips, so thick and heavy, were fashioned according to some ancient mould of beauty—some mould of beauty now forgotten—forgotten because that Greece drew forth Cytherea, from the flashing foam of the Ægean, and in her image created new forms of beauty, and made it a law among men that the short and proudly wreathed lip should stand for the sign and the main condition of loveliness through all generations to come. Yet still there lives on the race of those who were beautiful in the fashion of the elder world, and Christian girls of Coptic blood will look on you with the sad, serious gaze, and kiss you your charitable hand with the big pouting lips of the very Sphynx.

Laugh and mock if you will at the worship of stone idols, but mark ye this, ye breakers of images, that in one regard, the stone idol bears awful semblance of Deity—unchangefulness in the midst of change—the same seeming will, and intent for ever and ever inexorable! Upon ancient dynasties of Ethiopian and Egyptian Kings—upon Greek and Roman, upon Arab and Ottoman conquerors—upon Napoleon dreaming of an Eastern Empire—upon battle and pestilence—upon the ceaseless misery of the Egyptian race—upon keen-eyed travellers—

Herodotus yesterday, and Warburton to-day—upon
all and more this unworldly Sphynx has watched,
and watched like a Providence with the same earnest
eyes, and the same sad, tranquil mien.   And we, we
shall die, and Islam will wither away, and the Englishman straining far over to hold his loved India, will
plant a firm foot on the banks of the Nile and sit in
the seats of the Faithful, and still that sleepless rock
will lie watching and watching the works of the new
busy race, with those same sad earnest eyes, and the
same tranquil mien everlasting.   You dare not mock
at the Sphynx.

CHAPTER XXI

CAIRO TO SUEZ

THE ' Dromedary', of Egypt and Syria, is not the
two-humped animal described by that name in books
of natural history, but is in fact of the same family
as the camel, standing towards his more clumsy fellow-
slave in about the same relation as a racer to a cart-
horse.   The fleetness and endurance of this creature
are extraordinary.   It is not usual to force him into
a gallop, and I fancy, from his make, that it would
be quite impossible for him to maintain that pace for
any length of time; but the animal is on so large a
scale, that the jog-trot at which he is generally ridden
implies a progress of perhaps ten or twelve miles an
hour, and this pace, it is said, he can keep up inces-
santly without food, or water, or rest, for three whole
days and nights.

Of the two dromedaries which I had obtained for
this journey I mounted one myself, and put Dthemetri
on the other.   My plan was, to ride on with Dthemetri

to Suez as rapidly as the fleetness of the beasts would
allow, and to let Mysseri (then still remaining weak
from the effects of his late illness) come quietly on
with the camels and baggage.

The trot of the Dromedary is a pace terribly disagreeable to the rider, until he becomes a little accustomed to it; but after the first half hour I so far
schooled myself to this new exercise that I felt capable
of keeping it up (though not without aching limbs)
for several hours together. Now, therefore, I was
anxious to dart forward, and annihilate at once the
whole space that divided me from the Red Sea.
Dthemetri, however, could not get on at all: every
attempt at trotting seemed to threaten the utter
dislocation of his whole frame, and indeed I doubt
whether any one of Dthemetri's age (nearly forty, I
think) and unaccustomed to such exercise could have
borne it at all easily; besides, the dromedary which
fell to his lot was evidently a very bad one; he every
now and then came to a dead stop, and coolly knelt
down as though suggesting that the rider had better
get off at once, and abandon the experiment as one
that was utterly hopeless.

When for the third or fourth time I saw Dthemetri
thus planted, I lost my patience and went on without
him. For about two hours, I think, I advanced without once looking behind me. I then paused, and cast
my eyes back to the western horizon. There was no
sign of Dthemetri, nor of any other living creature.
This I expected, for I knew that I must have far out-
distanced all my followers. I had ridden away from
my party merely by way of humouring my impatience,
and with the intention of stopping as soon as I felt
tired, until I was overtaken. I now observed, however (this I had not been able to do whilst advancing
so rapidly), that the track which I had been following

was seemingly the track of only one or two camels. I did not fear that I had diverged very largely from the true route, but still I could not feel any reasonable certainty that my party would follow any line of march within sight of me.

I had to consider, therefore, whether I should remain where I was upon the chance of seeing my people come up, or whether I should push on alone, and find my own way to Suez. I had now learned that I could not rely upon the continued guidance of any track, but I knew that (if maps were right) the point for which I was bound bore just due East of Cairo, and I thought that, although I might miss the line leading most directly to Suez, I could not well fail to find my way sooner or later to the Red Sea. The worst of it was that I had no provision of food or water with me, and already I was beginning to feel thirst. I deliberated for a minute, and then determined that I would abandon all hope of seeing my party again in the desert, and would push forward as rapidly as possible towards Suez.

It was not without a sensation of awe that I swept with my sight the vacant round of the horizon, and remembered that I was all alone, and unprovisioned in the midst of the arid waste; but this very awe gave tone and zest to the exultation with which I felt myself launched. Hitherto, in all my wanderings I had been under the care of other people—sailors, Tatars, guides, and Dragomen had watched over my welfare; but now, at last, I was here in this African desert, and I *myself, and no other, had charge of my life*. I liked the office well; I had the greatest part of the day before me, a very fair dromedary, a fur pelisse, and a brace of pistols, but no bread, and worst of all, no water; for that I must ride,—and ride I did.

For several hours I urged forward my beast at a

rapid, though steady pace, but at length the pangs
of thirst began to torment me. I did not relax my
pace, however, and I had not suffered long, when a
moving object appeared in the distance before me.
The intervening space was soon traversed, and I
found myself approaching a Bedouin Arab, mounted
on a camel attended by another Bedouin on foot.
They stopped. I saw that there hung from the pack-
saddle of the camel one of the large skin water-flasks
commonly carried in the Desert, and it seemed to be
well filled. I steered my dromedary close up alongside of the mounted Bedouin, caused my beast to
kneel down, then alighted, and keeping the end of
the halter in my hand, went up to the mounted
Bedouin without speaking, took hold of his water-
flask, opened it, and drank long and deep from its
leathern lips. Both of the Bedouins stood fast in
amazement, and mute horror; and really if they had
never happened to see an European before, the ap-
parition was enough to startle them. To see for the
first time a coat and a waistcoat with the semblance
of a white human face at the top, and for this ghastly
figure to come swiftly out of the horizon, upon a fleet
dromedary—approach them silently, and with a de-
moniacal smile, and drink a deep draught from their
water-flask—this was enough to make the Bedouins
stare a little; they, in fact, stared a great deal—not
as Europeans stare with a restless and puzzled expression of countenance, but with features all fixed
and rigid, and with still, glassy eyes. Before they
had time to get decomposed from their state of
petrifaction, I had remounted my dromedary, and
was darting away towards the East.

Without pause or remission of pace, I continued
to press forward, but after a while, I found to my
confusion, that the slight track which had hitherto

guided me, now failed altogether. I began to fear that I must have been all along following the course of some wandering Bedouins, and I felt that if this were the case, my fate was a little uncertain.

I had no compass with me, but I determined upon the eastern point of the horizon as accurately as I could, by reference to the sun, and so laid down for myself a way over the pathless sands.

But now my poor dromedary, by whose life and strength I held my own, she began to show signs of distress; a thick clammy and glutinous kind of foam gathered about her lips, and piteous sobs burst from her bosom in the tones of human misery. I doubted, for a moment, whether I would give her a little rest or relaxation of pace, but I decided that I would not, and continued to push forward as steadily as before.

The character of the country became changed; I had ridden away from the level tracts, and before me now, and on either side, there were vast hills of sand and calcined rocks that interrupted my progress, and baffled my doubtful road, but I did my best. With rapid steps I swept round the base of the hills, threaded the winding hollows, and at last, as I rose in my swift course to the crest of a lofty ridge, Thalatta! Thalatta! the sea—the sea was before me!

It has been given me to know the true pith, and to feel the power of ancient pagan creeds, and so (distinctly from all mere admiration of the beauty belonging to Nature's works) I acknowledge a sense of mystical reverence when first I approached some illustrious feature of the globe—some coast-line of ocean—some mighty river or dreary mountain range, the ancient barrier of kingdoms. But the Red Sea! It might well claim my earnest gaze by force of the great Jewish migration which connects it with the history of our own religion. From this very ridge, it is likely enough, the panting Israelites first saw that shining inlet of the sea:—Ay! ay! but moreover, and best of all, that beckoning sea assured my eyes, and proved how well I had marked out the East for my path, and gave me good promise that sooner or later the time would come for me to drink of water cool and plenteous, and then lie down and rest. It was distant the sea, but I felt my own strength, and I had heard of the strength of dromedaries. I pushed forward as eagerly as though I had spoiled the Egyptians, and were flying from Pharaoh's police.

I had not yet been able to see any mark of distant Suez, but after a while I descried far away in the East, a large, blank isolated building. I made towards this, and in time got down to it. The building was a fort, and had been built there for the protection of a well contained within its precincts. A cluster of small huts adhered to the fort, and in a short time I was receiving the hospitality of the inhabitants, a score or so of people who sat grouped upon the sands near their hamlet. To quench the fires of my throat with about a gallon of muddy water, and to swallow a little of the food placed before me, was the work of a few minutes, and before the astonishment of my hosts had even begun to subside, I was pursuing my onward journey. Suez, I found, was still three hours distant, and the sun going down in the west warned me that I must find some other guide to keep me straight. This guide I found in the most fickle and uncertain of the elements. For some hours the wind had been freshening, and it now blew a violent gale; it blew— not fitfully and in squalls—but with such steadiness that I felt convinced it would blow from the same quarter for several hours; so when the sun set,

I carefully looked for the point whence the wind
came, and found that it blew from the very west—
blew exactly in the direction of my route. I had
nothing to do therefore but to go straight to leeward,
and this I found easy enough, for the gale was
blowing so hard, that, if I diverged at all from my
course, I instantly felt the pressure of the blast on
the side towards which I had deviated. Very soon
after sunset there came on complete darkness, but
the strong wind guided me well, and sped me too
on my way.

I had pushed on for about, I think, a couple of
hours after nightfall, when I saw the glimmer of a
light in the distance, and this I ventured to hope
must be Suez. Upon approaching it, however, I
found that it was only a solitary fort, and this
I passed by without stopping.

On I went, still riding down the wind, but at last
an unlucky misfortune befell me—a misfortune so
absurd that, if you like, you shall have your laugh
against me. I have told you already what sort of
lodging it is that you have upon the back of a camel.
You ride the dromedary in the same fashion; you
are perched, rather than seated, on a bunch of
carpets or quilts upon the summit of the hump. It
happened that my dromedary veered rather suddenly
from her onward course. Meeting the movement,
I mechanically turned my left wrist as though I
were holding a bridle rein, for the complete darkness
prevented my eyes from reminding me that I had
nothing but a halter in my hand. The expected
resistance failed, for the halter was hanging upon
that side of the dromedary's neck towards which
I was slightly leaning; I toppled over, head foremost,
and then went falling through air till my crown came
whang against the ground. And the ground too

was perfectly hard (compacted sand), but my thickly wadded head-gear (this I wore for protection against the sun) now stood me in good part, and saved my life. The notion of my being able to get up again after falling head-foremost from such an immense height, seemed to me at first too paradoxical to be acted upon, but I soon found that I was not a bit hurt. My dromedary had utterly vanished ; I looked round me, and saw the glimmer of a light in the fort which I had lately passed, and I began to work my way back in that direction. The violence of the gale made it hard for me to force my way towards the west, but I succeeded at last in regaining the fort. To this, as to the other fort which I had passed, there was attached a cluster of huts, and I soon found myself surrounded by a group of villanous, gloomy-looking fellows. It was sorry work for me to swagger and look big at a time when I felt so particularly small on account of my tumble and my lost dromedary, but there was no help for it ; I had no Dthemetri now to 'strike terror' for me. I knew hardly one word of Arabic, but somehow or other I contrived to announce it as my absolute will and pleasure that these fellows should find me the means of gaining Suez. They acceded, and having a donkey, they saddled it for me, and appointed one of their number to attend me on foot.

I afterwards found that these fellows were not Arabs, but Algerine refugees, and that they bore the character of being sad scoundrels. They justified this imputation to some extent on the following day. They allowed Mysseri with my baggage and the camels to pass unmolested, but an Arab lad belonging to the party happened to lag a little way in the rear, and him (if they were not maligned) these rascals stripped and robbed. Low indeed is the state of bandit morality, when men will allow the sleek traveller with well-laden camels to pass in quiet, reserving their spirit of enterprise for the tattered turban of a miserable boy.

I reached Suez at last. The British Agent, though roused from his midnight sleep, received me in his home with the utmost kindness and hospitality. Heaven! how delightful it was to lie on fair sheets, and to dally with sleep, and to wake, and to sleep, and to wake once more, for the sake of sleeping again!

CHAPTER XXII

SUEZ

I WAS hospitably entertained by the British Consul, or Agent, as he is there styled; he is the employé of the East Indian Company, and not of the Home Government. Napoleon, during his stay of five days at Suez, had been the guest of the Consul's father, and I was told that the divan in my apartment had been the bed of the great Commander.

There are two opinions as to the point where the Israelites passed the Red Sea; one is that they traversed only the very small creek at the northern extremity of the inlet, and that they entered the bed of the water at the spot on which Suez now stands,— the other that they crossed the sea from a point eighteen miles down the coast. The Oxford theologians who, with Milman their Professor,[1] believe that Jehovah conducted his chosen people without disturbing the order of Nature, adopt the first view,

[1] See Milman's *History of the Jews*. 1st edit. Family Library.

and suppose that the Israelites passed during an ebb
tide aided by a violent wind. One among many
objections to this supposition is, that the time of a
single ebb would not have been sufficient for the
passage of that vast multitude of men and beasts, or
even for a small fraction of it. Moreover, the creek
to the north of this point can be compassed in an
hour, and in two hours you can make the circuit of
the salt marsh over which the sea may have extended
in former times ; if therefore the Israelites crossed so
high up as Suez, the Egyptians, unless infatuated by
Divine interference, might easily have recovered their
stolen goods from the encumbered fugitives, by
making a slight detour. The opinion which fixes the
point of passage at eighteen miles distance, and from
thence right across the Ocean depths to the eastern
side of the sea, is supported by the unanimous tradition of the people, whether Christians or Mussulmans, and is consistent with Holy writ ; 'the waters
were a wall unto them on their right hand, *and on
their left*.' The Cambridge Mathematicians seem to
think that the Israelites were enabled to pass over
dry land by adopting a route not usually subjected
to the influx of the Sea ; this notion is plausible in a
mere hydrostatical point of view, but it is difficult to
reconcile it with the account given in Exodus, unless
we can suppose that the words 'sea' and 'waters'
are there used in a sense implying dry land.

Napoleon, when at Suez, made an attempt to follow
the supposed steps of Moses by passing the creek at
this point, but it seems, according to the testimony of
the people of Suez, that he and his horsemen managed
the matter in a way more resembling the failure of
the Egyptians, than the success of the Israelites.
According to the French account, Napoleon got out
of the difficulty by that warrior-like presence of mind

which served him so well when the fate of nations depended on the decision of a moment; he commanded his horsemen to disperse in all directions, in order to multiply the chances of finding shallow water, and was thus enabled to discover a line by which he and his people were extricated. The story told by the people of Suez is very different; they declare that Napoleon parted from his horse, got water-logged and nearly drowned, and was only fished out by the aid of the people on shore.

I bathed twice at the point assigned to the passage of the Israelites, and the second time that I did so, I chose the time of low water, and tried to walk across, but I soon found myself out of my depth, or at least in water so deep that I could only advance by swimming.

The dromedary which had bolted in the Desert was brought into Suez the day of my arrival, but the treasures attached to the saddle, including my pelisse and my dearest pistols, had disappeared; these things were of great importance to me at that time, and I moved the Governor of the town to make all possible exertions for their recovery; he acceded to my wishes as well as he could, and very obligingly imprisoned the first seven poor fellows he could lay his hands on.

At first the Governor acted in the matter from no other motive than that of courtesy to an English traveller, but afterwards, and when he saw the value I set upon the lost property, he pushed his measures with a degree of alacrity and heat which seemed to show that he felt a personal interest in the matter; it was supposed, either that he expected a large present in the event of succeeding, or that he was striving by all means to trace the property, in order that he might lay his hands on it after my departure.

I went out sailing for some hours, and when I returned I was horrified to find that two men had been
bastinadoed by order of the Governor, with a view to
force them to a confession of their theft. It appeared,
however, that there really was good ground for supposing them guilty, since one of the holsters was
actually found in their possession. It was said too
(but I could hardly believe it), that whilst one of the
men was undergoing the bastinado, his comrade was
overheard encouraging him to bear the torment without peaching. Both men, if they had the secret,
were resolute in keeping it, and were sent back to
their dungeon. I, of course, took care that there
should be no repetition of the torture, at least so long
as I remained at Suez.

The Governor was a thorough Oriental, and until
a comparatively recent period had shared in the old
Mahometan feeling of contempt for Europeans. It
happened, however, one day that an English gun-brig
had appeared off Suez, and sent her boats ashore to
take in fresh water. Now fresh water at Suez is a
somewhat scarce and precious commodity; it is kept
in tanks, and the largest of these is at some distance
from the place. Under these circumstances, the request for fresh water was refused, or at all events was
not complied with. The captain of the brig was a
simple-minded man, with a strongish will, and he at
once declared that if his casks were not filled in three
hours, he would destroy the whole place. ' A great
people indeed!' said the Governor—' a wonderful
people, the English!' He instantly caused every
cask to be filled to the brim from his own tank, and
ever afterwards entertained for our countrymen a high
degree of affection and respect.

The day after the abortive attempt to extract a
confession from the prisoners, the Governor, the Con-

sul, and I sat in council, I know not how long, with
a view of prosecuting the search for the stolen goods.
The sitting, considered in the light of a criminal
investigation, was characteristic of the East. The
proceedings began as a matter of course by the pro-
secutor's smoking a pipe and drinking coffee with
the judge, jury, and sheriff—that is, with the Governor, for in this one personage were vested almost all
the functions connected with the administration of
injustice. I got on very well with my host (this was
not my first interview), and he gave me the pipe from
his lips in testimony of his friendship. I recollect,
however, that my prime adviser, thinking me, I suppose, a great deal too shy and retiring in my manner,
entreated me to put up my boots and to soil the
Governor's divan, in order to inspire respect and
strike terror. I thought it would be as well for me
to retain the right of respecting myself, and that it
was not quite necessary for a well-received guest to
strike any terror at all.

Our deliberations were assisted by the numerous
attendants who lined the three sides of the room not
occupied by the divan. Any one of these who took
it into his head to offer a suggestion would stand
forward and humble himself before the Governor,
and then state his views; every man thus giving
counsel was listened to with some attention.

After a great deal of fruitless planning, the
Governor directed that the prisoners should be
brought in. I was shocked when they entered, for
I was not prepared to see them come *carried* into
the room upon the shoulders of others. It had
not occurred to me that their battered feet would
be too sore to bear the contact of the floor.
They persisted in asserting their innocence. The
Governor wanted to recur to the torture, but that

I prevented, and the men were lifted back to their dungeon.

One of the attendants now suggested a scheme—a scheme which seemed to me most childishly absurd, but nevertheless it was tried. A man went down to the dungeon with instructions to make the prisoners believe that he had gained permission to see them upon some invented pretext; and when the spy had thus won a little of their confidence, he was to attempt a sham treaty with them for the purchase of the stolen goods. This shallow expedient failed.

The Governor himself had not nominally the power of life and death over the people in his district, but he could if he chose send them to Cairo, and have them hanged there. I proposed that the prisoners should be *threatened* with this fate. The answer of the Governor made me feel rather ashamed of my effeminate suggestion: he said that if I wished it he would willingly threaten them with death, but he also declared that if he threatened, *he surely would make his words good.*

Thinking at last that nothing was to be gained by keeping the prisoners any longer in confinement, I requested that they might be set free. To this the Governor assented, though only, as he said, out of favour to me, for he had a strong impression that the men were guilty. I went down to see the prisoners let out with my own eyes. They were very grateful, and fell down to the earth kissing my boots. I gave them a present to console them for their wounds, and they seemed to be highly delighted.

Although the matter ended in a manner so satisfactory to the principal sufferers, there were symptoms of some angry excitement in the place; it was said that public opinion was much shocked at the fact that Mahometans had been beaten on account of

a loss sustained by a Christian. My journey was to
recommence the next day; and it was hinted that
if I persevered in my intention of going forward into
the Desert the people would have an easy and profit-
able opportunity of wreaking their vengeance on me.
If ever they formed any scheme of the kind, they at
all events refrained from any attempt to carry it into
effect.

One of the evenings during my stay at Suez was
enlivened by a triple wedding. There was a long,
and slow procession. Some carried torches, and
others were thumping drums, and firing pistols.
The bridegrooms came last, all walking abreast.
My only reason for mentioning the ceremony is, that
I scarcely ever in all my life saw any phenomena so
ridiculous as the meekness and gravity of those three
young men whilst being 'led to the altar'.

CHAPTER XXIII

SUEZ TO GAZA

THE route over the Desert from Suez to Gaza is
not frequented by merchants, and is seldom passed
by a traveller. This part of the country is less
uniformly barren than the tracts of shifting sand
that lie on the El Arish route. The shrubs yielding
food for the camel are more frequent, and in many
spots the sand is mingled with so much of productive
soil as to admit the growth of corn. The Bedouins
are driven out of this district during the summer
by the want of water, but before the time for their
forced departure arrives, they succeed in raising
little crops of barley from these comparatively fertile
patches of ground; they bury the fruit of their

labours, and take care so to mark the spot chosen,
that when they return, they can easily find their
hidden treasures. The warm dry sand stands them
for a safe granary. The country, at the time I
passed it (in the month of April) was pretty thickly
sprinkled with Bedouins expecting their harvest;
several times my tent was pitched alongside of their
encampments; but I have already told you all I
wanted to tell about the domestic—or rather the
castral—life of the Arabs.

I saw several creatures of the antelope kind in
this part of the Desert, and, one day, my Arabs
surprised in her sleep a young gazelle (for so I called
her), and took the darling prisoner. I carried her
before me on my camel for the rest of the day, and
kept her in my tent all night; I did all I could to
gain her affections, but the trembling beauty refused
to touch food, and would not be comforted; whenever she had a seeming opportunity of escaping, she
struggled with a violence so painfully disproportioned
to her fine delicate limbs, that I could not go on with
the cruel attempt to make her my own. In the
morning therefore, I set her loose, anticipating some
pleasure from the joyous bound with which, as I
thought, she would return to her native freedom.
She had been so stupefied, however, by the exciting
events of the preceding day and night, and was so
puzzled as to the road she should take, that she went
off very deliberately, and with an uncertain step.
She was quite sound in limb, but she looked so
idiotic that I fancied her intellect might have been
really upset. Never, in all likelihood, had she seen
the form of a human being until the dreadful moment when she woke from her sleep and found herself
in the gripe of an Arab. Then her pitching and
tossing journey on the back of a camel, and, lastly,

a *soirée* with me by candlelight! I should have been glad to know, if I could, that her heart was not broken.

My Arabs were somewhat excited one day by discovering the fresh print of a foot,—the foot, as they said, of a lion. I had no conception that the Lord of the forest (better known as a crest) ever stalked away from his jungles to make inglorious war in these smooth plains against antelopes and gazelles. I supposed that there must have been some error of interpretation, and that the Arabs meant to speak of a tiger. It appeared, however, that this was not the case; either the Arabs were mistaken, or the noble brute uncooped and unchained had but lately crossed my path.

The camels with which I traversed this part of the Desert were very different in their ways and habits from those that you hire on a frequented route. They were never led. There was not the slightest sign of a track in this part of the Desert, but the camels never failed to choose the right line. By the direction taken at starting, they knew the point (some encampment, I suppose) for which they were to make. There is always a leading camel (generally, I believe, the eldest) who marches foremost and determines the path for the whole party. When it happens that no one of the camels has been accustomed to lead the others, there is very great difficulty in making a start; if you force your beast forward for a moment, he will contrive to wheel and draw back, at the same time looking at one of the other camels with an expression and gesture exactly equivalent to 'après vous'. The responsibility of finding the way is evidently assumed very unwillingly. After some time, however, it becomes understood that one of the beasts has reluctantly consented to take the

lead, and he accordingly advances for that purpose.
For a minute or two he marches with great indecision,
taking first one line and then another, but soon, by
the aid of some mysterious sense, he discovers the
true direction, and thenceforward keeps to it steadily,
going on from morning to night.   When once the
leadership is established, you cannot by any persuasion, and scarcely even by blows, induce a junior
camel to walk one single step in advance of the
chosen guide.

On the fifth day I came to an oasis, called the
Wady el Arish, a ravine, or rather a gully ; through
this during the greater part of the year, there runs
a stream of water.   On the sides of the gully there
were a number of those graceful trees which the
Arabs call Tarfa.   The channel of the stream was
quite dry in the part at which we arrived, but at
about half a mile off some water was found, and this,
though very muddy, was tolerably sweet.   Here was
indeed a happy discovery, for all the water we had
brought from the neighbourhood of Suez was rapidly
putrefying.

The want of foresight is an anomalous part of the
Bedouin's character, for it does not result either from
reeklessness or stupidity.   I know of no human being
whose body is so thoroughly the slave of mind as
the Arab.   His mental anxieties seem to be for
ever torturing every nerve and fibre of his body,
and yet, with all this exquisite sensitiveness to the
suggestions of the mind, he is grossly improvident.
I recollect, for instance, that when setting out upon
this passage of the Desert, my Arabs (in order to
lighten the burthen of their camels), were most
anxious that we should take with us no more than
two days' supply of water.   They said that by the
time that supply was exhausted, we should arrive

at a spring which would furnish us for the rest of
the journey. My servants very wisely, and with
much pertinacity, resisted the adoption of this plan,
and took care to have both the large skins well
filled. We went on and found no water at all either
at the expected spring, or for many days afterwards,
so that nothing but the precaution of my own people
saved us from the very severe suffering which we
should have endured if we had entered upon the
Desert with only a two days' supply. The Arabs
themselves being on foot would have suffered much
more than I from the consequences of their im-
providence.

This want of foresight prevents the Bedouin from
appreciating at a distance of eight or ten days the
amount of the misery which he entails upon himself
at the end of that period. His dread of a city is one
of the most painful mental affections that I have ever
observed, and yet when the whole breadth of the
Desert lies between him and the town you are going
to he will freely enter into an agreement to *land* you
in the city for which you are bound. When, however, after many a day of toil, the distant minarets
at length appear, the poor Bedouin relaxes the
vigour of his pace—his steps become faltering and
undecided—every moment his uneasiness increases,
and at length he fairly sobs aloud, and embracing
your knees, implores, with the most piteous cries
and gestures, that you will dispense with him and
his camels, and find some other means of entering
the city. This, of course, one can't agree to, and
the consequence is, that one is obliged to witness and
resist the most moving expressions of grief and fond
entreaty. I had to go through a most painful scene
of this kind when I entered Cairo, and now the
horror which these wilder Arabs felt at the notion

of entering Gaza led to consequences still more distressing. The dread of cities results partly from a kind of wild instinct which has always characterized the descendants of Ishmael, but partly, too, from a well-founded apprehension of ill treatment. So often it befalls the poor Bedouin (when once entrapped between walls), to be seized by the Government authorities for the sake of his camels, that his innate horror of cities becomes really justified by results.

The Bedouins with whom I performed this journey were wild fellows of the Desert, quite unaccustomed to let out themselves or their beasts for hire, and when they found that by the natural ascendancy of Europeans they were gradually brought down to a state of subserviency to me, or rather to my attendants, they bitterly repented, I believe, of having placed themselves under our control. They were rather difficult fellows to manage, and gave Dthemetri a good deal of trouble, but I liked them all the better for that.

Selim, the chief of the party, and the man to whom all our camels belonged, was a fine, savage, stately fellow; there were, I think, five other Arabs of the party, but when we approached the end of the journey, they, one by one, began to make off towards the neighbouring encampments, and by the time that the minarets of Gaza were in sight, Selim, the owner of the camels, was the only one who remained; he, poor fellow, as we neared the town, began to discover the same terrors that my Arabs had shown when I entered Cairo. I could not possibly accede to his entreaties, and consent to let my baggage be laid down on the bare sands, without any means of having it brought on into the city. So at length when poor Selim had exhausted all his rhetoric of voice and action, and tears, he fixed his despairing eyes for a

minute upon the cherished beasts that were his only
wealth, and then suddenly and madly dashed away
into the farther Desert. I continued my course and
reached the city at last, but it was not without immense difficulty that we could constrain the poor
camels to pass under the hated shadow of its walls.
They were the genuine beasts of the Desert, and it
was sad and painful to witness the agony they suffered
when thus they were forced to encounter the fixed
habitations of men ; they shrank from the beginning
of every high narrow street as though from the
entrance of some horrible cave or bottomless pit ; they
sighed and wept like women. When at last we got
them within the courtyard of the Khan, they seemed
to be quite broken-hearted, and looked round piteously
for their loving master ; but no Selim came. I had
imagined that he would enter the town secretly by
night, in order to carry off those five fine camels, his
only wealth in this world, and seemingly the main
objects of his affection. But no—his dread of civilization was too strong ; during the whole of the three
days that I remained at Gaza he failed to show
himself, and thus sacrificed in all probability, not only
his camels, but the money which I had stipulated to
pay him for the passage of the Desert. In order,
however, to do all I could towards saving him from
this last misfortune, I resorted to a contrivance
frequently adopted by the Asiatics. I assembled a
group of grave and worthy Mussulmans in the courtyard of the Khan, and in their presence paid over the
gold to a Sheik well known in the place and accustomed to communicate with the Arabs of the Desert.
Then all present solemnly promised that, if ever Selim
should come to claim his rights, they would bear true
witness in his favour.

I saw a great deal of my old friend the Governor of

Gaza. He had received orders to send back all persons coming from Egypt, and force them to perform quarantine at El Arish; he knew so little of quarantine regulations, however, that his dress was actually in contact with mine, whilst he insisted upon the stringency of the orders which he had received. He was induced to make an exception in my favour, and I rewarded him with a musical snuff-box —a toy, which I had bought at Smyrna for the purpose of presenting it to any man in authority who might happen to do me an important service. The Governor was delighted with the gift, and in great exultation and glee he carried it off to his harem: soon, however, poor fellow, he returned with an altered countenance; his wives, he said, had got hold of the box, and had put it quite out of order. So short-lived is human happiness in this frail world!

The Governor fancied that he should incur less risk, if I remained at Gaza for two or three days more, and he wanted me to become his guest; I persuaded him, however, that it would be better for him to let me depart at once. He wanted to add to my baggage a roast lamb, and a quantity of other cumbrous viands, but I escaped with half a horse-load of leaven bread; this was very good of its kind, and proved a most useful present. The air with which the Governor's slaves affected to be almost breaking down under the weight of the gifts, reminded me of the figures one sees in some of the old pictures.

CHAPTER XXIV

GAZA TO NABLOUS

PASSING now once again through Palestine and Syria, I retained the tent which I had used in the Desert, and found that it added very much to my comfort in travelling. Instead of turning out a family from some wretched dwelling, and depriving them of rest without gaining rest for myself, I now, when evening came, pitched my tent upon some smiling spot within a few hundred yards of the village to which I looked for my supplies—that is, for milk, for bread (if I had it not with me), and sometimes also for eggs. The worst of it was that the needful viands were not to be obtained by coin, but only by intimidation. I at first tried the usual agent—money; Dthemetri, with one or two of my Arabs, went into the village near which I was encamped, and tried to buy the required provisions, offering liberal payment, but he came back empty-handed. I sent him again, but this time he held different language; he required to see the elders of the place, and, threatening dreadful vengeance, commanded them upon their responsibility to take care that my tent should be immediately and abundantly supplied. He was obeyed at once; and the provisions refused to me as a purchaser soon arrived, trebled or quadrupled, when demanded by way of a forced contribution. I quickly found (I think it required two experiments to convince me) that this peremptory method was the only one which could be adopted with success; it never failed. Of course, however, when the provisions have been actually obtained, you can, if you choose, give money exceeding the value of the provisions to *somebody*; an English—a thoroughbred English traveller will always do this (though it is contrary to the custom of the country), for the quiet (false quiet though it be) of his own conscience; but, so to order the matter that the poor fellows who have been forced to contribute, should be the persons to receive the value of their supplies, is not possible; for a traveller to attempt anything so grossly just as that, would be too outrageous. The truth is that the usage of the East in old times, required the people of the village at their own cost to supply the wants of travellers; and the ancient custom is now adhered to—not in favour of travellers generally—but in favour of those who are deemed sufficiently powerful to enforce its observance; if the villagers, therefore, find a man waiving this right to oppress them, and offering coin for that which he is entitled to take without payment, they suppose at once that he is actuated by fear (fear of *them*, poor fellows!), and it is so delightful to them to act upon this flattering assumption, that they will forgo the advantage of a good price for their provisions rather than the rare luxury of refusing for once in their lives to part with their own possessions.

The practice of intimidation, thus rendered necessary, is utterly hateful to an Englishman; he finds himself forced to conquer his daily bread by the pompous threats of the Dragoman, his very subsistence, as well as his dignity and personal safety, being made to depend upon his servant's assuming a tone of authority which does not at all belong to him. Besides, he can scarcely fail to see that, as he passes through the country, he becomes the innocent cause of much extra injustice—many supernumerary wrongs. This he feels to be especially the case when he travels with relays. To be the owner of a horse or a mule within reach of an Asiatic potentate, is to lead the life of the hare and the rabbit—hunted down and ferreted out. Too often it happens that the works of the field are stopped in the day-time, that the inmates of the cottage are roused from their midnight sleep, by the sudden coming of a Government officer; and the poor husbandman, driven by threats and rewarded by curses, if he would not loose sight for ever of his captured beasts, must quit all, and follow them: this is done that the Englishman may travel; he would make his way more harmlessly if he could, but horses or mules he *must* have, and these are his ways and means.

The town of Nablous is beautiful; it lies in a valley hemmed in with olive-groves, and its buildings are interspersed with frequent palm trees. It is said to occupy the site of the ancient Sychem. I know not whether it was there, indeed, that the father of the Jews was accustomed to feed his flocks, but the valley is green and smiling, and is held at this day by a race more brave and beautiful than Jacob's unhappy descendants.

Nablous is the very furnace of Mahometan bigotry; and I believe that only a few months before the time of my going there, it would have been madly rash for a man, unless strongly guarded, to show himself to the people of the town in a Frank costume; but since their last insurrection, the Mahometans of the place had been so far subdued by the severity of Ibrahim Pasha, that they dared not now offer the slightest insult to an European. It was quite plain, however, that the effort with which the men of the old school refrained from expressing their opinion of a hat and a coat was horribly painful to them. As I walked through the streets and bazaars, a dead silence prevailed; every man suspended his employment, and

gazed on me with a fixed, glassy look, which seemed
to say, ' God is good, but how marvellous and in-
scrutable are his ways that thus he permits this white-
faced dog of a Christian to hunt through the paths
of the faithful ! '

The insurrection of these people had been more
formidable than any other that Ibrahim Pasha had
to contend with ; he was only able to crush them
at last by the assistance of a fellow renowned for
his resources in the way of stratagem and cunning,
as well as for his knowledge of the country. This
personage was no other than Aboo Goosh (' the
father of lies ' [1]). The man had been suddenly taken
out of prison, and sent into his native hill-country,
with orders to procreate a few choice falsehoods and
snares for entrapping the rebellious mountaineers,
and he performed his function so well that he quickly
enabled Ibrahim to hem in and extinguish the insurrection ; he was rewarded with the Governorship
of Jerusalem, and this he held when I was there.
I recollect, by the by, that he tried one of his
stratagems upon me. I had not gone to see him
(as I ought in courtesy to have done) upon my
arrival at Jerusalem, but I happened to be the
owner of a rather handsome amber tchibouque-
piece ; this the Governor heard of, and having also
by some means contrived to see it, he sent me a
softly-worded message with an offer to buy the pipe
at a price immensely exceeding the sum I had given
for it. He did not add my tchibouque to the rest
of his trophies.

---

[1] This is an appellation not implying blame, but merit ; the
' lies ' which it purports to affiliate are feints and cunning
stratagems rather than the baser kind of falsehoods. The
expression, in short, has nearly the same meaning as the
English word ' Yorkshireman '.

There was a small number of Greek Christians
resident in Nablous, and over these the Mussulmans
held a high hand, not even allowing them to speak to
each other in the open streets; but if the Moslems
thus set themselves above the poor Christians of the
place, I, or rather my servants, soon took the as-
cendant over *them*. I recollect that just as we were
starting from the place, and at a time when a number
of people had gathered together in the main street to
see our preparations, Mysseri, being provoked at some
piece of perverseness on the part of a true Believer,
coolly thrashed him with his horsewhip before the
assembled crowd of fanatics. I was much annoyed
at the time, for I thought that the people would
probably rise against us. They turned rather pale,
but stood still.

The day of my arrival at Nablous was a *fête*—the
new year's day of the Mussulmans.[1] Most of the
people were amusing themselves in the beautiful
lawns and shady groves without the city. The men
were all remotely apart from the other sex. The
women in groups were diverting themselves and
their children with swings. They were so handsome
that they could not keep up their yashmaks; I believed that they had never before looked upon a man
in the European dress, and when they now saw in me
that strange phenomenon, and saw, too, how they
could please the creature by showing him a glimpse
of beauty, they seemed to think it more pleasant to
do this, than to go on playing with swings. It was
always, however, with a sort of zoological expression
of countenance that they looked on the horrible
monster from Europe; and whenever one of them
gave me to see for one sweet instant the blushing of

[1] The 29th of April.

her unveiled face, it was with the same kind of air as that with which a young timid girl will edge her way up to an elephant, and tremblingly give him a nut from the tips of her rosy fingers.

CHAPTER XXV

MARIAM

THERE is no spirit of Propagandism in the Mussulmans of the Ottoman dominions. True it is that a prisoner of war, or a Christian condemned to death, may on some occasions save his life by adopting the religion of Mahomet, but instances of this kind are now exceedingly rare, and are quite at variance with the general system. Many Europeans, I think, would be surprised to learn that which is nevertheless quite true, namely, that an attempt to disturb the religious repose of the Empire by the conversion of a Christian to the Mahometan faith is positively illegal; the event which now I am going to mention shows plainly enough that the unlawfulness of such interference is distinctly recognized even in one of the most bigoted strongholds of Islam.

During my stay at Nablous I took up my quarters at the house of the Greek 'Papa', as he is called, that is, the Greek Priest; the priest himself had gone to Jerusalem upon the business I am going to tell you of, but his wife remained at Nablous, and did the honours of her home.

Soon after my arrival, a deputation from the Greek Christians of the place came to request my interference in a matter which had occasioned vast excitement.

And now I must tell you how it came to happen,

as it did continually, that people thought it worth while to claim the assistance of a mere traveller, who was totally devoid of all just pretensions to authority or influence of even the humblest description, and especially I must explain to you how it was that the power thus attributed did really in some measure belong to me, or rather to my Dragoman. Successive political convulsions had at length fairly loosed the people of Syria from all their former rules of conduct, and from their old habits of reliance. Mehemet Ali's success in crushing the insurrection of the Mahometan population had utterly beaten down the head of Islam, and extinguished, for the time at least, those virtues and vices which spring from the Mahometan Faith. Success so complete as Mehemet Ali's, if it had been attained by an ordinary Asiatic potentate, would have induced a notion of stability. The readily bowing mind of the Oriental would have bowed low and long under the feet of a conqueror whom God had thus strengthened. But Syria was no field for contests strictly Asiatic—Europe was involved, and, though the heavy masses of Egyptian troops, clinging with strong gripe to the land, might seem to hold it fast, yet every peasant practically felt and knew that in Vienna, or Petersburgh, or London, there were four or five pale-looking men who could pull down the star of the Pasha with shreds of paper and ink. The people of the country knew, too, that Mehemet Ali was strong with the strength of the Europeans,—strong by his French General, his French tactics, and his English engines. Moreover, they saw that the person, the property, and even the dignity of the humblest European was guarded with the most careful solicitude. The consequence of all this was, that the people of Syria looked vaguely but confidently to Europe for fresh changes ; many would

fix upon some nation, France, or England, and stead-
fastly regard it as the arriving sovereign of Syria;
those whose minds remained in doubt equally contributed to this new state of public opinion—a state
of opinion no longer depending upon religion and
ancient habits, but upon bare hopes and fears.
Every man wanted to know,—not who was his
neighbour, but who was to be his ruler; whose feet
he was to kiss, and by whom *his* feet were to be
ultimately beaten. Treat your friend, says the pro-
verb, as though he were one day to become your
enemy, and your enemy as though he were one day
to become your friend. The Syrians went further,
and seemed inclined to treat every stranger as though
he might one day become their Pasha. Such was
the state of circumstances and of feeling which now
for the first time had thoroughly opened the mind
of Western Asia for the reception of Europeans and
European ideas. The credit of the English especially was so great that a good Mussulman flying
from the conscription or any other persecution, would
come to seek from the formerly despised hat that
protection which the turban could no longer afford;
and a man high in authority (as for instance the
Governor in command of Gaza), would think that
he had won a prize, or at all events a valuable lot-
tery ticket, if he obtained a written approval of his
conduct from a simple traveller.

Still, in order that any immediate result should
follow from all this unwonted readiness in the Asiatic
to succumb to the European, it was necessary that
some one should be at hand who could see, and would
push the advantage; I myself had neither the inclina-
tion, nor the power to do so; but it happened that
Dthemetri, who, as my Dragoman, represented me on
all occasions, was the very person of all others best

fitted to avail himself with success of this yielding
tendency in the Oriental mind. If the chance of
birth and fortune had made poor Dthemetri a tailor
during some part of his life, yet religion and the
literature of the Church which he served, had made
him a Man, and a brave Man too. The lives of his
honoured Saints were full of heroic actions provoking
imitation, and, since faith in a creed involves a faith
in its ultimate triumph, Dthemetri was bold from a
sense of true strength; his education too, though not
very general in its character, had been carried quite
far enough to justify him in pluming himself upon a
very decided advantage over the great bulk of the
Mahometan population, including the men in authority. With all this consciousness of religious and
intellectual superiority, Dthemetri had lived for the
most part in countries lying under Mussulman Governments, and had witnessed (perhaps too had suffered
from) their revolting cruelties; the result was that he
abhorred and despised the Mahometan faith and all
who clung to it. And this hate was not of the dry,
dull, and inactive sort; Dthemetri was in his sphere
a true Crusader, and whenever there appeared a fair
opening in the defences of Islam, he was ready and
eager to make the assault. Such feelings, backed by
a consciousness of understanding the people with
whom he had to do, made Dthemetri not only firm
and resolute in his constant interviews with men in
authority, but sometimes also (as you may know
already) very violent and even insulting. This tone,
which I always disliked, though I was fain to profit
by it, invariably succeeded; it swept away all resistance; there was nothing in the then depressed and
succumbing mind of the Mussulman that could oppose
a zeal so warm and fierce.

As for me, I of course stood aloof from Dthemetri's

crusades, and did not even render him any active
assistance when he was striving (as he almost always
was, poor fellow) on my behalf; I was only the
death's head and white sheet with which he scared
the enemy; I think, however, that I played this
spectral part exceedingly well, for I seldom appeared
at all in any discussion, and whenever I did, I was
sure to be white and calm.

The event which induced the Christians of Nablous
to seek for my assistance was this. A beautiful young
Christian, between fifteen and sixteen years old, had
lately been married to a man of her own creed.
About the same time (probably on the occasion of
her wedding) she was accidentally seen by a Mussulman Sheik of great wealth and local influence.
The man instantly became madly enamoured of her.
That strict morality so generally prevailing wherever
the Mussulmans have complete ascendancy prevented
the Sheik from entertaining any such sinful hopes as a
Christian might have ventured to cherish under the like
circumstances, and he saw no chance of gratifying his
love, except by inducing the girl to embrace his own
creed: if he could get her to take this step, her
marriage with the Christian would be dissolved, and
then there would be nothing to prevent him from
making her the last and brightest of his wives. The
Sheik was a practical man, and quickly began his
attack upon the theological opinions of the bride; he
did not assail her with the eloquence of any Imaums
or Mussulman Saints—he did not press upon her the
eternal truths of the 'Cow[1]', or the beautiful morality
of 'the Table[1]',—he sent her no tracts—not even a
copy of the holy Koran. An old woman acted as
missionary. She brought with her a whole basket-full

---

[1] These are the names given by the Prophet to certain
chapters of the Koran.

of arguments—jewels, and shawls, and scarfs, and all kinds of persuasive finery. Poor Mariam! she put on the jewels and took a calm view of the Mahometan Religion in a little hand-mirror—she could not be deaf to such eloquent earrings, and the great truths of Islam came home to her young bosom in the delicate folds of the Cashmere; she was ready to abandon her faith.

The Sheik knew very well that his attempt to convert an infidel was unlawful, and that his proceedings would not bear investigation, so he took care to pay a large sum to the Governor of Nablous in order to gain his connivance.

At length Mariam quitted her home, and placed herself under the protection of the Mahometan authorities. These men, however, refrained from delivering her into the arms of her lover, and kept her safe in a mosque until the fact of her real conversion (for this had been indignantly denied by her relatives) should be established. For two or three days the mother of the young convert was prevented from communicating with her child by various evasive contrivances, but not, it would seem, by a flat refusal. At length it was announced that the young lady's profession of faith might be heard from her own lips. At an hour appointed the friends of the Sheik and relatives of the damsel met in the mosque. The young convert addressed her mother in a loud voice, and said, 'God is God, and Mahomet is the Prophet of God, and thou, oh! my mother, art an infidel feminine dog!'

You would suppose that this declaration, so clearly enounced, and that, too, in a place where Mahometanism is, perhaps, more supreme than in any other part of the Empire, would have sufficed to confirm the pretensions of the lover. This, however, was not the

case. The Greek Priest of the place was despatched
on a mission to the Governor of Jerusalem (Aboo
Goosh), in order to complain against the proceedings
of the Sheik, and obtain a restitution of the bride.
Meanwhile the Mahometan authorities at Nablous
were so conscious of having acted unlawfully in con-
spiring to disturb the faith of the beautiful infidel,
that they hesitated to take any further steps, and
the girl was still detained in the mosque.

Thus matters stood when the Christians of the
place came and sought to obtain my aid.

I felt (with regret) that I had no personal interest
in the matter, and I also thought that there was no
pretence for my interfering with the conflicting claims
of the Christian husband and the Mahometan lover.
I declined to take any step.

My speaking of the husband, by the by, reminds
me that he was extremely backward about the great
work of recovering his youthful bride. The kinsmen
of the girl (they felt themselves personally disgraced
by her conduct) were vehement and excited to a high
pitch, but the Menelaus of Nablous was exceedingly
calm and composed.

The fact that it was no duty of mine to interfere
in a matter of this kind, was a very sufficient, and yet
a very unsatisfactory, reason for my refusal of all
assistance. Until you are placed in situations of this
kind, you can hardly tell how painful it is to refrain
from intermeddling in other people's affairs—to
refrain from intermeddling when you feel that you
can do so with happy effect, and can remove a load
of distress by the use of a few small phrases. Upon
this occasion, however, an expression fell from one
of the girl's kinsmen, which not only determined me
to abstain from interference, but made me hope that
all attempts to recover the proselyte would fail; this

person, speaking with the most savage bitterness, and with the cordial approval of all the other relatives, said that the girl ought to be beaten to death. I could not fail to see that if the poor child were ever restored to her family, she would be treated with the most frightful barbarity; I heartily wished, therefore, that the Mussulmans might be firm, and preserve their young prize from any fate so dreadful as that of a return to her own relations.

The next day the Greek Priest returned from his mission to Aboo Goosh; but the 'father of lies', it would seem, had been well plied with the gold of the enamoured Sheik, and contrived to put off the prayers of the Christians by cunning feints. Now, therefore, a second and more numerous deputation than the first waited upon me, and implored my intervention with the Governor. I informed the assembled Christians that since their last application I had carefully considered the matter. The religious question I thought might be put aside at once, for the excessive levity which the girl had displayed proved clearly that, in adopting Mahometanism, she was not quitting any other faith; her mind must have been thoroughly blank upon religious questions, and she was not, therefore, to be treated as a Christian straying from the flock, but rather as a child without any religion at all—a child incapable of imagining any truer worshippers than those who would deck her with jewels and clothe her in cashmere shawls.

So much for the religious part of the question. Well, then, in a merely temporal sense it appeared to me that (looking merely to the interests of the damsel, for I rather unjustly put poor Menelaus quite out of the question) the advantages were all on the side of the Mahometan match. The Sheik was in a higher station of life than the superseded husband, and had given the best possible proof of his ardent affection, by the sacrifices made and the risks incurred for the sake of the beloved object. I, therefore, stated fairly, to the horror and amazement of all my hearers, that the Sheik, in my view, was likely to make a capital husband, and that I entirely 'approved of the match'.

I left Nablous under the impression that Mariam would soon be delivered to her Mussulman lover. I afterwards found, however, that the result was very different. Dthemetri's religious zeal and hate had been so much excited by the account of these events, and by the grief and mortification of his co-religionists, that when he found me firmly determined to decline all interference in the matter, he secretly appealed to the Governor in my name, and (using, I suppose, many violent threats, and telling, no doubt, good store of lies about my station and influence) extorted a promise that the proselyte should be restored to her relatives. I did not understand that the girl had been actually given up whilst I remained at Nablous, but Dthemetri certainly did not desist from his instances until he had satisfied himself by some means or other (for mere words amounted to nothing) that the promise would be actually performed. It was not till I had quitted Syria, and when Dthemetri was no longer in my service, that this villanous though well-motived trick of his came to my knowledge ; Mysseri, who informed me of the step which had been taken, did not know it himself until some time after we had quitted Nablous, when Dthemetri exultingly confessed his successful enterprise. I know not whether the engagement extorted from the Governor was ever complied with. I shudder to think of the fate which must have befallen poor Mariam, if she fell into the hands of the Christians.

CHAPTER XXVI

THE PROPHET DAMOOR

For some hours I passed along the shores of the fair Lake of Galilee : then turning a little to the westward, I struck into a mountainous tract, and as I advanced thenceforward, the features of the country kept growing more and more bold. At length I drew near to the city of Safet. It sits proud as a fortress upon the summit of a craggy height ; yet, because of its minarets and stately trees, the place looks happy and beautiful. It is one of the holy cities of the Talmud ; and according to this authority, the Messiah will reign there for forty years before he takes possession of Sion. The sanctity and historical importance thus attributed to the city by anticipation render it a favourite place of retirement for Israelites ; of these it contains, they say, about four thousand, a number nearly balancing that of the Mahometan inhabitants. I knew by my experience of Tabarieh that a 'holy city' was sure to have a population of vermin somewhat proportionate to the number of its Israelites, and I therefore caused my tent to be pitched upon a green spot of ground at a respectful distance from the walls of the town.

When it had become quite dark (for there was no moon that night), I was informed that several Jews had secretly come from the city, in the hope of obtaining some help from me in circumstances of imminent danger ; I was also informed that they claimed my aid upon the ground that some of their number were British subjects. It was arranged that the two principal men of the party should speak for the rest, and these were accordingly admitted into

my tent.   One of the two called himself the British
Vice-Consul, and he had with him his consular cap ;
but he frankly said that he could not have dared to
assume this emblem of his dignity in the day-time,
and that nothing but the extreme darkness of the
night rendered it safe for him to put it on upon this
occasion.   The other of the spokesmen was a Jew of
Gibraltar, a tolerably well-bred person, who spoke
English very fluently.

These men informed me that the Jews of the place,
though exceedingly wealthy, had lived peaceably and
undisturbed in their retirement until the insurrection
of 1834; but about the beginning of that year a highly
religious Mussulman called Mohammed Damoor went
forth into the market-place, crying with a loud voice,
and prophesying that on the fifteenth of the following
June the true Believers would rise up in just wrath
against the Jews, and despoil them of their gold,
and their silver, and their jewels.   The earnestness
of the prophet produced some impression at the time,
but all went on as usual, until at last the fifteenth
of June arrived.   When that day dawned, the whole
Mussulman population of the place assembled in the
streets, that they might see the result of the prophecy.
Suddenly Mohammed Damoor rushed furious into
the crowd, and the fierce shout of the prophet soon
ensured the fulfilment of his prophecy.   Some of
the Jews fled, and some remained, but they who
fled and they who remained alike and unresistingly
left their property to the hands of the spoilers.   The
most odious of all outrages, that of searching the
women for the base purpose of discovering such
things as gold and silver concealed about their
persons, was perpetrated without shame.   The poor
Jews were so stricken with terror, that they submitted
to their fate, even where resistance would have been

easy. In several instances a young Mussulman boy, not more than ten or twelve years of age, walked straight into the house of a Jew, and stripped him of his property before his face, and in the presence of his whole family.[1] When the insurrection was put down, some of the Mussulmans (most probably those who had got no spoil wherewith they might buy immunity) were punished, but the greater part of them escaped; none of the booty was restored, and the pecuniary redress which the Pasha had undertaken to enforce for them had been hitherto so carefully delayed, that the hope of ever obtaining it had grown very faint. A new Governor had been appointed to the command of the place with stringent orders to ascertain the real extent of the losses, to discover the spoilers, and to compel immediate restitution. It was found that, notwithstanding the urgency of his instructions, the Governor did not push on the affair with any perceptible vigour; the Jews complained; and either by the protection of the British Consul at Damascus, or by some other means, had influence enough to induce the appointment of a special Commissioner—they called him 'the Modeer'—whose duty it was to watch for and prevent anything like connivance on the part of the Governor, and to push on the investigation with vigour and impartiality.

Such were the instructions with which some few weeks since the Modeer came charged; the result was that the investigation had made no practical advance, and that the Modeer, as well as the Governor, was living upon terms of affectionate friendship with Mohammed Damoor, and the rest of the principal spoilers.

[1] It was after the interview which I am talking of, and not from the Jews themselves that I learnt this fact.

Thus stood the chance of redress for the past, but the cause of the agonizing excitement under which the Jews of the place now laboured was recent, and justly alarming : Mohammed Damoor had again gone forth into the market-place, and lifted up his voice, and prophesied a second spoliation of the Israelites. This was grave matter ; the words of such a practical and clear-sighted prophet as Mohammed Damoor were not to be despised. I fear I must have smiled visibly, for I was greatly amused, and even, I think, gratified at the account of this second prophecy. Nevertheless, my heart warmed towards the poor oppressed Israelites, and I was flattered, too, in the point of my national vanity at the notion of the far-reaching link, by which a Jew in Syria, because he had been born on the rock of Gibraltar, was able to claim me as his fellow-countryman. If I hesitated at all between the ' impropriety ' of interfering in a matter which was no business of mine, and the ' infernal shame ' of refusing my aid at such a con-juncture, I soon came to a very ungentlemanly decision—namely, that I would be guilty of the ' impropriety ', and not of the ' infernal shame '. It seemed to me that the immediate arrest of Mohammed Damoor was the one thing needful to the safety of the Jews, and I felt sure (for reasons which I have already mentioned in speaking of the Nablous affair) that I should be able to obtain this result by making a formal application to the Governor. I told my applicants that I would take this step on the follow-ing morning ; they were very grateful, and were for a moment much pleased at the prospect of safety thus seemingly opened to them, but the deliberation of a minute entirely altered their views, and filled them with new terror ; they declared that any attempt or pretended attempt on the part of the

Governor to arrest Mohammed Damoor would certainly produce an immediate movement of the whole Mussulman population, and a consequent massacre and robbery of the Israelites. My visitors went out, and remained I know not how long consulting with their brethren, but all at last agreed that their present perilous and painful position was better than a certain and immediate attack, and that if Mohammed Damoor was seized, their second estate would be worse than their first. I myself did not think that this would be the case, but I could not of course force my aid upon the people against their will, and, moreover, the day fixed for the fulfilment of this second prophecy was not very close at hand ; a little delay, therefore, in providing against the impending danger, would not necessarily be fatal. The men now confessed that although they had come with so much mystery, and (as they thought) at so great risk to ask my assistance, they were unable to suggest any mode in which I could aid them, except, indeed, by mentioning their grievances to the Consul-General at Damascus. This I promised to do, and this I did.

My visitors were very thankful to me for my readiness to intermeddle in their affairs, and the grateful wives of the principal Jews sent to me many compliments, with choice wines and elaborate sweetmeats.

The course of my travels soon drew me so far from Safet, that I never heard how the dreadful day passed off which had been fixed for the accomplishment of the second prophecy. If the predicted spoliation was prevented, poor Mohammed Damoor must have been forced, I suppose, to say that he had prophesied in a metaphorical sense. This would be a sad falling off from the brilliant and substantial success of the first experiment.

CHAPTER XXVII

DAMASCUS

FOR a part of two days I wound under the base of the snow-crowned Djibel el Sheik, and then entered upon a vast and desolate plain rarely pierced at intervals by some sort of withered stem. The earth in its length and its breadth, and all the deep universe of the sky was steeped in light and heat. On I rode through the fire, but long before evening came, there were straining eyes that saw, and joyful voices that announced the sight—of Shaum Shereef—the 'Holy', the 'Blessed' Damascus.

But that which at last I reached with my longing eyes, was not a speck in the horizon, gradually expanding to a group of roofs and walls, but a long, low line of blackest green, that ran right across in the distance from East to West. And this, as I approached, grew deeper—grew wavy in its outline; soon forest trees shot up before my eyes, and robed their broad shoulders so freshly, that all the throngs of olives, as they rose into view, looked sad in their proper dimness. There were even now no houses to see, but minarets peered out from the midst of shade into the glowing sky, and kindling touched the sun. There seemed to be here no mere city, but rather a province, wide and rich, that bounded the torrid waste.

Until about a year or two years before the time of my going there, Damascus had kept up so much of the old bigot zeal against Christians, or rather against Europeans, that no one dressed as a Frank could have dared to show himself in the streets; but the firmness

and temper of Mr. Farren, who hoisted his flag in the
city as Consul-General for the district, had soon put
an end to all intolerance of Englishmen. Damascus
was safer than Oxford.[1] When I entered the city, in
my usual dress, there was but one poor fellow that
wagged his tongue, and him, in the open streets,
Dthemetri horse-whipped. During my stay I went
wherever I chose, and attended the public baths
without molestation. Indeed my relations with the
pleasanter portion of the Mahometan population
were upon a much better footing here than at most
other places.

In the principal streets of Damascus there is a path
for foot passengers raised a foot or two above the
bridle-road. Until the arrival of the British Consul-
General, none but a Mussulman had been allowed to
walk upon the upper way; Mr. Farren would not,
of course, suffer that the humiliation of any such
exclusion should be submitted to by an Englishman,
and I always walked upon the raised path as free
and unmolested as if I had been in Pall Mall. The
old usage was, however, maintained with as much
strictness as ever against the Christian Rayahs and
Jews; not one of these could have set his foot upon
the privileged path without endangering his life.

I was walking one day, I remember, along the
raised path, 'the path of the faithful', when a Christian

---

[1] An enterprising American traveller, Mr. Everett, lately
conceived the bold project of penetrating to the University of
Oxford, and this, notwithstanding that he had been in his
infancy (they being very young, those Americans) an Unitarian
preacher. Having a notion, it seems, that the ambassadorial
character would protect him from insult, he adopted the
stratagem of procuring credentials from his Government as
Minister Plenipotentiary at the Court of Her Britannic Majesty;
he also wore the exact costume of a Trinitarian, but all his
contrivances were vain; his infantine sermons were strictly
remembered against him; the enterprise failed.

Rayah from the bridle-road below saluted me with such earnestness, and craved so anxiously to speak and be spoken to, that he soon brought me to a halt; he had nothing to tell, except only the glory and exultation with which he saw a fellow Christian stand level with the imperious Mussulmans; perhaps he had been absent from the place for some time, for otherwise I hardly know how it could have happened that my exaltation was the first instance he had seen. His joy was great; so strong and strenuous was England (Lord Palmerston reigned in those days), that it was a pride and delight for a Syrian Christian to look up and say that the Englishman's faith was his too; if I was vexed at all that I could not give the man a lift and shake hands with him on level ground, there was no alloy in *his* pleasure; he followed me on, not looking to his own path, but keeping his eyes on me; he saw, as he thought and said (for he came with me on to my quarters), the period of the Mahometan's absolute ascendancy—the beginning of the Christian's. He had so closely associated the insulting privilege of the path with actual dominion, that seeing it now in one instance abandoned, he looked for the quick coming of European troops. His lips only whispered, and that tremulously, but his flashing eyes spoke out their triumph more fiercely. 'I, too, am a Christian. My foes are the foes of the English. We are all one people, and Christ is our King.'

If I poorly deserved, yet I liked this claim of brotherhood. Not all the warnings I heard against their rascality could hinder me from feeling kindly towards my fellow Christians in the East. English travellers (from a habit perhaps of depreciating sectarians in their own country) are apt to look down upon the Oriental Christians as being 'dissenters'

from the established religion of a Mahometan Empire.
I never did thus. By a natural perversity of disposition which nursemaids call contr*airiness*, I felt the
more strongly for my creed when I saw it despised
among men. I quite tolerated the Christianity of
Mahometan countries, notwithstanding its humble
aspect and the damaged character of its followers;
I went further, and extended some sympathy towards
those who, with all the claims of superior intellect,
learning, and industry, were kept down under the
heel of the Mussulmans by reason of their having *our*
faith. I heard, as I fancied, the faint echo of an
old Crusader's conscience, that whispered and said,
'Common cause!' The impulse was, as you may
suppose, much too feeble to bring me into trouble—
it merely influenced my actions in a way thoroughly
characteristic of this poor, sluggish century—that is,
by making me speak almost as civilly to the followers
of Christ as I did to their Mahometan foes.

This 'Holy' Damascus, this 'earthly paradise' of
the Prophet, so fair to the eyes, that he dared not
trust himself to tarry in her blissful shades—she is
a city of hidden palaces, of copses, and gardens, and
fountains, and bubbling streams. The juice of her
life is the gushing and ice-cold torrent that tumbles
from the snowy sides of Anti-Lebanon. Close along
on the river's edge through seven sweet miles of
rustling boughs and deepest shade, the city spreads
out her whole length; as a man falls flat, face forward
on the brook, that he may drink, and drink again;
so Damascus, thirsting for ever, lies down with her
lips to the stream, and clings to its rushing waters.

The chief places of public amusement, or rather, of
public relaxation, are the baths, and the great café.
This last is frequented at night by most of the wealthy
men of the city, and by many of the humbler sort; it

consists of a number of sheds, very simply framed and
built in a labyrinth of running streams—streams so
broken and headlong in their course that they foam
and roar on every side. The place is lit up in the
simplest manner by numbers of small, pale lamps,
strung upon loose cords, and so suspended, from
branch to branch, that the light, though it looks so
quiet amongst the darkening foliage, yet leaps and
brightly flashes, as it falls upon the troubled waters.
All around, and chiefly upon the very edge of the
torrents, groups of people are tranquilly seated.
They drink coffee, and inhale the cold fumes of the
narguilè; they talk rather gently the one to the
other, or else are silent. A father will sometimes
have two or three of his boys around him, but the
joyousness of an Oriental child is all of the sober
sort, and never disturbs the reigning calm of the
land.

It has been generally understood, I believe, that the
houses of Damascus are more sumptuous than those
of any other city in the East. Some of these—said
to be the most magnificent in the place—I had an
opportunity of seeing.

Every rich man's house stands detached from its
neighbours, at the side of a garden, and it is from
this cause, no doubt, that the city (severely menaced
by Prophecy) has hitherto escaped destruction. You
know some parts of Spain, but you have never, I
think, been in Andalusia; if you had, I could easily
show you the interior of a Damascene house, by referring you to the Alhambra, or Alcanzar of Seville.
The lofty rooms are adorned with a rich inlaying of
many colours, and illuminated writing on the walls.
The floors are of marble. One side of any room intended for noonday retirement is generally laid open
to a quadrangle, and in the centre of this is the

dancing jet of a fountain. There is no furniture that can interfere with the cool, palace-like emptiness of the apartments. A divan (that is, a low and doubly broad sofa) runs round the three walled sides of the room; a few Persian carpets (they ought to be called Persian rugs, for that is the word which indicates their shape and dimensions) are sometimes thrown about near the divan; they are placed without order, the one partly lapping over the other, and thus disposed, they give to the room an appearance of uncaring luxury; except these, there is nothing to obstruct the welcome air, and the whole of the marble floor, from one divan to the other, and from the head of the chamber across to the murmuring fountain, is thoroughly open and free.

So simple as this is Asiatic luxury!—The Oriental is not a contriving animal—there is nothing intricate in his magnificence. The impossibility of handing down property from father to son for any long period consecutively, seems to prevent the existence of those traditions by which, with us, the refined modes of applying wealth are made known to its inheritors. We know that in England a newly-made rich man cannot, by taking thought, and spending money, obtain even the same looking furniture as a Gentleman. The complicated character of an English establishment allows room for subtle distinctions between that which is *comme il faut*, and that which is not. All such refinements are unknown in the East —the Pasha and the peasant have the same tastes. The broad cold marble floor—the simple couch—the air freshly waving through a shady chamber—a verse of the Koran emblazoned on the wall—the sight and the sound of falling water—the cold fragrant smoke of the narguilè, and a small collection of wives and children in the inner apartments—all these, the

utmost enjoyments of the grandee, are yet such as to
be appreciable by the humblest Mussulman in the
empire.

But its gardens are the delight—the delight and
the pride of Damascus ; they are not the formal
parterres which you might expect from the Oriental
taste ; rather, they bring back to your mind the
memory of some dark old shrubbery in our northern
isle that has been charmingly *un-*'kept up' for many
and many a day.   When you see a rich wilderness of
wood in decent England, it is like enough that you
see it with some soft regrets.   The puzzled old woman
at the lodge can give small account of 'The family'.
She thinks it is 'Italy' that has made the whole
circle of her world so gloomy and sad.   You avoid
the house in lively dread of a lone housekeeper, but
you make your way on by the stables ; you remember
that gable with all its neatly nailed trophies of fitches,
and hawks, and owls, now slowly falling to pieces—
you remember that stable, and that, but the doors
are all fastened that used to be standing ajar—the
paint of things painted is blistered, and cracked—
grass grows in the yard—just there, in October
mornings, the keeper would wait with the dogs and
the guns—no keeper now ; you hurry away, and gain
the small wicket that used to open to the touch of a
lightsome hand—it is fastened with a padlock—(the
only new looking thing)—and is stained with thick,
green damp—you climb it, and bury yourself in the
deep shade, and strive but lazily with the tangling
briars, and stop for long minutes to judge, and
determine whether you will creep beneath the long
boughs, and make them your archway, or whether
perhaps you will lift your heel, and tread them down
underfoot.   Long doubt, and scarcely to be ended,
till you wake from the memory of those days when

the path was clear, and chase that phantom of a muslin sleeve that once weighed warm upon your arm.

Wild as that, the nighest woodland of a deserted home in England, but without its sweet sadness, is the sumptuous garden of Damascus. Forest trees, tall and stately enough, if you could see their lofty crests, yet lead a tussling life of it below, with their branches struggling against strong numbers of bushes and wilful shrubs. The shade upon the earth is black as night. High, high above your head, and on every side all down to the ground, the thicket is hemmed in, and choked up by the interlacing boughs that droop with the weight of roses, and load the slow air with their damask breath.[1] There are no other flowers. Here and there, there are patches of ground made clear from the cover, and these are either carelessly planted with some common and useful vegetable, or else are left free to the wayward ways of Nature, and bear rank weeds, moist-looking, and cool to your eyes, and freshening the sense with their earthly and bitter fragrance. There is a lane opened through the thicket, so broad in some places, that you can pass along side by side—in some, so narrow (the shrubs are for ever encroaching) that you ought, if you can, to go on the first, and hold back the bough of the rose tree. And through the sweet wilderness a loud rushing stream flows tumbling along, till it is halted at last in the lowest corner of the garden, and there tossed up in a fountain by the side of the simple alcove. This is all.

Never for an instant will the people of Damascus attempt to separate the idea of bliss from these wild gardens and rushing waters. Even where your best affections are concerned, and you—wise preachers

[1] The rose trees which I saw were all of the kind we call 'damask'; they grow to an immense height and size.

abstain and turn aside when they come near the
mysteries of the happy state, and we (wise preachers
too), we will hush our voices, and never reveal to
finite beings the joys of the 'Earthly Paradise'.

CHAPTER XXVIII

PASS OF THE LEBANON

'THE ruins of Baalbec!' Shall I scatter the vague
solemn thoughts, and all the airy phantasies which
gather together, when once those words are spoken,
that I may give you instead, tall columns, and measure-
ments true, and phrases built with ink?—No, no;
the glorious sounds shall still float on as of yore, and
still hold fast upon your brain with their own dim
and infinite meaning.

The pass by which I crossed the Lebanon is like,
I think, in its features to that of the Foorca in the
Bernese Oberland. For a great part of the way, I
toiled rather painfully through the dazzling snow, but
the labour of ascending added to the excitement with
which I looked for the summit of the pass. The time
came. There was a minute, and I saw nothing but
the steep, white shoulder of the mountain; there was
another minute, and that the next, which showed me
a nether heaven of fleecy clouds — clouds floating
along far down in the air beneath me, and showed me
beyond, the breadth of all Syria west of the Lebanon.
But chiefly I clung with my eyes to the dim steadfast
line of the sea which closed my utmost view. I had
grown well used of late to the people and the scenes
of forlorn Asia—well used to tombs and ruins, to
silent cities and deserted plains, to tranquil men, and
women sadly veiled; and now that I saw the even

plain of the sea, I leapt with an easy leap to its yonder
shores, and saw all the kingdoms of the West in that
fair path that could lead me from out of this silent
land straight on into shrill Marseilles, or round by the
pillars of Hercules, to the crash and roar of London.
My place upon this dividing barrier was as a man's
puzzling station in eternity, between the birthless
Past, and the Future that has no end.   Behind me
I left an old and decrepit World—Religions dead and
dying—calm tyrannies expiring in silence—women
hushed, and swathed, and turned into waxen dolls
—Love flown, and in its stead mere Royal, and
'Paradise', pleasures.—Before me there waited glad
bustle and strife—Love itself, an emulous game—
Religion a Cause and a Controversy, well smitten and
well defended—men governed by reasons and suasion
of speech—wheels going—steam buzzing—a mortal
race, and a slashing pace, and the Devil taking the
hindmost—taking *me*, by Jove (for that was my inner
care), if I lingered too long, upon the difficult Pass
that leads from Thought to Action.

I descended, and went towards the West.

The group of Cedars, remaining on this part of
the Lebanon, is held sacred by the Greek Church,
on account of a prevailing notion that the trees were
standing at the time when the Temple of Jerusalem
was built.   They occupy three or four acres on the
mountain's side, and many of them are gnarled in a
way that implies great age, but except these signs I
saw nothing in their appearance or conduct that
tended to prove them contemporaries of the cedars
employed in Solomon's temple.   The final cause to
which these aged survivors owed their preservation,
was explained to me in the evening by a glorious old
fellow (a Christian Chief), who made me welcome in
the valley of Eden.   In ancient times the whole range

of the Lebanon had been covered with cedars, and
as the fertile plains beneath became more and more
infested by Government officers and tyrants of high
and low estate, the people by degrees abandoned them,
and flocked to the rugged mountains for protection,
well knowing that the trouble of a walk up hill would
seriously obstruct their weak and lazy oppressors.
The cedar forests gradually shrank under the axe of
the encroaching multitudes, and seemed at last to be
on the point of disappearing entirely, when an aged
chief, who ruled in this district, and who had witnessed
the great change effected even in his own life-time,
chose to say that some sign or memorial should be
left of the vast woods with which the mountains had
formerly been clad, and commanded accordingly that
this group of trees (a group probably situated at the
highest point to which the forest had reached) should
remain untouched. The Chief it seems was not moved
by the notion I have mentioned as prevailing in the
Greek Church, but rather by some sentiment of veneration for a great natural feature,—a sentiment akin,
perhaps, to that old and earthborn Religion which
made men bow down to creation, before they had yet
learnt to know and worship the Creator.

The Chief of the valley in which I passed the night
was a man of large possessions, and he entertained
me very sumptuously ; he was highly intelligent, and
had had the sagacity to foresee that Europe would
intervene authoritatively in the affairs of Syria.
Bearing this idea in mind, and with a view to give
his son an advantageous start in the ambitious career
for which he was destined, he had hired for him a
teacher of Italian, the only accessible European tongue.
The tutor, however (a native of Syria), either did not
know, or did not choose to teach the European form
of address, but contented himself with instructing his

pupil in the mere language of Italy. This circumstance gave me an opportunity (the only one I ever
had, or was likely to have [1]) of hearing Oriental
courtesies expressed in an European tongue. The boy
was about twelve or thirteen years old, and having
the power of speaking to me without the aid of an
interpreter, he took a prominent part in the hospitable
duties of the day. He did the honours of the house
with untiring assiduity, and with a kind of gracefulness which by mere description can scarcely be made
intelligible to those who are unacquainted with the
manners of the Asiatics. The boy's address resembled
a little that of a highly polished and insinuating
Roman Catholic Priest, but had more of girlish gentleness. It was strange to hear him gravely and slowly
enunciating the common and extravagant compliments of the East in good Italian, and in soft, persuasive tones. I recollect that I was particularly
amused at the gracious obstinacy with which he
maintained that the house and the surrounding estates
belonged, not to his father, but to me. To say this
once, was only to use the common form of speech,
signifying no more than our sweet word ' welcome ';
but the amusing part of the matter was that whenever, in the course of conversation, I happened to
speak of his father's mansion or the surrounding
domain, the boy invariably interfered to correct my
pretended mistake, and to assure me once again with a
gentle decisiveness of manner that the whole property
was really and exclusively mine, and that his father
had not the most distant pretensions to its ownership.

I received from my host some good information
respecting the people of the mountains, and their
power of resisting Mehemet Ali. The Chief gave me

[1] A Dragoman never interprets in terms the courteous
language of the East.

very plainly to understand that the Mountaineers being dependent upon others for bread and gunpowder (the two great necessaries of martial life), could not long hold out against a power occupying the plains and commanding the sea ; but he also assured me, and that very significantly, that, if this source of weakness were provided against, *the Mountaineers were to be depended upon* ; he told me that, in ten or fifteen days, the Chiefs could bring together some fifty thousand fighting men.

CHAPTER XXIX

SURPRISE OF SATALIEH

WHILST I was remaining upon the coast of Syria, I had the good fortune to become acquainted with the Russian Sataliefsky [1], a General Officer who in his youth had fought and bled at Borodino, but was now better known among Diplomats by the important trust committed to him at a period highly critical for the affairs of Eastern Europe. I must not tell you his family name ; my mention of his title can do him no harm, for it is I, and I only, who have conferred it, in consideration of the military and diplomatic services performed under my own eyes.

The General, as well as I, was bound for Smyrna, and we agreed to sail together in an Ionian brigantine. We did not charter the vessel, but we made our arrangement with the captain upon such terms that we could be put ashore upon any part of the coast that we might choose. We sailed, and day after day the vessel lay dawdling on the sea with calms and feeble breezes for her portion. I, myself, was well

---

[1] A title signifying Transcender or Conqueror of Satalieh.

repaid for the painful restlessness occasioned by slow weather, because I gained from my companion a little of that vast fund of interesting knowledge with which he was stored—knowledge a thousand times the more highly to be prized, since it was not of the sort that is to be gathered from books, but only from the lips of those who have acted a part in the world.

When after nine days of sailing or trying to sail, we found ourselves still hanging by the mainland to the north of the Isle of Cyprus, we determined to disembark at Satalieh, and to go on thence by land. A light breeze favoured our purpose, and it was with great delight that we neared the fragrant land, and saw our anchor go down in the bay of Satalieh within two or three hundred yards of the shore.

The town of Satalieh[1] is the chief place of the Pashalik in which it is situate, and its citadel is the residence of the Pasha. We had scarcely dropped our anchor, when a boat from the shore came alongside with officers on board. These men announced that strict orders had been received for maintaining a quarantine of three weeks against all vessels coming from Syria, and they directed accordingly that no one from the vessel should disembark. In reply, we sent a message to the Pasha, setting forth the rank and titles of the General, and requiring permission to go ashore. After a while the boat came again alongside, and the officers, declaring that the orders received from Constantinople were imperative and unexceptional, formally enjoined us in the name of the Pasha to abstain from any attempt to land.

I had been hitherto much less impatient of our slow voyage than my gallant friend, but this opposition made the smooth sea seem to me like a prison

---

[1] Spelt 'Attalia' and sometimes 'Adalia' in English books and maps.

from which I must and would break out. I had an
unbounded faith in the feebleness of Asiatic Potentates, and I proposed that we should set the Pasha at
defiance.   The General had been worked up to a state
of most painful agitation by the idea of being driven
from the shore which smiled so pleasantly before his
eyes, and he adopted my suggestion with rapture.

We determined to land.

To approach the sweet shore after a tedious voyage,
and then to be suddenly and unexpectedly prohibited
from landing—this is so maddening to the temper,
that no one who had ever experienced the trial would
say that even the most violent impatience of such
restraint is wholly inexcusable. I am not going to
pretend, however, that the course we chose to adopt
on the occasion can be perfectly justified. The
impropriety of a traveller's setting at naught the
regulations of a foreign state is clear enough, and
the bad taste of compassing such a purpose by mere
gasconading is still more glaringly plain. I knew
perfectly well that, if the Pasha understood his duty,
and had energy enough to perform it, he would order
out a file of soldiers the moment we landed, and cause
us both to be shot upon the beach, without allowing
more contact than might be absolutely necessary for
the purpose of making us stand fire ; but I also firmly
believed that the Pasha would not see the befitting
line of conduct nearly so well as I did, and that even
if he did know his duty, he would hardly succeed in
finding resolution enough to perform it.

We ordered the boat to be got in readiness, and the
officers on shore seeing these preparations, gathered
together a number of guards ; these assembled upon
the sands ; we saw that great excitement prevailed,
and that messengers were continually going to and
fro between the shore and the citadel.

Our Captain, out of compliment to his Excellency, had provided the vessel with a Russian war-flag, and during our voyage he had been in the habit of hoisting it alternately with the Union Jack. We agreed that we would attempt our disembarkation under this the Russian standard. I was glad to have it so resolved, for I should have been sorry to engage the honoured flag of England in an affair like this. The Russian ensign was therefore committed to one of the sailors, and the man honoured with this charge took his station at the stern of the boat. We gave particular instructions to the Captain of the brigantine, and when all was ready, the General and I, with our respective servants, got into the boat, and were slowly rowed towards the shore. The guards gathered together at the point for which we were making, but when they saw that our boat went on without altering her course, *they ceased to stand very still*; none of them ran away, or even shrank back, but they looked as if *the pack were being shuffled*, every man seeming desirous to change places with his neighbour. They were still at their post, however, when our oars went in, and the bow of our boat ran up—well up upon the beach.

The General was lame by an honourable wound received at Borodino, and could not without some help get out of the boat; I, therefore, landed the first. My instructions to the Captain were attended to with the most perfect accuracy, for scarcely had my foot indented the sand when the four six-pounders of the brigantine quite gravely rolled out their brute thunder. Precisely as I had expected, the guards, and all the people who had gathered about them, gave way under the shock produced by the mere sound of guns, and we were all allowed to disembark without the least molestation.

We immediately formed a little column, or rather,
as I should have called it, a procession, for we had no
fighting aptitude in us, and were only trying, as it
were, how far we could go in frightening full-grown
children.   First marched the sailor with the Russian
flag of war bravely flying in the breeze; then came
the General and I; then our servants; and, lastly, if
I rightly recollect, two more of the brigantine's crew.
Our flag-bearer so exulted in his honourable office,
and bore the colours aloft with so much of pomp and
dignity, that I found it exceedingly hard to keep a
grave countenance.   We advanced towards the castle,
but the people had now had time to recover from the
effect of the six-pounders (only, of course, loaded with
powder), and they could not help seeing, not only the
numerical weakness of our party, but the very slight
amount of wealth and resource which it seemed to
imply; they began to hang round us more closely;
and just as this reaction was beginning, the General
(he was perfectly unacquainted with the Asiatic
character) thoughtlessly turned round, in order to
speak to one of the servants.   The effect of this slight
move was magical; the people thought we were going
to give way, and instantly closed round us.   In two
words, and with one touch, I showed my comrade the
danger he was running, and in the next instant we
were both advancing more pompously than ever.
Some minutes afterwards there was a second appearance of reaction, followed again by wavering and
indecision on the part of the Pasha's people, but at
length it seemed to be understood that we should go
unmolested into the audience hall.

Constant communication had been going on between
the receding crowd and the Pasha, and so, when we
reached the gates of the citadel, we saw that preparations were made for giving us an awe-striking

reception. Parting at once from the sailors and our servants, the General and I were conducted into the audience hall; and there, at least, I suppose the Pasha hoped that he would confound us by his greatness. The hall was nothing more than a large whitewashed room. Oriental potentates have a pride in that sort of simplicity, when they can contrast it with the exhibition of power; and this the Pasha was able to do, for the lower end of the hall was filled with his officers. These men (in number, as I thought, about fifty or sixty) were all handsomely, though plainly, dressed in the military frock-coats of Europe; they stood in mass, and so as to present a hollow, semi-circular front towards the end of the hall at which the Pasha sat; they opened a narrow lane for us when we entered, and as soon as we had passed they again closed up their ranks. An attempt was made to induce us to remain at a respectful distance from his Mightiness; to have yielded in this point would have been fatal to our success—perhaps to our lives; but the General and I had already determined upon the place which we should take, and we rudely pushed on towards the upper end of the hall.

Upon the divan, and close up against the right-hand corner of the room, there sat the Pasha—his limbs gathered in—the whole creature coiled up like an adder. His cheeks were deadly pale, and his lips perhaps had turned white, for without moving a muscle the man impressed me with an immense idea of the wrath within him. He kept his eyes inexorably fixed as if upon vacancy, and with the look of a man accustomed to refuse the prayers of those who sue for life. We soon discomposed him, however, from this studied fixity of feature, for we marched straight up to the divan, and sat down, the Russian close to the Pasha, and I by the side of the Russian. This act astonished the attendants, and plainly disconcerted the Pasha ; he could no longer maintain the glassy stillness of his eyes, and evidently became much agitated. At the feet of the Satrap there stood a trembling Italian ; this man was a sort of medico in the potentate's service, and now, in the absence of our attendants, he was to act as an interpreter. The Pasha caused him to tell us that we had openly defied his authority, and had forced our way on shore in the teeth of his officers.

Up to this time I had been the planner of the enterprise, but now that the moment had come when all would depend upon able and earnest speechifying, I felt at once the immense superiority of my gallant friend, and gladly left to him the whole conduct of this discussion ; indeed he had vast advantages over me, not only by his superior command of language and his far more spirited style of address, but also in his consciousness of a good cause, for, whilst I felt myself completely in the wrong, his Excellency had really worked himself up to believe that the Pasha's refusal to permit our landing was a great outrage and insult. Therefore, without deigning to defend our conduct, he at once commenced a spirited attack upon the Pasha. The poor Italian Doctor translated one or two sentences to the Pasha, but he evidently mitigated their import ; the Russian, growing warm, insisted upon his attack with redoubled energy and spirit ; but the medico, instead of translating, began to shake violently with terror, and at last he came out with his 'non ardisco', and fairly confessed that he dared not interpret fierce words to his master.

Now then, at a time when everything seemed to depend upon the effect of speech, we were left without an interpreter.

But this very circumstance, though at first it ap-

peared so unfavourable, turned out to be advantageous.
The General, finding that he could not have his words
translated, ceased to speak in Italian, and recurred to
his accustomed French; he became eloquent: no one
present, except myself, understood one syllable of what
he was saying, but he had drawn forth his passport,
and the energy and violence with which, as he spoke,
he pointed to the graven Eagle of all the Russias,
began to make an impression; the Pasha saw at his
side a man, not only free from every the least pang of
fear, but raging, as it seemed, with just indignation,
and thenceforward he plainly began to think that in
some way or other (he could not tell how) he must
certainly have been in the wrong.   In a little time he
was so much shaken that the Italian ventured to resume his interpretation, and my comrade had again
the opportunity of pressing his attack upon the Pasha;
his argument, if I rightly recollect its import, was to
this effect :—'If the vilest Jews were to come into
the harbour, you would but forbid them to land, and
force them to perform quarantine; yet this is the
very course, O Pasha, which your rash officers dare
to think of adopting with *us*!—those mad and
reckless men would have actually dealt towards a
Russian General Officer and an English Gentleman
as if they had been wretched Israelites! Never,
never will we submit to such an indignity. His
Imperial Majesty knows how to protect his nobles
from insult, and would never endure that a General
of his army should be treated in matter of quarantine
as though he were a mere Eastern Jew!' This
argument told with great effect; the Pasha fairly
admitted that he felt its weight, and he now only
struggled to obtain such a compromise as might partly
save his dignity; he wanted us to perform a quarantine of one day for form's sake, and in order to show

his people that he was not utterly defied; but finding that we were inexorable, he not only abandoned his attempt, but promised to supply us with horses.

When the discussion had arrived at this happy conclusion, tchibouques and coffee were brought, and we passed, I think, nearly an hour in friendly conversation. The Pasha, it now appeared, had once been a prisoner of war in Russia; during his captivity he could not have failed to learn the greatness of the Czar's power, and it was this piece of knowledge perhaps which made him more alive than an untravelled Turk might have been to the force of my comrade's eloquence.

The Pasha now gave us a generous feast; our promised horses were brought without much delay; I gained my loved saddle once more, and when the moon got up and touched the heights of Taurus, we were joyfully winding our way through the first of his rugged defiles.

THE END